MOSES AND THE
DEUTERONOMIST

MOSES and the DEUTERONOMIST

*A Literary Study of
the Deuteronomic History*

Part One

DEUTERONOMY
JOSHUA
JUDGES

ROBERT POLZIN

The Seabury Press · New York

1980
The Seabury Press
815 Second Avenue
New York, N.Y. 10017

Library of Congress Cataloging in Publication Data
Polzin, Robert.
Moses and the Deuteronomist.
Includes bibliographical references.
1. Bible. O.T. Deuteronomy—Criticism,
interpretation, etc. 2. Bible. O.T. Joshua—
Criticism, interpretation, etc. 3. Bible. O.T.
Judges—Criticism, interpretation, etc. I. Title.
BS1275.2.P64   222   80-17189
ISBN O-8164-0456-9
ISBN O-8164-2284-2 (pbk.)

Portions of chapter 1 and the early part of chapter 2 also appear
in "Reporting Speech in the Book of Deuteronomy: Toward a
Compositional Analysis of the Deuteronomic History," in *Tradi-
tions of Transformation: Turning-Points in Biblical Faith*, edited by
Jon D. Levenson and Baruch Halpern, published by Eisenbrauns
(Winona Lake, Ind., 1980). They are reprinted with permission.

For Jonathan and David

CONTENTS

PREFACE

Biblical critics have been so busy juggling the concepts of myth and history that they have ignored the most obvious feature of biblical narrative: it tells a story. Hans Frei aptly describes this situation as "the eclipse of biblical narrative" (1974). From the eighteenth century onwards, historical analysis of the kind that Frei documents has been unable to handle realistic or historylike narrative, and the result has been the standard commentary that misses the narratological dimensions of the text in an erudite, indeed encyclopedic, search for ostensive or ideal reference. But something happens to a story's meaning when an exegete, for the sake of philological or conceptual analysis, removes the serpentine skin of a text that makes it cohere as a narrative. Narrative meaning slips away.

One way to preserve a story's meaning is to tell another story in its interpretation. The reader will notice at the end of this book a detailed table of contents that is a kind of narrative index. It highlights the story-line in my interpretation of the Deuteronomic History, wherein I attempt to get at one understanding of its meaning by taking its narrative aspects seriously, an enterprise quite different from the usual referential search. Much more in tune with my approach is Frank Kermode's recent *The Genesis of Secrecy: On the Interpretation of Narrative* (1979). Surely the time has come to end a centuries-old eclipse of biblical narrative, and Kermode's study masterfully begins this process as he focuses on the New Testament, especially the Gospel of Mark. The present volume is an attempt to do the same in Old Testament studies with a literary interpretation of the first three books of the Deuteronomic History.

Right from the start I want to emphasize that not all parts of this interpretive story are equally plausible, even to myself. As the postscript states, everything about my interpretation is provisional, yet some parts are more provisional than others. Rather than leave blanks in those parts of my story that resisted narration, I chose to move it along for the sake of continuity. But as is the case with every story, continuity, albeit necessary, is always illusory. Thus, for example, I am less satisfied with my account of Joshua 10 than the homogeneous manner of my interpretive account might indicate. Nevertheless I feel confident that much of my story-line "fits" the Deuteronomic narrative. I do hope to complete this story with another volume in the not too distant future. By then it should be better known how important it may be to hear the conclusion.

I am also conscious that some readers might mistakenly detect a triumphant tone in my claim that the Deuteronomist might be described as a proto-Gadamerian, as if this would afford some kind of sacred corroboration of a contemporary hermeneutic option. However, I do want to point out that if I believe such an affinity between an ancient and modern perspective to exist, I do not intend to claim by this that such perspectives are therefore more plausible or "closer to the truth" than others.

Finally, the story I tell in no way denies the existence of interpolations throughout the Deuteronomic History. It may be that my literary struggle with the entire text may help identify the more likely examples.

ACKNOWLEDGMENTS

I began this book in the summer of 1977. Since then its rapid completion is largely the result of a generous leave fellowship awarded me by the Social Sciences and Humanities Research Council of Canada. I am indebted to the Research Council for making possible what the Canadian-American exchange rate had made exceedingly improbable and for always being sympathetic and responsive to my changing needs. Most of this book was written at the University of California, Irvine, where I enjoyed the facilities of the School of Criticism and Theory and the gracious hospitality of its Director, University Professor Murray Krieger. The School's secretary, Betty Terrell, was always available to help a sojourning family cope with the dreamland quality of Southern California.

All or substantial portions of my manuscript were read and commented on by Robert Alter, Wolfgang Iser, Murray Krieger, and Stephen Wilson. I am grateful to them for generous response and helpful suggestions. They shamelessly encouraged the literary proclivities of a scholar trained in historical criticism. I gratefully acknowledge basic insights into the Book of Judges shared with me through an unpublished paper by Jamie Scott. From the beginning, my project has had the encouragement of James Ackerman, David Robertson, and Matitiahu Tsevat. My wife, as always, deserves special credit for her constant help and support. And lastly, this book is dedicated to my two sons, now six and four, who know a good story when they hear one.

One

CRITICISM AND CRISIS
WITHIN BIBLICAL STUDIES

The Immediate Context

Exegetical scholars are agreed only that historical criticism, the best method of discovering the literal sense, cannot be given up. (Krentz, 1975:72)

. . . we have to conclude that historical exegesis is suspect of obscurantism. Could it be that its methodological preunderstanding is at odds with the contemporary cultural preunderstanding? (Patte, 1976:10)

The very first question that today confronts anyone who attempts to analyze biblical material in a scholarly context is: Should one's approach be primarily historical or literary, diachronic or synchronic? Recent claims of some biblical scholars, especially those employing various versions of literary structuralism emanating from France, tend to cast serious doubt upon the hitherto secure consensus of modern biblical studies concerning the fundamental role of historical criticism. Thus we find Patte the structuralist versus Krentz the historian in the above quotations.

The problem is semantic in a double sense: not only is it a question of which approach best helps us "discover the literal sense," as Krentz puts it, but there is also the problem of whether a-historical literary approaches to the study of the Bible may accurately be designated "scholarly." Since recent structural studies claim not to be based on the findings of modern historical criticism, and yet claim to be as scientifically rigorous as (so Patte, 1976:19), or even more rigorous than (so Doty, 1973:119–21), their historical counterparts, there appears to be a fundamental dispute as to what constitutes scholarly study of the Bible.

On the other hand, the structuralist claim of methodological rigor is contradicted by representative historical critical statements. For example, we read that "there can be for us no scholarly access to the Bible without a knowledge of the circumstances of its formation" (Kaiser, 1975:13).

I would like to spell out in this introductory chapter the personal context out of which the present study derives. It seems to me that if there is a crisis in biblical scholarship today it does not consist in the present, almost healthy tension between historical and literary criticism but rather in the destructive self-image both may mistakenly have concerning their status as scholarly disciplines modeled after the natural sciences. The diachronic/synchronic question, of itself, presents us merely with a *problem* that in no sense approaches the monumental dimensions of the crisis about which I will speak shortly. As I have stated elsewhere (Polzin, 1977:16–18), diachronic and synchronic study of the Bible, historical critical and literary structural approaches, possess a complementary relationship to each other. Neither constitutes, a priori, the fundamental basis for the other's existence, neither occupies by intrinsic right an academic throne to which the other must bring its conclusions for scholarly approbation, for a scientific *nihil obstat*. Nevertheless, we shall see below that this complementary relationship does allow an operational priority to literary analysis at the preliminary stages of research.

The battle which now seems to be increasingly waged in biblical journals and at biblical conferences is similar to that which has been going on for decades among (literary) literary critics ever since the postwar emergence in North America of the so-called New Critics such as Frye, Wimsatt, and Beardsley. Using terminology employed by Said (1976) and Krieger (1976), we may say that with the onset of French literary structuralism these postwar critics are now the "old" New Critics, while modern scholars such as Barthes, Kristeva, Greimas, and Todorov have become the "new" New Critics. How the dispute with the "old" New Critics ran its course may offer some insights for biblical scholars as to the probable outcome of the emerging confrontation between established historical critics and a boisterous, vociferous, but not altogether unified group of younger scholars of the Bible who now appear to be challenging their predecessors.

Within literary circles, one can find a convenient account of past and present battles between literary *history* and literary *criticism* in the excellent volumes of the journal *New Literary History*. A helpful analysis of what such battles entail, and how they may be profitably resolved, is Istvan Soter's article on "The Dilemma of Literary Science"

(*NLH* 1970:85–100). The position outlined there offers a number of helpful insights into the present condition of biblical studies and represents, with some few exceptions, the general operational context within which the present study has been written.

It might be useful for me now to introduce two assertions that describe the main elements of my synchronic/diachronic assumptions and a third that articulates what I believe to be the real crisis in biblical scholarship today.

1. A historical critical analysis of biblical material is necessary for an *adequate* scholarly understanding of what it means.

There is no need, of course, to defend such a view before the vast majority of biblical scholars who might read the present pages. For indeed historical criticism is *the* cornerstone of modern biblical studies. But there are some biblical scholars who, influenced by the "old" and "new" New Critics, forcefully proclaim that one need not attend to the historical context of a work in order to discover a whole range of acceptable meanings that it contains. What Northrop Frye writes of Boehme, many younger biblical scholars are now writing of the Bible:

> It has been said of Boehme that his books are like a picnic to which the author brings the words and the reader the meaning. The remark may have been intended as a sneer at Boehme, but it is an exact description of all works of literary art without exception. (Quoted in Strickland, 1977:86)

Since some parts of the Bible may be considered to be at least in the running for the title "literary art," the question arises how important it is to determine by historical means what a biblical author or editor might have meant when he wrote or compiled his work. Some structuralists and most New Critics would assert that he who has embarked upon such a quest has fallen prey to "the intentional fallacy." (For views, pro and con, see Molina, 1976.)

Perhaps the best known defense of the proposition that the intentional fallacy is itself a fallacy is *Validity in Interpretation,* by E. D. Hirsch. (One can also consult Hirsch, 1976.) For those who are familiar with Hirsch's thorough discussions, and are in fundamental agreement with his repudiation of the hermeneutical views of New Critics and structuralists alike, the present defense of biblical historical criticism will appear modest—indeed even unnecessary. In any case, I propose to indicate my position without recourse to Hirsch's arguments because I am not entirely comfortable with them. Above all, as Geoffrey Strickland points out, largely in defense of Hirsch, the latter argues his case mainly "on the grounds of common sense" (Strickland, 1977:86). Now this is precisely the defense to which the biblical historical critics traditionally and mostly implicitly have had recourse, and M. Tsevat argues very persuasively that "arguments based on common sense as such have little or no place in the sciences, the humanities included" (1975:217).

I have no space here to develop lines of argument that would defend historical criticism's traditional emphasis on extra-textual context, but let me at least indicate the direction it would take. First, I would defend such a position by invoking arguments drawn from extended debates within modern linguistics, especially those which oppose Chomsky's a priori ignoring of extra-linguistic context in linguistic analysis.[1] Thus transformational grammar has held in linguistics what the New Critics and some French structuralists have proposed in literary criticism: the rejection *in principle* of factors of real-life context in the interpretation of literary texts. Recognition by biblical scholars of this linguistic debate would have the salutary effect of broadening and deepening their own discussions on the relatively rare occassions that they get down to fundamental consideration of methodological principles.

A second line of argument that could be invoked against the principled rejection of the social context as irrelevant to the interpretation of texts comes paradoxically from certain Russian formalist and sociological literary theorists who have had essential roles in the development of modern-day literary structuralism of the Russian rather than the French variety. If a typical historical critical approach to the study of the Bible can state,

> To hear and understand the witness of the biblical books correctly, it is necessary to know at what times and in what circumstances they came into existence. This involves a knowledge of the history, religion, and theology of Israel and Judaism, as well as of the world from which they grew (Kaiser, 1975:2),

a Russian theorist in 1930 can emphasize with italics such statements as,

> *The immediate social situation and the broader social milieu wholly determine—and determine from within, so to speak—the structure of an utterance.* (Voloshinov, 1973:86)

> *Verbal communication can never be understood and explained outside of this connection with a concrete situation.* (Voloshinov, 1973:95)

The difference between Kaiser's and Voloshinov's largely similar positions is that the Russian theorist's is not simply an assertion, but a conclusion reached by means of convincing literary argument and analysis. The impression one gets from reading certain structuralists is that the first task which the historical exegete feels obliged to undertake, namely, to use "every linguistic tool at his disposal to determine the sense the text had for its writer and first audience (the *sensus literalis sive historicus*)" (Krentz, 1975:39), is a linguistically naive and misguided point of view. On the other hand, even though the historical critic's impulse may rightly be termed precipitous, whole schools of modern semioticians and structuralists would themselves consider the rejection of linguistically relevant situations by some of their colleagues as myopic. It is important, therefore, here at the beginning, not to place all structuralists in the same hermeneutical basket.

2. A competent literary analysis of biblical material is necessary for even a *preliminary* scholarly understanding of what this ancient text means.

We may begin by reaffirming Robert Alter's assessment of modern biblical studies:

> It is a little astonishing that at this late date there exists virtually no serious literary analysis of the Hebrew Bible. By serious literary analysis I mean the manifold varieties of minutely discriminating attention to the artful use of language, to the shifting play of ideas, conventions, tone, sound, imagery, narrative viewpoint, compositional units, and much else; the kind of disciplined attention, in other words, which through a whole spectrum of critical approaches has illuminated, for example, the poetry of Dante, the plays of Shakespeare, the novels of Tolstoy. (Alter, 1975:70)

The defensive reaction to this article, represented by the published letters of a number of biblical scholars in a later issue of *Commentary*, serves to confirm Alter's view that biblical scholars have little acquaintance with even elementary forms of disciplined literary analysis. Alter's pessimistic opinion is shared by David Robertson (1977:87), and biblical critics would do well to listen to such literary critics, especially where the nature and scope of literary criticism, and its role within biblical scholarship, are concerned.

The present study assumes that the above assessment accurately represents the state of biblical scholarship today. It further assumes that this literary lacuna is a primary reason why historical critical analyses of biblical material have so often produced disappointing and inadequate results. If adequate historical studies of literary texts operationally depend upon the existence of competent literary studies of such texts, we may have here a plausible reason for a good number of failures in historical critical understanding of biblical material. It remains now to describe in what sense literary criticism may be spoken of as having an operational priority over historical criticism.

The question of the sequence of literary versus historical investigations of literary texts is, of course, one that has been discussed at great length in literary circles. In the study of literature, what comes first from a methodological point of view: a historical (genetic or diachronic) approach or a descriptive (synchronic or literary critical) approach? This is the dilemma of literary science, as I. Soter describes it (1970). The answer which informs the present study assumes that scholarly understanding of biblical material results from a *circular* movement that begins with a literary analysis, then turns to historical problems, whose attempted solution then furnishes further refinements and adaptations of one's literary critical conclusions.[2] The priority of synchrony (in the dynamic sense emphasized especially by the Russian structuralists) over diachrony is not in rank but only in operation. Thus we are still allowed to call both approaches truly complementary: each must eventually take the other's conclusions into account. What is primarily emphasized here is *where one begins.* As Soter writes:

> We must put an end to the dilemma, but this is possible only if we start from the book as an artistic creation, i.e., we must give priority to critical-aesthetic considerations and only afterwards turn to historical problems. . . . Of course, "priority" in this sense is not priority in rank, since criticism starting from the literary product, and historical research returning to it, are both secondary seen from the point of view of the book itself. (1970:94)

The reasons for assuming such a sequence in procedures is admirably and succinctly given by Krystyna Pomorska (1971). She points out that if we move in the opposite direction, basing synchronic analyses on historical studies, "we always run a risk of applying ready-made theories to something not suited to them" (276). In order to gain an intimate knowledge of the literary work, we must make it the starting point of our efforts:

> A literary work represents a complex phenomenon whose *process* is as significant as its ontological nature. But it seems impossible to study the process before knowing the nature of the product. (276)

Impossible, at least, before having a *preliminary* understanding of the literary composition of the work as *product.*

The great Russian literary theorist Mikhail Bakhtin agrees with the sequence we are describing. In discussing why he does a literary critical analysis of Dostoevsky's work before tackling historical questions, he admits that such a preliminary literary investigation does need to be deepened by historical perspectives. Nevertheless, "without such a preliminary orientation, historical investigations degenerate into a disconnected series of chance comparisons" (1973:230, n.4).

3. Both literary and historical criticism of the Bible uncover hermeneutical principles within the text that appear to be at fundamental odds with prevailing views on the nature of historical and literary scholarship, views based upon the supposed similarity of both disciplines to the natural sciences.

This assertion is in essential agreement with the hermeneutic views of H. G. Gadamer in his classic work *Truth and Method*, and helps to explain why I believe a crisis exists within biblical studies today. My position deals with the contradictory situation scholarship finds itself in when it compares *what* the Bible characteristically claims is the road to a correct understanding of God's word and *how* scholarship is supposed to have arrived at its own understanding of these claims. The "what" and the supposed "how" are paradoxically contradictory in the sense that scholarly principles of interpretation reveal a biblical message which implicitly challenges the validity of the hermeneutic principles which many scholars use.

If the scholar pays attention to the referential aspects of the biblical text—and it is my opinion that he can do so in the name of scholarship—he seems forced to make a decision about the hermeneutic principles he will use in his study. For the scholar who confronts the question whether the Bible has some kind of claim on him, any literary or historical criticism modeled after the supposed objectivity of the natural sciences will be seen to operate according to hermeneutic principles that are in conflict with the message and spirit of the biblical text: the message that this scholarship uncovers would reject the very method by which it is uncovered.

A discussion of this assertion is all the more necessary today since it is in basic conflict with the usual explanations of the theological significance of "scholarly" (read here "historical") disciplines of the Bible:

> It cannot be disputed that the Introduction to the Old Testament is an auxiliary discipline of theology. . . . Introduction, together with the other historical disciplines prepares for an understanding of the scriptures which will lead to the word of God, to which it bears witness, being heard in our time. (Kaiser, 1975:13)

We are thus led to believe that the better able one is to subject the Bible to the whole array of modern historical disciplines, the better can be one's preparation for understanding of what the word of God *says*.

Whether one's ideal be ecclesiastical or scholarly or a combination of both, a basic dilemma is posed by the belief that the primary task of the biblical historian is to hear the biblical message in the sense it had for its writer and first audience (Krentz, 1975:39): once one subjects a biblical text to a literary or historical analysis, the conclusion is often inescapable that the typically biblical approach to the word of God it uncovers is apparently opposed to such an understanding of the scholarly task. To study the Bible with such an uninvolved and "objective" stance is still to discover a message that was apparently not meant to be understood in such a way. One can even phrase the dilemma in structuralist jargon: the result of this kind of decoding of the text is the recovery of an original message that reads, "Do not decode this in the way you have."[3]

But are we not forced to examine the biblical text from a historical critical point of view if we want to reconstruct what the writer or editor meant and what his audience first understood? Do we not run the risk of interpreting the text in an overly subjective and contemporary way if we ignore the historical critical approach? As Krentz writes, "Historical study prevents too rapid modernizing" (1975:65). What is at issue here is whether the *need* one feels to concentrate the search for a text's meaning on the author's original situation and intent may not in fact itself be a contemporary and subjective element in the discussion. If this be so, then by trying to avoid contemporary subjectivity in such a way (by this kind of biblical criticism) one has already surrendered to one of the most pervasive of contemporary biases: the supposed greater objectivity of the historical critical mode of interpretation.

If above I have defended scholarship's *need* for both literary and historical criticism, I mean to suggest here that such arguments in their behalf are often misused in support of the supposed greater objectivity of a scholarly mode of interpretation based upon the natural sciences as models. But what the Bible teaches and what this view of modern scholarship teaches, about how best to interpret messages as fundamentally assertive as those in the Bible are plainly at odds with one another. And for all those who view this kind of scholarship as the handmaid of religion or as "the basement of theology" (Kaiser, 1975:13), the clear result of putting it into practice, by a scholarly application of literary and historical criticism, is to infuse these disciplines with a self-destruct mechanism.

The first two assertions of this section discuss the twofold direction of a scholarly understanding of the Bible. The present assertion actually addresses the question of whether much of today's historical and literary critical self-understanding is adequate from a biblical point of view. The answer would seem to be no, and this is precisely what constitutes

the present crisis. For so many to believe that they are actually understanding the Bible's claims *on its own terms,* when in fact they are not,
represents a true crisis in scholarship.

There are those who would not dream of asking the question I have
just raised. For those who believe that an impersonal, uninvolved scholarship is necessary even to assess the biblical message—necessary at
least in the sense that one must first correctly perceive a message before
one can assess it—there is no room left for the possibility that biblical
messages might justifiably assess such a view of scholarship. Scholarship
for these individuals involves a contract which includes a self-justifying
clause that reads, "Attitudes toward the text that question the fundamental role of an uninvolved impersonal criticism are critically unacceptable. But critically unacceptable approaches to the Bible are too
subjective to be taken seriously. Therefore one can safely ignore such
attitudes." Catch 22. There apparently exists academic as well as religious fundamentalism, scholarly as well as theological dogmatism.

I can illustrate my general position by referring to a specific biblical
book. For many, the Deuteronomic History is a literary unity and the
Book of Deuteronomy is its programmatic introduction. As the word of
God through Moses, this book is presented as the blueprint according
to which the history narrated in the following books, Joshua–2 Kings, is
to be interpreted. It might be useful, therefore, to see briefly how
various words of God are interpreted by Moses and the narrator in the
Book of Deuteronomy.

Moses is portrayed in Deuteronomy as the pre-eminent interpreter of
God's words. The story describes only one instance of divine speech
that was heard by the people of Israel, the decalogue of 5:6–21. All the
other words of God, even those directly quoted by the narrator in
chapters 31, 32, and 34, are not heard by the people, but are transmitted to them through the intervention of Moses primarily and, in a few
scattered instances, through that of the elders of Israel, the Levitical
priests, and the narrator himself.

In Deuteronomy, Moses is pictured in his addresses as interpreting
speeches that had taken place prior to his interpretive words. As
5:28–31 brings out, Moses carries out this practice as an introduction
and as a conclusion to God's further commands of chapters 12–26.
Thus Moses is pictured as setting the Deuteronomic lawcode *in context*
by, among other things, interpreting past words, especially those of
God's. What is immediately obvious here is the absolutely authoritarian,
or at least authoritative, nature of Moses' interpretive function.

It is true that Moses takes care to situate, in time and in space, the
past events and speech that he reports:

"The LORD our God said to us in Horeb . . ." (1:6)
"At that time I said to you . . ." (1:9)

This practice agrees with that of the narrator whose framing narrative in Deuteronomy situates the words of Moses in time and space: when, where, and in what circumstances Moses spoke the words reported in the book. Indeed this contextualizing practice of Moses and the narrator helps to create a factual tone in the narrative that invests it with an aura of historicity which must have been as obvious to the book's first audience as it is to us.

When Moses, for example, rehearses in his first address what of importance had been said and done before arriving in Moab, the stated location of Moses' addresses, his audience could supply whatever contextual information was part of their common experience. But what they could not do was to supplement his account with anything that had to do with the *content* of God's words to Moses or Israel, since only Moses is described as having heard these words (except for the decalogue). Moreover, since God had told Moses alone,

"I will tell you all the commandments and the statutes and the ordinances which you shall teach them . . ." (5:31),

only Moses is pictured as directly authorized by God to *interpret* his words. And, more to the point, when Moses in chapter 5 recounts this authenticating command of God's, no one in his audience is in a position to institute an investigation into whether Moses was reporting accurately God's words of authorization; after all, we are told in the book that only Moses heard these words.

The principal role of Moses, as seen in the Book of Deuteronomy, is hermeneutic: he is the book's primary declarer (*maggîd*) and teacher (*melammed*) of God's word. He not only declares what God has said, he teaches or interprets what the divine words mean for Israel. And he is pictured as doing so in an authoritative manner that was consonant with the status he is pictured as enjoying within the Israelite community.

Even if we confine our illustrative remarks to the Book of Deuteronomy, it is still obvious here at the beginning of the history that by the end of the book the narrator has also established *his* authoritative role as *maggîd* and *melammed* of Moses' words. And the narrator accomplishes the establishment of his authority amazingly enough while remaining mostly in the background of his narrative: the reporting speech of the narrator comprises only about fifty-six verses of the book.

He will, of course, come to the foreground with the preponderantly reporting narrative of Joshua–2 Kings. Indeed, what is obvious, even on a first reading of the history, is that in the narrator's reporting words, comprising the bulk of Joshua–2 Kings, we have some kind of authoritative interpretation of the words of Moses insofar as they affect the subsequent history of Israel.

In both cases of the reporting of God's words—that is, in the case of Moses' reporting of God's words, and in the case of the narrator's reporting of Moses' words—both the declaration and interpretation of those words are accomplished in an authoritative manner that is completely at odds with the reasoned approach to them that is the result of historical and literary scholarship modelled on the natural sciences. The clear hermeneutic principles of Deuteronomy, admittedly sketched here in an elementary way in anticipation of the following chapters, have profound implications for the role of scholarly interpretation of the biblical text.

If the Deuteronomic History tells a story in which certain past events are considered important for men's lives, it follows that when a literary and historical analysis of this work helps us understand, in a more profound way and in greater detail, what that story meant to its original audience, one effect of this scholarly retelling of the Deuteronomic story is to cast doubt on a scholarship that re-tells these stories but deliberately refuses to *apply* them, in Gadamer's sense of application. The manner in which Moses is described as interpreting God's words in the Book of Deuteronomy, and the manner in which the narrator interprets Moses' words in Joshua–2 Kings, seem to be at odds with the manner in which many scholars "interpret" the narrator's words in the Deuteronomic History. There is, of course, no a priori necessity for scholars to accept the biblical view on how the word of God is to be interpreted, but let them at least recognize that an impersonal and uninvolved interpretation does not in fact "hear the biblical message in the sense it had for its writer and first audience."[4]

When Noth, for example, concludes that a gifted individual wrote the Deuteronomistic History in the middle of the sixth century, probably somewhere in Palestine, and when Noth believes that the theme of this author's work was one of unrelieved and irreversible doom, we may say with some accuracy that the words of one so-called historian, the Deuteronomist, have been studied and interpreted by the standards of another historian, Martin Noth. But suppose we were to reverse the situation—and there appears to be no reason why we should be forbidden to do so—and ask what would be the case were Noth's historical work to be judged by the hermeneutical standards of the Deuteronomist? This type of reverse question is certainly not original, and some scholars pondering the respective roles of the historical and theological sciences have had something valuable to say on this matter. One has only to think of the important little work by Peter Stuhlmacher (1977), in contrast to Gerhard Maier's flawed attempt (1977), to realize that the problem must be faced squarely by biblical scholars lest the present crisis continue.

If it is true that biblical texts, which themselves most often report and interpret previous discourses to later audiences, do not exhibit the least concern to establish, in any manner that deserves to be called similar to that of an uninvolved and nonapplied scholarship, the sense which these previous traditions had for their original audiences, then of what value is this kind of scholarship for determining the biblical message? For clearly in such a case what the biblical message tells such a critic, even though that message is established by the biblical critic, is the relatively useless role of this kind of criticism in dealing with the crucial topics with which the Bible is typically concerned.

I believe that these cautionary remarks apply equally well to literary criticism of the Bible. Although I hope that the analysis that follows will be of interest to other scholars, it does not escape the dilemma expounded above. From a methodological point of view, literary criticism can claim for itself no greater sensitivity to the biblical message than historical criticism. The following pages simply represent the personal record of one scholar's attempt to understand, interpret, and apply the brilliant statement that is the Deuteronomic History. In a concluding postscript I intend to reflect upon my understanding of the Deuteronomic History as an example of hermeneutical application.

> Both the critic and the historian thus emerge from the self-forgetfulness to which they had been banished by a thinking for which the only criterion was the methodology of modern science. Both find their true ground in effective historical consciousness. (Gadamer, 1975:305)

Historical Critical Work on the Deuteronomic History

In Otto Kaiser's summary of the state of the art concerning the Deuteronomic History (1975:115–75), we find the following assessment concerning views on the prehistory of the Books of Samuel:

> Attention to the problem of the layers of Deuteronomistic and pre-Deuteronomistic redactions, which today is again strongly to the fore, is likely to be especially fruitful for future scholarship. (160)

The basic perspective according to which the present study proceeds is very much opposed to Kaiser's view. For if I have been at pains, here at the beginning, to underline my conviction that historical critical analysis is essential to an adequate scholarly understanding of the Deuteronomic History, it is my pessimistic view that almost two centuries of research on Deuteronomy and the other books it introduces—research that began with de Wette's ground-breaking work on Deuteronomy (1805) and culminated in Martin Noth's modern classic (1967)—have produced no hypothesis that can be described as historically or literarily adequate.

There seem to be two general reasons why the results of all this scholarly effort have been so disappointing, apart from the general hermeneutical criticism we advanced in the preceding section. First, an unacceptable proportion of criteria by which scholars have dated their material in literary, form, tradition, and redaction critical studies have proven to be either invalid or vastly inadequate for the task assigned to them: the construction of a reasonable hypothesis concerning the historical process that led to the formation of the Deuteronomic History. It would take a separate monograph to flesh out this position in some detail; it will remain, however, simply an assertion of the present study. The second reason is perhaps more important, since it can be seen to be in large part a cause of the first: historical criticism of the Bible is, after more than a century, something of a disappointment precisely because "literary criticism of biblical texts is still in its infancy" (Robertson, 1977:87). (The implication I have given to Robertson's assessment is mine, not his.)

First, if we may agree with the opinion that the importance of von Rad's contributions "for the whole of subsequent Old Testament scholarship on Deuteronomy cannot be too highly stated" (Kaiser, 1975:120), von Rad's historical critical method may thus offer us a classic example of why modern historical critical research on the Deuteronomic History has not fared better. (We are limiting ourselves here to judgments about research on the history of the text and traditions of the Bible, rather than on the history which it narrates, although the two are necessarily connected according to the hermeneutic stance I am taking.) Von Rad's crucial contribution to Deuteronomic research is based first of all upon his essay, "The Form-critical Problem of the Hexateuch" (1966; published originally in 1938). The heart of this provocative hypothesis concerns the original separation of the so-called Settlement and Sinai traditions presently found in the Hexateuch. The plausibility of such a separation rests almost completely on his ability to order diachronically the various reflexes of the

historical creeds he claimed to have found in Deuteronomy 6 and
26, Joshua 24, and elsewhere in the Bible. I have dealt elsewhere in
some detail with the failure of von Rad's diachronic criteria to
achieve their purpose (Polzin, 1977:153–76), and will offer only one
example of the invalidity of his dating procedures.

Von Rad's thesis would be convincing only if the historical creeds of
Deuteronomy 6, 26, and Joshua 24 indeed could be shown to be the
oldest representatives in the Bible of credal accounts of the saving acts
of God. But to prove his point von Rad appeals to that ubiquitous
guideline "the shorter a genre representative is, the older it probably
is." Now, since Deuteronomy 6, 26, and Joshua 24 are more concise
versions of the genre "historical creed" as regards both form and content, it follows that these versions, which omit mention of the Sinai
traditions (as opposed, say, to Neh 9) represent that early stage of
Israel's traditions when Settlement and Sinai stories were separate,
whereas Nehemiah 9 and the Hexateuch in its final form represent later
stages when both traditions had been combined.

The invalidity of the "shorter is older" guideline used in historical
critical study now seems fairly clear from modern studies such as Lord
(1968; first published in 1960) and Culley (1976:1–32). It remains a
puzzle why more recent works such as Koch (1969) still invoke the
principle.

The use of guidelines as questionable as the one just mentioned is by
no means an exceptional case in modern research on the biblical text.
The mere mention of such classic works as Wellhausen's *Prolegomena*
(1965; first published in 1878) and Noth's *A History of Pentateuchal
Traditions* (1972; first published in 1948) causes one to reflect: if the
best and most influential representatives of modern biblical scholarship
often base their arguments on weak and inadequate diachronic guidelines, what must be the case with works of lesser quality? The state of
affairs in Deuteronomic studies is symptomatic of the larger situation in
biblical studies in general.[5]

Another example of a questionable guideline commonly used for
separating earlier and later blocks of material in Deuteronomy is the
designation of the Deuteronomic style as characteristically employing
the second person singular, and of the Deuteronomistic style as characteristically using the second person plural (e.g., Kaiser, 1975:129–31).
In the following chapters, we will not employ the customary terminological distinction between "Deuteronomic" and "Deuteronomistic,"
since it rests upon the acceptance of specific historical critical conclusions; one may consult Cross (1973:274, n.1) for an explanation of the
distinction.

Typical of the hypotheses that result from the use of such guidelines is A. Weiser's hypothesis of six stages in the formation of the Books of Samuel, a view which Kaiser believes is "the most coherent picture" drawn on the subject (Kaiser, 1975:158–60).

If there is a present consensus that Deuteronomy–2 Kings in its present form constitutes a unified "Deuteronomistic History," it is also true that scholars have not even been able to agree on such fundamental aspects of this Deuteronomistic editing as, for example, whether its basic thematic proclamation is one of "unrelieved and irreversible doom" (Noth's view as characterized by Cross, 1973:275) or rather one which consists of a combination of punishment and hope (thus von Rad, Wolff, and Cross, with recipes that vary the sequencing and proportion of each of the two main thematic ingredients). One can certainly agree with Cross when he writes that "fresh attempts to examine the history of the Deuteronomistic tradition, while casting much light on the Deuteronomistic corpus, leave many embarrassing contradictions and unresolved problems" (1973:278). Not the least embarrassment for historical scholarship is the lack of agreement, after so prolonged an investigation, on the basic thematic thrust of the supposed Deuteronomistic editing.

The fundamental questions concerning the Deuteronomic History—of two editions or one, of a thematic profile either of irreversible doom or of destruction muted by grace—appear no closer to a solution now than they have been in the past. It remains to be seen whether Cross's thesis on the structure of the Deuteronomistic History (1973:274–89) may not in fact be the clearest picture we have so far.

Second, my remarks above on the operational priority of literary analysis find an unfortunate confirmation in modern studies on the Deuteronomic History by offering a plausible reason why men of genius such as Martin Noth have produced studies that, however sophisticated they may appear to be historically, must be termed inadequate from a preliminary literary critical point of view. Perhaps this helps us understand why, for example, Noth's critical reading of the Deuteronomistic History rejects one of its most obvious features. For Noth "astonishingly enough assumed that the purpose of this great undertaking was a purely negative one" (Kaiser, 1975:172). Whatever may be said of Noth's historical critical analysis, the function of a literary investigation of a work must be able to explain, not deny, its obvious features. And certainly its admixture of destruction and hope is an obvious and essential feature, one that later studies such as von Rad's, Wolff's, and Cross's have been quick to point out. We shall see in the next chapter how the Deuteronomic theme of conditional hope is inextricably woven into the

programmatic introduction to the Deuteronomic History, the Book of
Deuteronomy.

The present study, therefore, will not allude to previous critical
treatments of the Deuteronomic History with any frequency. It starts
afresh with a preliminary literary analysis and attempts to work its way
through the text without tackling the usual historical questions that
have been the primary focus of previous analyses. It seeks to define the
distinctive qualities of the work as a preliminary orientation to further
historical investigation:

> This operation consisting of going from the inner world of a work
> to its historical "ambience" and back to the work, demands a close
> cooperation between literary criticism and literary history, between
> aesthetics and history, which adds richness to both disciplines
> which receive support from each other. (Soter, 1970:96)

Modern Literary Criticism and Ancient Israelite Narrative

A compositional or perspectival approach recently has been shown to
offer a number of valuable insights in the area of literary criticism.[6] One
could object that literary approaches such as those underlying the present study are entirely inappropriate for textual material so obviously
editorialized over generations, perhaps even over centuries. After all, it
will be pointed out, to look for the "basic ideological stance" of recognized literary works such as those authored by well-known literary ar-
tists like Dostoevsky or Tolstoy under vastly better known historical
circumstances than those under which the biblical authors or editors
worked is an entirely different enterprise than that which confronts the
interpreter of biblical texts. Even if one concedes, for the sake of argument, the operational priority of literary over historical criticism, is it
not still likely that rhetorical approaches fashioned for modern western
literary texts would be unable to produce acceptable results when
applied to ancient Near Eastern texts such as the so-called
Deuteronomic History? Is this not a sound literary, historical, even
scholarly attitude to take when confronted with an enterprise such as
the present study? If, for example, genres differ from culture to culture, then surely literary approaches, even assumed to be relatively
successful when used to untangle the meaning of one culture's messages as found in historically verified "literary unities," are doubly suspect if they are rashly taken over for an analysis of texts that are not
only from vastly different cultures but also are obviously the result of a
long process of editoral reworking. Such an argument demands at least
a few prefatory words.

It is easier to respond to this argument than one who has been trained in the historical critical approach to biblical texts might assume. If we recognize that modern scholarly study of the Bible is itself largely a response to the challenges which the emerging "science" of historiography presented to students of the Bible in the nineteenth century (see on this the excellent essay of Miles, 1977), we must also recognize that the modern critical study of the Bible has not until recently been seriously challenged by sophisticated proponents of modern literary or hermeneutic studies. In fact the biblical scholar who may find it easy to ignore or even to confidently criticize present efforts to subject the Bible to serious literary study is actually not so well equipped as he may imagine to take a definite stand on the issue.

Indeed, it is true that the main lines of modern biblical research have rarely produced sustained and serious reflections on questions about how one culture differs from another, and how these differences affect, and are reflected in, the literate and literary artifacts of those cultures.[7] Moreover, it is becoming increasingly clear to those both within and without biblical studies that form or genre criticism, as it has developed since Gunkel's time, is, despite superficial similarities, a vastly different enterprise than is the study of genres outside the biblical disciplines. So the historical critical challenge to literary analyses such as the present attempt does formulate concerns that are theoretically important and appropriate. However, it is equally true that the proponents of such a challenge possess no greater authority, insight, or erudition to answer the questions or respond to the concerns they pose than those scholars to whom the challenge is proposed, apart from the normal differentials between individual scholars. What may be "historically" perceptive may be "literarily" myopic, and vice versa.[8]

When we reflect upon the disjointed nature of many biblical passages and upon precipitous explanations of widespread editorial activity within it, it is worthwhile to remember that, whatever the historical process that gave rise to the present text, the compositional technique used to analyze these texts should be judged and evaluated primarily by the results it achieves. One can of course assume that wholesale editorial activity is the origin of most of the complicated shifts in perspective so obvious at many points in the biblical text.[9] If, on the other hand, we assume that many gaps, dislocations, and reversals in the biblical text may profitably be viewed as the result of the use (authorial or editorial) of several different viewpoints within the narrative, then, whether the present text is the product either of a single mind or of a long and complicated editorial process, we are still responsible for making sense of the present text by assuming that the present text, in more cases than previously realized, does make sense. A particular biblical passage "makes sense" if it repeats compositional patterns already encountered in what precedes it and foreshadows perspectives that lie ahead.[10]

The Deuteronomic History

That corpus of the Hebrew Bible that stretches from the Book of Deuteronomy through 2 Kings is called the Deuteronomic History. It consists of seven books: Deuteronomy, Joshua, Judges, 1–2 Samuel, and 1–2 Kings. The analysis that follows aims at segmenting the first three books of this corpus into a number of basic units that allow it to exhibit more obviously the various points of view that make up its compositional structure. The term "composition" therefore has to do with the relationships of various points of view, on a number of levels, that make up a literary work. I will assume from the start that the Deuteronomic History is a unified literary work; I do not base this assumption upon previous historical critical analyses. By the term "Deuteronomist" I mean that person or persons, functioning in an authorial or editorial role, and responsible for the final form of the Deuteronomic History. There may actually have been no single individual or recognizable group to whom this term refers. I use it heuristically to designate that imagined personification of a combination of literary features that seem to constitute the literary composition of the Deuteronomic History. For me, the text creates the Deuteronomist's features as much as it creates those of Moses. The Deuteronomist is the "implied author" of this work.[11]

One way to get at a useful framework within the text is to attend to the various shifts that occur within the text and within the various levels of the text. These shifts often indicate the implied author's devices for framing his work and, once identified, can help us understand how he may be said to manipulate and program his readers' responses. The various points of view realized in the text are represented there in a number of ways that are interrelated, and an attempt to articulate a framework is the first step in analyzing what a text or its author seems to be saying. To much of what is written, its "author" does not subscribe. He may, for example, be offering up a position to ridicule. A framework helps us distinguish an author's stated position from statements he transmits for various other reasons.[12]

If we begin with V. N. Voloshinov's demonstration (1973) of the crucial importance of "reported speech" in language analysis, we are immediately able to segment the Deuteronomic History into two basic units which, although not quantitatively balanced, are amazingly complementary from a compositional point of view. It has long been emphasized that basic to the viewpoint of the Deuteronomist is "that system of prophetic prediction and its exactly observed fulfilment which pervades the whole work of this writer" (von Rad, 1966:208–9). If we apply this obvious aspect of the Deuteronomist's position to his work *in toto,* we see that a compositional device occurring innumerable times within it—that is, first the word of God is reported by a prophet, then a description of events follows with the explicit statement that these events happened "according to the word of God" (or a statement similar in meaning)—appears to be operating in the relationship between the two largest segments of the work. The first segmentation of the Deuteronomic History results in separating the Book of Deuteronomy from Joshua–2 Kings. We thereby see that Deuteronomy, in that it is almost totally a number of Mosaic speeches, functions as an expression of the prophetic word of God, and that Joshua–2 Kings mainly recounts events that constitute "its exactly observed fulfilment."

The balanced nature of this first division is seen when one applies Voloshinov's distinction between reporting and reported speech to the two basic sections of the Deuteronomic History. The Book of Deuteronomy contains thirty-four chapters. Almost all of the book consists of reported speech, mostly in direct discourse and mostly of Moses, whereas only about fifty-six verses are reporting speech, the Deuteronomic narrator's, which forms the context for Moses's direct utterances. On the other hand, Joshua–2 Kings is predominantly reporting speech, that of the narrator, with a significantly smaller amount of reported speech scattered throughout. (However, here the disproportion between reporting and reported speech is not as great as in Deuteronomy.) In Deuteronomy, reported speech of its hero is emphasized; in Joshua–2 Kings, the reporting speech of its narrator is dominant. It is as though the Deuteronomist is telling us in Deuteronomy, "Here is what God has prophesied concerning Israel," but in Joshua–2 Kings, "This is how God's word has been exactly fulfilled in Israel's history from the settlement to the destruction of Jerusalem and the Exile."

Another significant aspect of the relationship between Deuteronomy on the one hand and Joshua–2 Kings on the other is seen in the internal arrangement of reporting and reported speech within each of the two segments themselves. In Joshua–2 Kings it is not enough to chronicle Israel's continual disobedience and the countless disastrous events that resulted from such disobedience. As von Rad has detailed for us with regard to 1–2 Kings (1966:205–21), the narrative systematically singles out the reported speech of prophets who periodically arise to announce to various individuals the punishing word of God. Thus, for example, intermittent recurring reported prophetic speech interrupts the narrative at least eleven times in 1–2 Kings (von Rad, 1966:208–12), apparently to reinforce what appears to be the general point of view of Joshua–2 Kings taken as a whole: how Israel's history is dependent upon the word of God that is the Book of Deuteronomy. In Joshua–2 Kings, the reporting narrator is intermittently supported in his basic story of Israel's history by the occasional reported words of various prophets. The preponderant reporting narrative of the narrator and the intermittent reported speech of a number of prophets within the narrative help to articulate the same evaluative point of view.

When we look at the Book of Deuteronomy, the relationship between the reporting narration and reported prophetic speech is reversed. Reported prophetic speech absolutely predominates, with reporting narration at a minimum and on occasion a confusing interruption. We will discuss this last point in detail when we discuss the composition of Deuteronomy, but for now it is enough to underline how the respective roles of narrator's word and prophetic word in Deuteronomy form a mirror image of their roles in Joshua–2 Kings. In Deuteronomy the unobtrusive reporting speech of the retiring narrator reinforces and supports here and there the preponderant reported speech of the greatest prophet of them all, Moses. In Joshua–2 Kings, lesser prophets occasionally appear to reinforce by their reported speech the now preponderant and highly visible reporting speech of the narrator.

If we first divide up the Deuteronomic History into Deuteronomy on the one hand and Joshua–2 Kings on the other, the concept of reported speech, primarily in the form of direct discourse, allows us to see that in the first section, according to quantity and distribution, Moses' words are to the narrator's words as, in the second section, the narrator's words are to the words of a number of lesser prophets. The significance of this first compositional relationship will become apparent as we further analyze each of the two main sections of the Deuteronomic History.

The distribution of reported speech and its reporting context has helped form a preliminary criterion that allowed us both to segment the text into its two largest main sections and to discover a couple of complementary relationships between these sections. This criterion can now be used to help us articulate a central problem confronting any attempt at a literary interpretation of the Deuteronomic History: *wherein does the ultimate semantic authority of this complex lie?* By the phrase "ultimate semantic authority" we mean the basic ideological and evaluative point of view of a work (Bakhtin, 1973), the unifying ideological stance of a work's "implied author." Do we find it in the speech of the narrator, forming the slight frame of the Book of Deuteronomy and the main body of Joshua–2 Kings, or is it present in the reported speech both of

Moses, forming the bulk of Deuteronomy, and of other mouthpieces of God scattered throughout the rest of the history?

Another way to express the problem is this: there are two kinds of speech in the Deuteronomic History, the word of the narrator and the reported words of those individuals who form part of his story. What is immediately obvious, and to be expected, from even a superficial reading of the text is that among the figures in the story preeminent place is given to the figure of God himself, and that the preeminent speech the Deuteronomic narrator reports is speech purported to be from God himself. Therefore, is the implied author's stance to be found in the words of the narrator or in the words of God found in the narrative? Or, as a third possibility, is it found somehow synthesized both in the narration that quantitatively predominates and in the quoted words of God that are quantitatively much less dominant in the Deuteronomic History?

All three of the possibilities just mentioned assume that the Deuteronomic History is indeed a *monologue,* that is, its ideological evaluation is carried out from a single dominating point of view which subordinates all others in the work. The Deuteronomic History, viewed as the juxtaposition of two principal utterances, that of its narrator and that of God, is constructed as an utterance within an utterance: the reported word of God is found within the reporting word of the narrator. Stated in these terms, the ideological composition of this work appears to be overtly monologic, since the immediate obvious message of the narrator is, "God has said 'such and such' to Israel, and the events of Israel's history have happened in the way I am now describing them: as a fulfillment of God's word." This is the narrator's obvious conclusion about the history of Israel. He says to the reader, "In terms of what God and myself say, 'I and the Father are one.' "

Bakhtin summarizes the characteristics of a novel that is basically monological in structure; his words are equally valid for a work such as the Deuteronomic History:[13]

> How and in what elements of the verbal whole is the author's ulti-
> mate semantic authority realized? For the monologic novel this
> question is very easily answered. Whatever types of word the
> novelist-monologist may introduce and whatever their composi-
> tional distribution may be, the author's interpretations and evalua-
> tions must dominate all others and must comprise a compact and
> unambiguous whole. (1973:168)

Viewed from this perspective, the central authority figure of the history is God and, consequently, the prophets of God within the narrative who are described as reporting his words. In addition, since the history purports to show how this divine speech has been verified in history, we may say that the narrator's general position may be understood as one that is in agreement with the ideological positions of the central authority figures of his story. It is apparent therefore that if the Deuteronomic History is viewed as the intersection of two words, God's and the narrator's, the overall picture presented therein is one in which, concerning the ideological plane, the narrator's word is presented as subordinate to God's word which the narrator reports. The Deuteronomic History is not the intersection of two equally weighted words, but the conjoining of God's word to the narrator's word in a dominant to subordinate relationship respectively.

When we inquire further into the overtly monologic structure of the history on the plane of ideology, we find that the question is not quite so simply answered. For even if we can say that the narrator clearly intends to subordinate his position to the word of God which he reports to us, we still must inquire what precisely does God say within the work, and how precisely is his word said to be fulfilled in it? For clearly even a monologue may contain a variety of ideas and viewpoints that may or may not compete with one another with equal weight or authority. This raises the question of whether the history, as an overt monologue in which the Deuteronomist has subordinated his narrator's voice to God's voice as its echo, actually may contain a *hidden dialogue* within the word of God itself and/or within the "subordinate" word of the narrator. There is not just one utterance of God but a number of them reported to have been said by God throughout the historical period covered by the narrative. There is not just one utterance of the narrator interpreting God's word, but a number of them.[14]

Therefore the possibility exists that, whatever may be the obvious monologic composition of the Deuteronomic History taken as a unity, a closer reading of the text may reveal a hidden dialogue between competing voices within the various utterances of God both in themselves and as interpreted by the Deuteronomic narrator. Bakhtin describes theoretically what would be the case if a work were indeed a true dialogue:

> The weakening or destruction of the monological context occurs only when two equally and directly object-oriented utterances come together. Two equally and directly object-oriented words within a single context cannot stand side by side without dialogically intersecting, regardless of whether they corroborate one another or on the contrary contradict one another, or have any other sort of dialogical relationship (the relationship of question and answer, for example).

> Two equal-weighted words which speak to the same subject, once
> they have come together, must become oriented one to the other.
> Two embodied thoughts cannot lie side by side like two objects—
> they must come into inner contact, i.e., must enter into a semantic
> bond. (1973:156)

In the light of what I have argued earlier in this chapter, an attempt to answer such a basic question as whether we have in the history a monologue or a dialogue, in the sense employed by Bakhtin, ought not, at first, be based upon the historical critical approaches of modern biblical scholarship. From a methodological point of view, historical criticism is ill-suited for beginning attempts at understanding the important questions that an interpretation of the Deuteronomic History involves, however necessary such approaches are for an adequate understanding. Therefore, the present study begins at a point that is operationally prior to the kinds of historical critical stances that up to now have divided biblical scholars on the structure of the Deuteronomic History, e.g., the question of the existence and description of at least two editions of this work. For, whatever might be the Deuteronomic History's genesis, what we are now asking is where does a close compositional reading of this work place it within the dynamic poles of a dialogue on one hand and a monologue on the other? Whatever the answer may turn out to be, no help is at this preliminary point relevant, since both a predominantly dialogic and a predominantly monologic ideology could conceivably be the final result of either one or more editions of the Deuteronomic History. At the same time, I fully recognize that historical critical analyses are methodologically useful, indeed necessary to further refine and even, in some cases, alter preliminary approximations of a dialogic or monologic composition of our text.

It does seem clear that even with regard to the overtly monologic nature of the Deuteronomic History, it would be too simplistic to say that the ultimate semantic authority is to be found solely in the words of God reported in the history, or solely in the words of the narrator that form the controlling narrative. For clearly, even though the narrator assumes that his words are subordinate to God's words, by the very fact that he "takes over" what God has said and uses it for his own purposes, to this extent he is subordinating God's words to his own. Therefore, it seems that we would be more faithful to an intuitive first impression of the work to assume that ultimate semantic authority, be it predominantly monologic or dialogic, will be found somehow synthesized in the narration that quantitatively predominates, but by authorial plan is subordinate, and in the quoted words of God that are quantitatively subordinate, but by authorial plan dominant.

Another way of describing the position just stated would be to say the following: the ultimate semantic authority of a work, the implied author's "intention,"[15] a text's basic ideological perspective, can be realized not only by a narrator's direct word, but as Bakhtin puts it, "with the help of the words of others, created and distributed in a specific way as belonging to others" (1973:155). Moreover, if it is possible to find the author's voice in the words of others, conversely it is also possible to find in the author's words, or in those of his narrator, reflections of points of view that are subordinate or even contrary to his basic ideological position. In other words, the specific composition of a work on the ideological plane is not always concurrent with its composition on less basic levels such as the phraseological level of reporting/reported speech.

The above point is especially relevant to our discussion of the compositional structure of the Deuteronomic History in general and of its two basic sequential sections in particular.[16] An adequate explanation of the Deuteronomic History's framework must begin to delineate which of its utterances are single-voiced and which are double-voiced, on a number of compositional planes. Moreover, on the basic plane of a work's ideology, a proposed framework ought to be able to describe which of the text's utterances or words express its dominant ideological voice(s), which its subordinated or dependent ideological voice or voices, and which utterances express both kinds of voices. Furthermore, the framework constructed ought to illuminate the various relationships between competing voices of whatever level in the text, and between various levels themselves, that is, the concurrence or not of the compositional structure of different planes.

The basic requirements of an adequately constructed framework are further complicated by the object we are investigating. The Deuteronomic History is an especially complex arrangement of messages within a message, so that it would be especially helpful to construct a satisfactory description of how its internal messages interrelate to form that message we call the Deuteronomic History.

Two

THE BOOK OF
DEUTERONOMY

Moses and the Deuteronomic Narrator
as Hero and "Author" of the Book

1. Concerning the attribution of utterances in Deuteronomy, most of the book is a series of direct quotations of Moses. Within this body of Mosaic utterances, in one instance, 27:1–8, Moses and the elders of Israel speak as one in direct discourse, and in another instance in the same chapter, 27:9–10, Moses and the Levitical priests are quoted in direct discourse. In all other cases in the reporting of Moses' words, Moses speaks alone. In addition, the Deuteronomic narrator, like Moses, is able to quote God in direct discourse: five times toward the end of the book, 31:14b, 16b–21, 23b; 32:49–52; and 34:4b.

The book is more than just Moses' utterances within the narrator's utterances: Moses' utterances continually quote, with direct discourse, other utterances, as for example throughout chapters 2 and 3 which are mostly various quotations within a quote. Here Moses is quoted by the narrator as quoting a number of others. Each of these cases can be described as an utterance (of the person quoted by Moses) within an utterance (of Moses) within an utterance (of the narrator).

It is sometimes more complicated than this. For example, 1:28 has the narrator quoting Moses quoting Israel quoting Israel's scouts at Kadesh-Barnea. And in 2:4–5; 32:26, and 40–42, we find the narrator quoting Moses quoting Yahweh quoting himself, all in direct discourse. In such cases, we have examples of an utterance within an utterance within an utterance within an utterance.

The varying complexities of quotes within quotes that make up most of Deuteronomy is further enhanced by a complicated temporal scheme relating the quotes to their context. At first, Moses' words look mostly to past events and past statements, as in the first address of Moses in 1:6–4:40. Then in his second address, 5:1b–28:68, Moses starts to turn his attention to the future, and a much larger proportion of other people's utterances found within this address express what they will, should, or should not say in the future, e.g., 6:20–25; 7:17; 9:4. Then in the third address of Moses, 29:2–31:6, whenever Moses quotes anyone directly, it is their *future* utterances he quotes, coinciding with the almost complete orientation of this address toward the distant future. Finally, the group of Moses' sayings that ends the book's collection of his utterances, 31:7–33:29, also emphasizes the future in its quotes, as 31:17b and 32:37–42 show.

The temporal relations of Moses' inclusion of utterances within his own utterances is occasionally even more complex, as for example in 9:26–29. In this pericope the narrator is quoting Moses who, in the valley of Beth-Peor, is quoting what he (Moses) had said at Horeb to the effect that he had prayed that the Egyptians would not say "such and such" at some time subsequent to the events at Horeb.

One of the immediate results of this exceedingly complex network of utterances within utterances is the deliberate representation in Deuteronomy of a vast number of intersecting statements, sometimes in agreement with one another, sometimes interfering with one another. This enables the book to be the repository of a plurality of viewpoints, all working together to achieve an effect on the reader that is multidimensional. We should not be surprised that such a sophisticated work has come down to us from the first millennium B.C.E. This complex intersecting of viewpoints deserves to be taken seriously and analyzed carefully by the modern reader.

The immediate hero of the book is Moses as the spokesman of God. The only other person who is quoted by the narrator is God. (We have already mentioned that Moses speaks with the elders of Israel in 27:1–8, and that he speaks with the Levitical priests in 27:9–10.) Thus there are only two direct voices[1] which the narrator asks us to attend to in the book: Moses' and God's. Deuteronomy may be described therefore as the speech of the Deuteronomic narrator in which he directly quotes only two figures in the story, predominantly Moses and sometimes God.

As far as Moses is concerned, none of the words of God which he quotes are described as also having been heard by the people, except for the decalogue (5:6–21). In fact, in chapter 5, Moses makes the point that only when God spoke the decalogue was he heard by the people: all the other words of God were deliberately avoided by the people as directly heard words, and were to be transmitted indirectly to them through Moses reporting. As for the narrator, he like Moses directly reports God's words. In 31:14b he relates, in direct discourse, God's words to Moses; he does so again in 31:16b–21; 32:49–52; and 34:4b. He also directly reports God's words to Joshua in 31:23b. *In all these cases, he is a privileged observer and reporter of God's words, just as he describes Moses describing himself to be in chapter 5.* The point is unavoidable that only two personages in the book directly hear and relate God's words (apart from the decalogue): Moses and the Deuteronomic narrator.

2. If only Moses and the narrator are privileged to hear God's word in the book, and even though Moses reports the bulk of God's words found therein, only the words of God that are reported by the narrator are *immediately* reported there. The preponderance of God's words found in Deuteronomy are on another level, a secondary or mediate level. That is, the narrator quotes Moses as quoting God. One might therefore begin one's analysis of the book by articulating a problem similar to the one made at the end of the last chapter concerning the entire Deuteronomic History. There it was asked whether the ideological position of the Deuteronomist as implied author is to be found in the words of God or in the words of the Deuteronomic narrator. Here we may ask an analogous question. How reliable a narrator do we have here, and how is his voice related to the voice of the book's implied author?

The emphasis in Deuteronomy is on the legislative and judicial word of God, and the conveyors of this word are two: Moses and the narrator. In interpreting the book, do we understand Moses' word as subordinate to the narrator's, or is the narrator's word subordinate to that of Moses? The narrator might be said to be the main carrier of the implied author's ideological stance since he alone conveys to us Moses' conveying of the words of God that constitute most of the book. But if so, one notices that, as vehicle for the book's ultimate semantic authority (he alone can tell us what Moses says that God says to the reader of the book), the narrator seems at great pains to impress upon his reader that it is Moses, and Moses alone, who possessed the type of reliable authority to convey accurately and authoritatively the direct words of God that form most of the book. We find ourselves in a dilemma: we are asked by the narrator to accept his assertion that "there has not arisen a prophet since in Israel like Moses, whom the LORD knew face to face . . ." (34:10), at the same time as it is only the Deuteronomic narrator who knows Moses face to face! If the path to God is through Moses, the path to Moses is through the text's narrator. Does the reader interpret the reported words of Moses by means of the reporting context: "Moses was God's greatest prophet, therefore believe *him* when he says . . ."? Or does one interpret the reporting words of the narrator by means of the reported words of Moses: "Moses said such and such, therefore believe *me,* as narrator, when I say . . ."?

In our brief introductory remarks to the Deuteronomic History above, we made the assumption that ultimate semantic authority in the work, that is, the implied author's main ideological stance, probably should be looked for both in the words of God and in the words of the narrator. We can apply this assumption to the Book of Deuteronomy itself by stating that the ultimate ideological stance of the book ought to be looked for both in the reporting words of the narrator, its "author's" spokesman, and in the reported words of Moses, its hero. We may note that in Deuteronomy we find both the narrator and Moses utilizing the formula that is the basic constituent of the whole history: "God said 'such and such'; therefore this event happened precisely to fulfill His word." For example, Moses is quoted as saying:

> "And the LORD heard your words and was angered, and he swore, 'Not one of these men of this evil generation shall see the good land which I swore to give to your fathers . . .' " (1:34–35)

In the next chapter, Moses is then quoted as saying:

> "And the time from our leaving Kadesh-Barnea until we crossed the brook Zered was thirty-eight years, until the present generation, that is, the men of war, had perished from the camp *as the LORD had sworn to them.*" (2:14; emphasis added)

We find the Deuteronomist employing the same compositional device in the narrator's portions of Deuteronomy. Thus the narrator says,

> And the LORD said to Moses, "This is the land of which I swore to Abraham, to Isaac, and to Jacob, 'I will give it to your descendants.' I have let you see it with your eyes but you shall not go over there" (34:4),

to which he immediately adds in 34:5:

> So Moses the servant of the LORD died there in the land of Moab, *according to the word of the LORD.* (emphasis added)

These pericopes illustrate very well how elements of the ultimate semantic stance of the Book of Deuteronomy (as of the whole history), to which is subordinated everything else in the text, are to be found both in the utterances of the narrator and in the utterances of Moses as hero of the book.

We may expect to find characteristics of the narrator's speech in the hero's speech, and vice versa, on any or all compositional planes of the book. Both words will be "double-voiced," and to this extent the question must be raised about Deuteronomy which was previously raised about the whole Deuteronomic History: if it is clear that this book is an overt monologue (its narrator is clearly stating, "As far as our basic stance is concerned, Moses and I are one."), to what extent may we characterize the book, in its compositional structure, as a hidden dialogue or even as a hidden polemic? Are there competing and equally weighted points of view represented in Deuteronomy on a number of compositional planes? Concerning the ideological plane of the book, the four pericopes quoted above show that it is probably misguided to attribute dominant viewpoints solely to the narrator or solely to Moses. It is possible, I believe, to determine by careful rhetorical analysis elements of the text that can be said to belong to the ultimate ideological stance of the book, just as one can discover and describe other elements that are clearly subordinate to this viewpoint.

The Reporting Speech of Deuteronomy:
The Narrator's Direct Utterances

The reporting context of Deuteronomy comprises only about fifty-six verses: 1:1–5; 2:10–12, 20–23; 3:9, 11, 13b–14; 4:41–5:1a; 10:6–7, 9; 27:1a, 9a, 11; 28:69; 29:1a; 31:1, 7a, 9–10a, 14a, 14c–16a, 22–23a, 24–25, 30; 32:44–45, 48; 33:1; 34:1–4a, 5–12. The remainder of the book is composed of utterances of various individuals, mostly Moses, reported in direct discourse.

1. What is the position of the Deuteronomic narrator and what is his voice like?[2] The obvious relation of reporting to reported speech shows that, on the phraseological plane at least,[3] Moses' words are to some extent subordinated to the narrator's. Although the narrator has deliberately put himself in the background and Moses in the foreground, the narrator's word, for very specific reasons, remains visibly separate on the surface of the text. Since the book's surface is constructed mostly in two voices, and since the implied author could have chosen completely to merge his narrator's voice with the voice of his hero, as seems to be the case in the Book of Qoheleth, it is clear that Deuteronomy emphasizes, even on the phraseological plane, a distinction between the word of Moses and the word of the narrator. What are the implications of such an arrangement?

The most obvious functions of the narrator's words are that they situate the words of Moses in time and space (when, where, and in what circumstances Moses spoke the words reported by the narrator), and that they define the preeminent position Moses held as leader and legislator of his people. It is also clear that the narrator does not attempt to interpret the words of Moses to any great extent in the Book of Deuteronomy. This is to be expected since the other main section of the history, Joshua–2 Kings, so clearly and so often indicates that it functions as the Deuteronomist's main interpretation of the word of Moses found in Deuteronomy. The *overt* function of the narrator's direct utterances in Deuteronomy is to represent to his readers the word of Moses as preeminent, and Moses himself as the greatest prophet in Israel's history.

On the other hand, there are clear indications, even within the brief scope of fifty-six verses, that the content and distribution of the narrator's direct utterances serve to exalt his importance as one who is as necessary to his contemporaries as Moses was to his, and to legitimize that self-serving claim by means obvious and subtle. We now want to explain how, within the narrator's apparently monologic utterances, there are in fact two ideological perspectives that interfere with one another to such an extent that the narrative carries within itself (just as Moses' utterances do) a hidden tension concerning the preeminence of Moses.

Most of the narrator's words provide a suitable frame for the words of Moses in that the former do not distract the reader, either by their quantity or in their emotional power, from attending to the preponderantly powerful words of the book's hero. Examples of the narrator's respectful reticence are found in 1:1–5 and 4:41–48 in the first Mosaic address, 5:1a and 28:69 (Hebrew versification) in the second address, and 29:1a in the third.

But there are other words of the narrator which in fact serve to "break frame" (Goffman, 1974), either by distracting the reader away from Moses' main message through the insertion of a number of apparently pedantic, explanatory side-remarks, or else by simply interrupting Moses' words without apparent reason, such as within Moses' third short address: "So Moses continued to speak these words to all Israel, saying . . ." (31:1). What do these narrative "interruptions" of Moses' speech mean?

A typical explanation of these occasional frame-breaks points to some sort of editorial activity aimed at (haphazardly) bringing the text up-to-date, either by explaining archaic terms for contemporary readers or by artificially adding other words of Moses that the editor felt were sufficiently important (thus, e.g., von Rad, 1966:79–80). If it cannot be decided whether these verses indicate the activity of an author or rather of an editor, an argument for their not being crude or haphazard interruptions of the text can still be articulated. Historical critical explanations of these verses as crude editorial additions may be considered premature, since it can be plausibly argued that such frame-breaks perform an integral and important function in the text. Rather than indications of sloppy editorial tampering, these breaks in the text serve to represent the narrator's subtle but powerful claim to his audience to be the sole authentic interpreter of Moses' words. Let us look at some of these passages.

2. In Moses' first address, 1:6–4:40, the text abruptly shifts from Moses' utterance to the narrator's comment, and back again, five times. For example, in chapter 2, Moses is recalling to the Israelites how they had avoided passing through Edom at the command of the LORD, and had turned toward Moab. Then the text suddenly shifts to another voice:

> The Emim formerly lived there [Moab], a people great and many and tall as the Anakim; like the Anakim they were also known as Rephaim, but the Moabites call them Emim. The Horites also lived in Seir formerly, but the sons of Esau settled in their stead: as Israel did to the land of their possession which the LORD gave to them. (2:10–12)

Four other interruptions, similar in pedantic tone and content, appear in this first address: 2:20–23; 3:9, 11, 13b–14. What strikes one immediately is how relatively minor appears to be those points of Moses' speech that the Deuteronomist feels important enough to interrupt with explanatory background information from his narrator. Somehow, what Moses at this point is saying is especially important to the Deuteronomist's audience, and so the text is interrupted with information whose contemporary importance is indicated within these interruptions by phrases such as, ". . . even to this day" (2:22); "is it [Og's bedstead] not in Rabbah of the Ammonites?" (3:11); and ". . . Havvoth-jair, as it is to this day" (3:14). Given these verses' nature as explanations of relatively minor aspects of Moses' speech, why are they there at all, if we are to assume that they are not disruptive to the text?

As Uspensky brings out (1973:148) and Booth (1961:passim) amply illustrates, shifts such as these often indicate an author's device for manipulating and programming his readers' responses. Specifically then, even if we might have lost, over the ages, historical information that would help us see the importance that the content of these interruptions might have had to the Deuteronomist and his audience, it still must be pointed out here that frame-breaks of this kind are a frequent device by which an author/editor, even of an ancient work, may *involve* his readers more in his message. In the case of Deuteronomy, this would involve shifting the reader back and forth a number of times between the "that day" of Moses and the "this day" of the Deuteronomist. By breaking frame five times, the Deuteronomist may very well be forcing the reader to shift back and forth a number of times between narrated past and narrator's present.

We are suggesting that the Deuteronomic narrator is pictured here as subtly reinforcing the *difference* between Moses' audience and his own audience so that the latter, while attending focally to Moses' powerful authority and message, is subsidiarily and intermittently kept aware of the distance between the two audiences. These frame-breaks force the Deuteronomic audience to shift from a subsidiary awareness that they are descendants of these earlier Israelites, and therefore distant hearers of Moses' teaching, to a momentary focal awareness of this situation, and then back again to the continuing focal awareness of the earlier context of the story.

By chapter 4, principally by means of these five breaks, the reader of the Deuteronomist's day has begun to *feel*, inchoately and almost without being aware of it, what he will by the end of the book consciously apprehend, that the book's author, through his narrator, is as important to him as Moses was to those earlier Israelites.

We can be more specific than this. The function of these frame-breaks appears to be a chief means by which the narrator begins to program his audience to realize that he is indeed the Moses of his generation. In this first address Moses looks to the past and invokes it as the interpretant for his audience's present and future. If we may anticipate briefly our analysis of the utterances of Moses to make a point, we will see that the perspective of Moses' first address involves a shifting back and forth between "the day that you stood before the LORD your God at Horeb" (4:10) and the "this day" when "I set before you . . . this law in Moab" (4:8). Moses uses "that day" at Horeb to help him cement "this day's" interpretation of that law. We are suggesting that just as Moses is described as doing this explicitly in his first address, so also the Deuteronomist, by taking Moses' "this day" and transforming it into "that day" (1:3) when Moses set forth the law, uses it to cement "this day's," that is, the Deuteronomist's interpretation of Moses' law, namely, the history from Joshua to 2 Kings as recounted by his narrator.

The deliberate comparison made between how Moses taught and how the Deuteronomic narrator teaches is all the more impressive when we consider that he here implies it by subtle compositional means rather than by bald and bold statements. When we come to our analysis of Moses' addresses, we will see that this same comparison between Moses and the narrator is much more boldly stated. The difference is instructive. Given the overt message of the history, "Moses was the greatest prophet of God: I the narrator am just his interpreter," if the narrator is to convey to his audience an analogous status in regard to Moses as interpreter of the Law, he will be more inclined to represent such a point of view more or less clearly through *Moses'* utterances, while leaving to his own utterances more subtle ways of manipulating his audience in the same direction.

The implication of the foregoing analysis is that parts of the narrative which serve either as a frame for the Mosaic utterances or as a statement of Moses' eminence are to be distinguished from other parts of that narrative which break frame in order to prepare the reader to accept authorial claims for eminence, or at least for a status equal in his own generation to Moses' status in the latter's generation.

3. The frame-breaks that interrupt Moses' second address (5:1b–28:68) also function as interruptions designed to put the narrator on the same level as Moses, and even to *limit* the authority of Moses. The first interruption occurs in 10:6–9. Here, after the narrator relates information about Israel's itinerary and about Aaron's death in vv. 6 and 7, we read:

> *At that time* the LORD set apart the tribe of Levi to carry the ark of the covenant of the LORD, to stand before the LORD to minister to him and to bless in his name *to this day.* Therefore Levi has no portion or inheritance with his brothers; the LORD is his inheritance, as the LORD your God said to him. (10:8–9; emphasis added)

There are a number of features worth noting in this frame-break, besides the function it has of jolting the reader back to a focal awareness of another time and circumstance. In v. 8, the italicized words recall the typical Mosaic device of using "that day" to clarify "this day"; only in this example it is not clear who is supposed to be employing the device. Second, the list of levitical functions, to carry the ark, to stand before the LORD to minister to him, to bless, seems to be a summary of God's words, here apparently rendered in indirect discourse which continues on into v. 9. Then, in v. 9b, "as the LORD your God said to him" suddenly shifts the report into direct discourse again, as the phrase, "the LORD your God" shows. Vv. 8 and 9 sound very much like a continuation of Moses' speech in v. 5. On the other hand, the phrases, "At that time . . . to this day," are ambiguous enough to make us wonder whether in fact vv. 8 and 9 are a continuation of the frame-break of vv. 6 and 7.

The very ambiguity of vv. 8 and 9 serves to underline what we have been noticing all along: the utterance of Moses and the utterance of the narrator are in many respects indistinguishable. Both employ the device, "God said such and such; such and such an event fulfills God's word." As we have already noted, 1:34–35 and 2:14 have Moses speaking this way, and 34:4–5 has the narrator speaking in exactly the same way. Again, as we have seen, since both use the "that day . . . this day" device in their utterances, v. 8 could have been spoken by Moses just as well as by the narrator. We should point out here that v. 9b, if attributed to the narrator, would be a rare instance in Deuteronomy of the narrator's speech employing "quasi-direct discourse" (cf. Voloshinov, 1973:137–59). Here, the presence of "as the LORD your God said to him" does not indicate the narrator's utterance (since he never uses the second person to indicate the audience for whom he is writing) but rather Moses' reported speech in some kind of direct discourse. Vv. 8 and 9 are a good example of how the voices of Moses and narrator echo one another.

Chapter 27 contains three narrative interruptions:

> Now Moses and the elders of Israel commanded the people . . .
>   (27:1a)
> And Moses and the levitical priests said to all Israel . . . (27:9a)
> And Moses charged the people the same day . . . (27:11)

It is possible to regard chapter 27 as an obvious and awkward interruption of Moses' second address only if one forgets that the whole book shows signs of an intricately planned composition. What is important here is that Moses speaks in conjunction with the elders of Israel and with the levitical priests. If we have faith in the deliberate compositional complexity of the book, we are led to see the frame-breaks of 27:1a, 9a as further diminishing the uniqueness of Moses' authority at a key place in the text.

The frame-break of 27:11 is similar to the frame-break within the third address, 31:1. Both appear to continue the Deuteronomist's practice of shifting the reader back periodically to the narrator's present in order to reinforce the reader's experience that it is the narrator who is the vital link between Moses and the "this day" of the reporting speech.

Within the narrator's direct utterances, it is by means of the distribution of the frame-breaks we have just discussed that the unique status of Moses, emphasized in the other parts of the reporting narrative, is undermined. The narrator's utterances are spoken in two ideological voices which interfere with one another: an overt, obvious voice that exalts Moses and plays down its own role, and a hidden voice that will soon exalt itself at the expense of Moses' uniqueness.

4. In summary, our analysis of the distribution and content of the various "authorial" interruptions by the narrator in Moses' three addresses indicates a subtle but effective strategy on the part of the Deuteronomist gradually to diminish the unique status of his hero at the very same time as the retrospective elements of Moses' own utterances are enhancing that status. Already by the end of Moses' first address, during which we hear Moses deftly rehearsing past events and utterances to prepare his audience to heed "the statutes and the ordinances which I teach you" (4:1), the Deuteronomist by means of five narrative interruptions of apparently inconsequential nature is beginning to accustom his audience to listen to his narrator's voice, a voice that also rehearses past events and utterances as a means of inclining his audience to heed what *he* is teaching them.

In Moses' second address, a series of narrative interruptions further the process of diminishing Moses' unique status at the same time as it is being augmented by the account of his magisterial actions and utterances. In 10:6–9 the normal signals that up to now have so clearly separated reported from reporting speech in the book are so muted that it is not possible to say for sure whether vv. 8 and 9 are the reporting utterance of the narrator or the reported word of Moses. The effect of this compositionally is to reinforce in yet another way what has been accomplished by the previous frame-breaks. Once again brought back by 10:6–7 to a brief focal awareness that it is the narrator who is transmitting the words of Moses, not Moses speaking directly, the reader of 10:8–9 now experiences the narrator's utterance and the hero's word as indistinguishable in tone, style, and content: the voice of the Deuteronomic narrator merges for a brief moment with Moses'.

By the time we reach the last word of the narrator in the book, 34:5–12, we are well disposed to interpret this first explicit and direct evaluation of Moses' unique status in the proper perspective. The soft, still voice of the narrator has deftly drawn attention to itself throughout the book with such subtle persistence that when we come to the words that frame the end of the narrative, and read therein,

> And there has not arisen a prophet since in Israel like Moses, whom the Lord knew face to face . . . (34:10),

we are tempted to disagree and to say in reply:

> On the contrary, the Lord our God *has* raised up for us a prophet like Moses from among us, and God *has* put His words in his mouth, and he *has* spoken to us all that God commands him. And whoever of us do not give heed to God's words, which this latter prophet speaks in his name, God will require it of us.

This dissenting reply to 34:10, which comes to us somehow through the book itself, is expressive of another voice which has entered into a gentle but effective dialogue with the first. The author's narrative frame-breaks have allowed us to introduce this other voice.

The dissenting reply I have just quoted above is actually adapted from the words of *Moses* in 18:15–18. We are thus led into a consideration of the reported speech of Moses. Here too, as 18:15–18 illustrates, what appears to be the monologic word of the greatest prophet of them all perhaps contains a hidden dialogue between two "Mosaic" voices, to some degree in conflict. The first, most obvious Mosaic voice functions in exactly the same way as 34:10 does in the reporting context: to exalt the hero of Deuteronomy and to subordinate its "author." At the same time, a second Mosaic voice speaks in the book to exalt the narrator at the expense of Moses' uniqueness, just as the frame-breaks do within the reporting context. The main question there as here is whether these two voices are of equal weight.

Reported Speech in Deuteronomy:
The First Address of Moses (1:6–4:40)

A study of this size is not able to deal in a systematic way with all the utterances of Moses; rather we will selectively discuss those utterances which seem to illustrate the compositional relationships inherent in the book and important for our understanding of the subsequent history.
1. Within Moses' first address, there is a series of texts that immediately stands out in relation to the reporting context. Moses speaks the following to Israel:

> "The LORD *was angry with me also because of you,* and said, 'You shall not go in there.' " (1:37)

> "But the LORD *was angry with me because of you,* and would not hearken to me . . ." (3:26)

> "Furthermore the LORD *was angry with me because of you,* and he swore that I should not cross the Jordan, and that I should not enter the good land which the LORD your God gives you for an inheritance. For I must die in this land, I must not go over the Jordan; but you shall go over and take possession of that good land." (4:21–22; all emphasis added)

We have already seen that the narrator in 34:1–5 quotes God to the same effect and describes the fulfillment of God's word in the death of Moses in Moab. In the Mosaic utterances, a motive is given for God's angry decision: Moses suffers "because of Israel." On the other hand, the reporting context of 34:1–5 does not give any reason for God's decision. As such, the Mosaic versions are more condemnatory of Moses' fate than is the reporting narrative of chapter 34. Is there something significant in these variations? We have already seen that, as a framing (and not a frame-breaking) narrative for the reported words of Moses, 34:1–12 functions overtly to represent Moses as preeminently unique, the greatest prophet in Israel's history (34:10–12). This voice, however, is in some tension with another narrative voice (found especially in the frame-breaks) which seems to diminish Moses' uniqueness in favor of the narrator.

Since we may presume to find in the reported speech of Deuteronomy reflexes of these two reporting voices in gentle polemic with one another, we can at this point accept as a working hypothesis that 1:37; 3:26–27; and 4:21–22 are all reflections in the corpus of Mosaic utterances of that point of view which denies the unique status of Moses in the reporting narrative. There is in all three pericopes a mention of God's *anger* with Moses because of some wrongdoing (on Israel's part, on Moses' part, or on both parts). He, like Israel, must suffer: that is God's *judgment*. On the other hand, chapter 34 speaks only of God's *decision* without reference to anger or motive. The distinction is crucial for our understanding of the points of view represented by these two Deuteronomic voices in conflict: one supports the uniqueness of Moses and exalts his status as much as possible; the other tends to diminish his unique status. We shall now see how these two voices are found in the Mosaic utterances through a variety of interesting contexts.

There is definite indication that the dialogue about the unique status of Moses vis-a-vis other prophets is intimately connected with a dialogue about the unique status of Israel vis-a-vis other nations. Moses speaks in 4:32–34:

> "For ask now . . . whether such a great thing as this has ever happened or was ever heard of. Did any people ever hear the voice of a god speaking out of the midst of the fire, as you have heard, and still live? Or has any god ever attempted to go and take a nation for himself from the midst of another nation, by trials, by signs, by wonders, and by war, by a mighty hand and an outstretched arm, and by great terrors, according to all that the LORD your God did for you in Egypt before your eyes?"

At stake here certainly is the uniqueness of Israel's deity; there is no other beside him. But almost as important is the question of divine election of Israel, an election that makes Israel unique among nations because of God's special treatment.

But another Mosaic voice sounds in our ears, one which tends to *diminish* the unique character of God's election of Israel. What God has done for Israel, he has also done on behalf of other nations:

> ". . . do not contend with [the sons of Esau] . . . because I have given Mount Seir to Esau as a possession." (2:5)

> "And the LORD said to me, 'Do not harass Moab or contend with them in battle, for I will not give you any of their land for a possession, because I have given Ar to the sons of Lot for a possession.'" (2:9)

> ". . . and when you approach the frontier of the sons of Ammon, do not harass them or contend with them, for I will not give you any of the land of the sons of Ammon as a possession, because I have given it to the sons of Lot for a possession." (2:19)

So apparently Israel is no more unique than the sons of Esau and Lot insofar as they have all received special treatment from Yahweh with regard to the gift of land! These texts tend to diminish the uniqueness of Israel as the elect of the LORD, whereas in 4:32–34 Israel's unique status is dominant.

The conflict about the status of Israel, apparent in the Mosaic quotations of God's words, finds expression in the reporting context of the book precisely at the two narrative frame-breaks that we have already mentioned in connection with the authorial voice tending to diminish Moses' unique status as *the* prophet of God. We thus have a startling correlation: the voice that tends to diminish Moses' status tends to diminish Israel's uniqueness also.

When we discussed the frame-breaks, 2:10–12, 20–23, the importance of the information that interrupts Moses' speech was not apparent; it should be now. For example, when the reporting speech of Deuteronomy states,

> but the LORD destroyed [the Zamzummim] before [the Ammonites]; and they dispossessed them, and settled in their stead; as he did for the sons of Esau, who live in Seir, when he destroyed the Horites before them, and they dispossessed them, and settled in their stead to this day (2:21–22),

the *content* of this reporting utterance (which interrupts the reported word of Moses) implies that Israel is not unique, at the same time as the *placement* of this utterance, as explained in conjunction with other frame-breaks discussed above, reinforces the nonuniqueness of Moses by focusing on the narrator as an equally important spokesman of God. A tentative correlation between the two conflicting voices both in the reporting and reported utterances of Deuteronomy is this: the voice which exalts the unique status of Moses vis-a-vis other prophets also emphasizes the unique status of Israel vis-a-vis other nations; on the other hand, the voice which diminishes the unique status of Moses also diminishes the unique status of Israel.

There is another aspect of this central Deuteronomic dialogue which elements of Moses' first address already illustrate. In the discussion of the Deuteronomic texts that relate God's refusal to allow Moses to enter the land, 1:37; 3:26–27; and 4:21–22 were seen on one hand to diminish Moses' status by emphasizing God's anger with him and subsequent punishment; on the other hand 34:1–5, which is part of the concluding narrative frame tending to exalt Moses' status, speaks only of God's *decision* to bar Moses from the land and does not refer to divine anger or motivation. The difference here appears to be the reflection of two voices in dialogue with one another. The one voice expresses an adverse decision by God as a punishment of some type: "God was angry with me because of you." The other voice, by omitting such a reference, formulates an adverse decision by God as unrelated to retributive justice: "I have let you see it . . . but you shall not go over there." The relevance of these two points of view in relation to the meaning of the Exile of Israel should be obvious.

If we apply this hint to a number of utterances found in Moses' first address, we come to a tentative conclusion: those utterances which emphasize the uniqueness of Moses or Israel tend also to emphasize hope through the grace and mercy of God, whereas those utterances that diminish Moses' or Israel's unique status tend also to emphasize law and God's retributive justice.

In these remarks on Moses' first address, we have so far only treated aspects of its composition on the ideological plane, the plane of ultimate semantic authority. We want now to discuss aspects of the surface composition of the first address in order to relate it to the dialogue so far evident on the ideological plane.

2. At the beginning of this chapter, we gave examples of the complicated phraséological and temporal scheme apparent in Moses' addresses. Moses' first address is, by more than half, *his* reporting of past speech in direct discourse, usually what he, Yahweh, or Israel had said in the past. Moses' narration of *events*, past, present, or future, forms less than half of his first address which is almost equally divided between chapters 1 to 3 on the one hand and chapter 4 on the other. *Chapter 4 stands off from the first three chapters not only by its references to future rather than past events and utterances, but also by the fact that its reported* *speech is predominantly in indirect discourse, whereas the reported speech in chapters 1 to 3 was overwhelmingly in direct discourse.*

A convenient illustration of the shift from direct discourse in chapters 1 to 3 to indirect discourse in chapter 4 is seen in *how* Moses reports God's words denying him access to the land. Whereas we read in chapters 1 and 3,

> The LORD . . . said, "You shall not go in there." (1:37)

> And the LORD said to me, ". . . for you shall not go over this Jordan" (3:26–27),

in chapter 4 we read:

> Furthermore, the LORD . . . swore that I should not cross the Jordan, and that I should not enter the good land which the LORD your God gives you for an inheritance. (4:21)

This shift from direct to indirect discourse is not haphazard. There are basic compositional reasons for such differences and we may here usefully refer to Voloshinov's ground-breaking analysis of reported speech (1973).[4] He brilliantly shows for one thing that:

> Analysis is the heart and soul of indirect discourse. (129)

Without being able to enter into the manner in which Voloshinov establishes this conclusion in detail, we can still utilize it to formulate the compositional structure of Moses' first address on the phraseological and temporal planes: in chapters 1 to 3 Moses mainly *reports* the past so that in chapter 4 he may *analyze* it in relation to the present and the future. At first, Moses concentrates on giving us as "factual" an account of the past as possible, so that in chapter 4 he may concentrate on analyzing and responding to the facts of the past as a key to present and future action.[5] It is because Moses is pictured as busy commenting and responding to the past that his third report of God's refusal to allow him to enter the land switches naturally, and not accidentally, to indirect discourse in chapter 4. It is no accident, therefore, that chapter 4 of Moses' first address (4:1–40) contains only one and a half verses of reported speech in direct discourse (4:6b, 10). There are important compositional reasons for this, not the least of which is that Moses is being described here as using these temporal and phraseological points of view to advance the ideological positions of the first address.

We may therefore describe Moses' first address as composed of two sections: 1) a "factual" look to the past expressed predominantly by reported speech in direct discourse (Deut 1–3); and 2) an analytical, evaluative response to the past as a means of indicating its full significance for his audience's subsequent history in the land and (eventually) in exile (Deut 4:1–40). What is immediately evident is that this description nicely fits the basic compositional structure of the Deuteronomic History as we have initially divided it: 1) the Deuteronomist's "factual" look at the past, framed predominantly in the reported speech of Moses expressed in direct discourse (the Book of Deuteronomy); and 2) the Deuteronomist's analytical, evaluative response to that past by means of indicating its full significance for *his* audience's subsequent history in the land and (eventually) in exile (Josh–2 Kgs).

A final comment on the composition of Moses' first address. Since our analysis of its temporal and phraseological composition has shown that reporting is dominant in the first part and analytic evaluation predominant in the second part, we would therefore expect the two conflicting ideological voices of the book to be represented in more or less extended relief and with clear-cut contours in chapter 4, and this is precisely the case. 4:1–39 neatly divides into two extensive evaluative sections. The first section, vv. 1 to 28, describes Israel's subsequent history in terms of sin, judgment, exile, and ends in a note of despair:

> And there you will serve gods of wood and stone, the work of men's hands, that neither see nor hear, nor eat nor smell. (4:28)

To be noted in 4:1–28 is an emphasis on the nonuniqueness of Moses (4:21–22: Moses is punished along with the other Israelites) and a diminution of the unique status of Israel (4:19: even though he has reserved Israel for himself, God has still allotted the host of heaven "to all the peoples under the whole heaven"). Coupled with this egalitarian tendency in depicting Moses and Israel is an emphasis on the *retributive* aspect of the covenant, starkly expressed in the formula:

> For the LORD your God is a devouring fire, a jealous God. (4:24)

The other voice of Deuteronomy's evaluative dialogue with itself is found in extensive form in vv. 29 to 39. To be noted in this section is its overwhelming emphasis on the unique status of Israel, seen in terms of the LORD's inexplicable choice of them as his very own and not in terms of any just claim Israel could lay on him (4:32–39). Such a view of Israel's status vis-a-vis God is succinctly expressed in a hope-filled formula that is in explicit phraseological contrast with 4:24:

> for the Lord your God is a merciful God; he will not fail you or
> destroy you or forget the covenant with your fathers which he
> swore to them. (4:31)

The contours of each Deuteronomic voice in this chapter are not
perfectly clear-cut, however. The voice of judgment is overwhelmingly
present in vv. 1 to 28, yet the voice of election and grace is still heard
within, although it seems to be used against itself, as it were. After
Moses tells the people in v. 6 that their obedience to God's law will
constitute wisdom and understanding in the eyes of other peoples, he
states:

> For what great nation is there that has a god so near to it as the
> Lord our God is to us *whenever we call upon him?* (4:7; emphasis
> added)

In the next verse, Moses returns to the theme that Israel is unique in
the righteousness of the laws they possess. V. 7 indeed sounds like the
voice of grace and election found in the second section, vv. 29 to 39. It
rejoices in the special status of Israel among the nations. But it is an
utterance here used against itself. As its immediate context, 4:6–8,
shows, the relative intimacy that Israel enjoys with their god—an intimacy greater than that shared by other nations with their gods—is
understood to be legal and retributive in nature. Israel is a paragon of
one nation's intimacy with their god precisely by the righteousness of
the laws they have and by their success in keeping them. Surely at this
point in the dialogue the voice of judgment is trying to turn the utterance of an opposing point of view against itself.

Moreover, just as the first part of chapter 4 is basically retributive
even though it contains an utterance that more suitably belongs to a
voice of mercy and grace, the second section, vv. 29 to 39, also contains
an utterance that belongs more appropriately to the voice of retribution, even though the section as a whole is overwhelmingly representative of a voice that invokes the patriarchal covenant of mercy and grace.
The apparently discordant utterance is found in v. 30:

> When you are in tribulation and all these things come upon you in
> the latter days, you will return to the Lord your God *and obey his
> voice.* (emphasis added)

Although a far distant fate of grace and hope is finally predicted here in
Moses' first address, the prediction is prefaced by a prior state of obedience, and thus of retributive justice. We shall see further on in our

analysis of Moses' second address that the bracketing of utterances of mercy and grace with neutralizing statements of a retributive nature is a consistent pattern in the Book of Deuteronomy.

The two voices of a dialogue here in Moses' own speech, even as it was present in the reporting context of the narrator's utterances, are found conjoined but still in tension in the final verse of Moses' first address:

> Therefore you shall keep his statutes and his commandments, which I command you this day, that it may go well with you, and with your children after you, and that you may prolong your days in the land . . . (4:40)

We are again back to the Deuteronomic voice of retributive justice according to which Israel's fate depends in large part on their obedience to the covenant. But this is only one voice in an apparent dialogue, and the first address of Moses ends with a refrain that contains the other voice of unconditional and inexplicable election:

> . . . which the LORD your God gives you *forever*. (4:40; emphasis added)

So far, compositional analysis has indicated that traces of a dialogue are implicit on every level of the book. Therefore, as we proceed, we should not be surprised to see that the interplay of the two voices involved in this dialogue is an essential constituent, rather than a secondary addition to, the ultimate semantic authority that unifies not only Deuteronomy but, as we shall see, the entire Deuteronomic History. It remains to be seen whether this "dialogue" is real or only a device utilized by a monologic author.

The Second Address of Moses (5:1b–28:68)

The reporting context of 4:41–43 provides a concluding frame to Moses' first address, while 4:44–5:1a constitutes the introductory frame to Moses' second, main address. Like the introduction to Moses' first address (1:1–5), the author's framing context here situates the words of Moses in space and time, giving the circumstances in which Moses' reported speech was uttered. These details selectively repeat information found in the previously reported speech of Moses.

The core of the second address is the so-called Deuteronomic law-code (12:1–26:15). Before I undertake my central task of examining those utterances within this second address whose phraseological, psychological, and temporal composition have an important bearing on our understanding of the ideological composition of the book, I want to give an illustration of the various ways in which the surface planes of an utterance may be related to its deeper ideological plane within the overall composition of a work.

Certain aspects of utterances' phraseological, temporal, or psychological composition may affect their deeper ideological point of view; other aspects may not. Deuteronomy 5:1–5 illustrates both cases. The first few verses of Moses' second address offer us a good example of how variation on the plane of phraseology, or on another surface plane, in some cases is concurrent with a shift in point of view on the ideological plane, yet in other cases is not. The terminology employed here is drawn from Uspensky (1973). Basic to his approach are the following points:

i. The most basic point of view of a work is *ideological* or evaluative; it comprises that system of viewing the world according to which the work is conceptually unified. It is the "ultimate semantic authority" of a work, in Bakhtin's terms. Often this level is the least accessible to formalization, for its analysis relies to a degree on intuitive understanding.

ii. The *phraseological* plane appears to be coextensive with "the plane of expression" in Hjelmslev's terms (1961), or similar to the signifier aspect of the verbal sign in de Saussure's terms (1966). Since Uspensky makes the point that this plane is often the only one on which we can detect changes in the author's position, I think it is safe to infer that this plane refers to the surface of the text in general and to the opposition there of reported to reporting speech in particular, and that the other surface planes refer to specific aspects of the phraseological plane which are considered important enough by Uspensky to merit the designation of a special term.

iii. The *spatio-temporal* plane involves the location in time and space from whose perspective an author, narrator, or character speaks in a work. In Deuteronomy the temporal plane has more relevance than the spatial plane. As this analysis of Deuteronomy is meant to illustrate, the multiplicity of temporal points of view in a work is often quite complex.

iv. The *psychological* plane involves whether the author or narrator describes what a person says or does from a point of view that is internal or external to the person described, to the person speaking, or to the person or persons spoken to. If, for example, an author transmits information that is generally not accessible to the normal onlooker, he is taking an internal psychological point of view. Most often, these psychological elements are conveyed by distinct phraseological elements of a text.

v. It is to be emphasized once again that the composition of a work on one plane may or may not concur with its composition on another plane.

We may now proceed to 5:1–5, in which Moses speaks to Israel:

> Hear, O Israel, the statutes and the ordinances which *I* speak in *your* hearing this day, and *you* shall learn them and be careful to do them. (2) The LORD *our* God made a covenant with *us* in Horeb. (3) Not with *our* fathers did the LORD make this covenant, but with *us*, who are all of *us* here alive this day. (4) The LORD spoke with *you* face to face at the mountain, out of the midst of the fire, (5) while *I* stood between the LORD and *you* at that time, to declare to *you* the word of the LORD; for *you* were afraid because of the fire, and *you* did not go up into the mountain . . . (emphasis added)

There is a clear phraseological alternation in Moses' utterances here between an "I vs. you" form in vv. 1, 4 and 5, and an "our/us" form in vv. 2 and 3. One might well ask whether a shift is thereby indicated on other surface planes as well. Also do these surface shifts involve an ideological shift as well?

It is easy to see that this phraseological shift also involves a change of perspective on the psychological plane. Moses alternates his point of view between one who presents himself as above his hearers in special knowledge and one who emphasizes shared experiences with his fellow Israelites. The choice of the "I vs. you" form indicates a distinction between speaker and listener, and Moses thereby speaks from the position of his self-consciousness as declarer-teacher of God's word. The use of the "our/us" form indicates no such distinction, and emphasizes a shared status between speaker and hearer. The *teacher* imparts knowledge which his hearers are not presumed to know; the *fellow Israelite* speaks of matters experienced in common with his hearers. The shift involves an overt presentation of the prophetic status of Moses as opposed to a status shared with his fellow Israelites. The question naturally arises whether this phraseological/psychological shift in perspective necessarily indicates, at this point, a shift on the ideological plane as well, especially since we have by now discovered in the book hints of an ideological dialogue that does involve the question of Moses' unique status.

If we build upon our previous analysis of chapter 4, we shall see that this phraseological shift from the "I vs. you" form to the "our/us" form does not *necessarily* involve utterances belonging to differing ideologies. Let us see why this is so.

In 4:1–28, which emphasizes retributive justice and the nonuniqueness of Moses, Moses exhorts the Israelites not to forget "the covenant of the LORD your God, which he made with you" (4:23). On the other hand, in the second part of the chapter, which emphasizes grace, free election, and the uniqueness of Israel (4:29–39), Moses reminds the people that God will not "forget the covenant with your fathers which he swore to them" (4:31). When we add to this the information found in 5:2–3, namely, that the covenant made "with us in Horeb" was "not with our fathers," we are able, thus far in our reading of the book, to come to two conclusions about the concurrence of the phraseological and the ideological planes of 5:1–5:

i. It is clear from chapters 4 and 5 that the phraseological distinction between "covenant with you" and "covenant with your fathers" in chapter 4, and "covenant in Horeb" and "covenant with our fathers" in chapter 5 involves an ideological distinction as well. A speaker's overt identification with the covenant made at Horeb indicates an ideological point of view *concentrating* on retributive justice and the nonuniqueness of Moses and Israel. On the other hand, a speaker's identification with the covenant made with our/your fathers seems to involve an ideological viewpoint *centering* on mercy, grace, and the unique statuses of Moses and Israel.

ii. Nevertheless, *either* covenant is spoken of as:

"with *you*" (4:23) or "with *us*" (5:2): Horeb Covenant
"with *your* fathers" (4:31) or "with
our fathers" (5:3)   Patriarchal Covenant

We can see immediately that the retributive ideology can alternate between the "I vs. you" form and the "our/us" form. For example, the retributive voice alternates between an "I vs. you" form in 4:23 and an "our/us" form in 5:2–3. This voice, therefore, may be exercising the same phraseological shift within chapter 5 itself which it does between chapters 4 and 5. Although chapters 4 and 5 do not give us enough information, we may assume that the ideological voice of grace or mercy also speaks in both the "I vs. you" and the "our/us" tones. Therefore, in 5:1–5 the phraseological alternation between the "I vs. you" and the "our/us" forms has significance on the psychological plane but not necessarily on the ideological plane.

An inference can be drawn from the preceding analysis: since the phraseological shift of the forms we have been discussing (between "your" and "our") involves a psychological shift but not necessarily an ideological one, both voices of the basic dialogue about Moses' unique status as prophet of God appear to be in general agreement at least concerning Moses' role as one who both declares (*lᵉhaggîd*) and teaches (*lᵉlammed*) God's word. Moreover, both voices seem to be in agreement that this prophetic role does not inhibit them from describing Moses as speaking from the point of view of his self-perception as an Israelite, sharing the same knowledge and experience as his fellow Israelites. *The conflict over Moses' unique role centers rather on whether there could ever be another prophet like him.* As we by now have seen in a number of different contexts, the Deuteronomist's constant and obvious exaltation of Moses paradoxically contributes to the ultimate exaltation of the one who quotes him throughout the Book of Deuteronomy, the Deuteronomic narrator himself.

The Surface Composition of the Second Mosaic Address

1. Whereas Moses' first address is, by more than half, *his* reporting of speech in *direct* discourse, over half of his second address, i.e., the lawcode of chapters 12–26, consists of his reporting of speech in a manner other than by direct discourse. More specifically, if we limit ourselves to Moses' reporting of God's words, Moses' utterances shift between addresses from a concentration on reporting God's words in direct discourse to a concentration on reporting them in a manner that largely destroys the contours which heretofore have distinguished God's words from Moses'. The importance of this distinction in depicting Moses in his practice of reporting the word of God is great. Since the Deuteronomic lawcode is phrased as a direct address of Moses to the people, it is this compositional fact that makes it much more difficult to decide, with any clear-cut boundaries, which utterances are meant to represent the reported speech of God, which are the commenting and responding reactions of Moses himself, and which utterances combine both.

In Moses' first address it was much easier to distinguish between Moses' *declaring* God's word and his *teaching* or *interpreting* that word. Thus, that address divided itself neatly into chapters 1 to 3 on one hand (Moses the *maggîd*) and chapter 4 on the other (Moses the *mᵉlammed*). In the second address, these two Mosaic functions are much more synthetically combined. This is true in the Mosaic utterances that frame the lawcode: chapters 5:1–11:32 and 26:16–28:68 contain proportionately far fewer quotations of God in direct discourse than the first address; this is also true of the Deuteronomic lawcode itself which quotes the LORD in direct discourse only in 17:16b and 18:17–20.

These two functions of Moses' role as mouthpiece of God—to declare and to interpret his word—correspond neatly to aspects of how we receive or accept another speaker's speech (Voloshinov:117–21). On the one hand, the basic tendency in reacting to another's speech "may be to maintain its integrity and authenticity; a language may strive to forge hard and fast boundaries for reported speech" (119). On the other hand, the basic tendency might be to infiltrate "reported speech with authorial retort and commentary in deft and subtle ways . . . to obliterate its boundaries" (120).

For example, large, clear-cut blocks of reported speech in direct discourse normally will be indicative of the first tendency, and Moses' first address illustrates this situation. On the other hand, his second address, with its wholesale shift away from the reporting of God's words in direct discourse, together with its abundance of commentary and response, illustrates the second tendency. When we couple these facts with the authoritative source of the utterances Moses is reporting (*God* spoke them), we see that there is an immediate build-up in the phraseological composition of the book concerning Moses' status as a mouthpiece of God. In the first address, Moses is depicted mostly as reporting God's word by respecting the clear-cut boundaries of that speech through the predominant use of direct discourse; in the second address, reports of God's word in direct discourse almost completely disappear. God is only quoted in direct discourse nine times in twenty-four chapters: 5:6–21, 28–31; 9:12, 13–14, 23; 10:1–2, 11; 17:16; 18:17–20. Most of these cases occur in Moses' reporting context. Given the tendency of the second address to synthesize reporting and reported voices, these few direct utterances seem therefore to have an important function which we will attempt to identify below.

Other aspects of the second address's phraseological composition can be mentioned here. Moses is described as framing the reported words of God by means of his reporting utterances of 5:1–11:32 and 26:16–28:68. One can analyze the speech of a *character* of a work in the same way as one analyzes the speech of an author or a narrator of a work. Just as we first analyzed the reporting utterances of the narrator of Deuteronomy, and are now analyzing the reported utterances of its hero, Moses, so in turn each of Moses' addresses may be analyzed from the point of view of the *reporting* utterances of Moses as well as from the point of view of the *reported* utterances they contain. Within the second address, Moses' reporting frames are to the lawcode of 12–26 what in the book itself the narrator's reporting frames are to all of Moses' addresses contained therein. Stated in this way, we can see that the over-all composition of Deuteronomy is one in which we read how Moses is described as declaring and interpreting the word of God as a panoramic preview of how the Deuteronomic narrator will describe and interpret the word of Moses in Joshua–2 Kings.

2. There is an aspect of the second address which confirms our interpretation of Moses' more intense depiction there as declarer and interpreter of God's words. Although the phrases "God of *our* fathers" or "*our* God" appears at least twenty-three times in the book, we find them only once in the lawcode, which overwhelmingly prefers the "I vs. you" form, and therefore the lawcode predominantly employs phrases such as "your God." Thus, although Moses' utterances are many times longer in the second address than in the first, the first address describes Moses as using the "our" form eleven times, but only twice does he directly use this form in the second address. This is an indication of a psychological shift between the two addresses. Moses at chapter 5 leaves off speaking to his audience sometimes as a fellow Israelite, and henceforth (apart from 5:2 and 6:4) speaks only from the viewpoint of his role as teacher, insofar as the "I vs. you" and "our/us" forms are concerned.

The predominant *psychological* viewpoint of the second address is immediately set up by the content of chapter 5, whose main intent is to describe the circumstances that led to the privileged information Moses transmits in his utterances. All the Israelites heard the voice of God giving the ten words, but only Moses, at the elders' request and God's command, hears God's further words to be reported to the rest of the people. This is the main psychological perspective of the second address.

The second address's *temporal* composition is predominantly future-oriented, just as the first address was predominantly past-oriented. The temporal orientation of the second address is divided up into utterances that address the context of Israel's *immediate* future in the land (the lawcode), and utterances that describe the *distant* future of punishment and devastation (e.g., chapter 28). The immediate past is sometimes addressed, as in chapter 5 and in chapters 9 and 10. But even in these cases, it appears to be an opportunity to draw some concrete lesson about the future that is motivating Moses' references. Thus chapter 5 prepares us for Moses' authoritative pronouncement of the lawcode; and chapters 9 and 10 describe past circumstances that explain why God will allow a disobedient people to possess the land.

The Ideological Problems of the Second Address

At first reading, Moses' second address would seem to contradict the tentative conclusion we reached as a result of our analysis of his first address. The conclusion reached there was that the Deuteronomic voice which tends to emphasize the uniqueness of Moses or Israel tends also to emphasize hope through the grace and mercy of God, whereas those utterances that appear to diminish Moses' or Israel's unique status tend also to emphasize law and God's retributive justice. But Moses' second address is filled with utterance upon utterance that exalt and emphasize Moses' and Israel's unique statuses. The cumulative effect of these statements appears to be that there will never be another prophet like Moses and that no nation has enjoyed such a special status with the LORD as Israel. And all this in the unremitting context of God's retributive justice and covenant of law with Israel. This context appears to contradict the tentative conclusions we reached in our analysis of the first address.

It is no surprise that this address, which contains an extensive law-code of fifteen chapters, would be dominated by an ideological voice concerned above all with retributive justice and a covenant of law, rather than with mercy and a covenant of grace. What *is* surprising is that such a block of material, so obviously dominated in this way, also succeeds by a number of interlocking devices in diminishing the unique statuses of Moses and Israel at the same time as it unceasingly employs utterances that seem to exalt them. This paradox is what we want to describe from a compositional point of view. The easier part of our task will be to describe how extensively the unique statuses of Moses and Israel are advanced in the second address. (The frequency and intensity of Moses' rhetoric concerning God's retributive justice is so great in the second address that it will be assumed in the following discussion.)

The obvious way in which Moses' unique status vis-a-vis other prophets is not only underlined but also advanced in the second address is by Moses' account of his commissioning by God in chapter 5. Whereas in the first address Moses only states that the LORD had commanded him to teach the Israelites commandments and ordinances (e.g., 4:5), here at the beginning of his second address he describes the circumstances which led up to this command and reports the actual command in direct discourse. After the people approach Moses and request him to "hear all that the LORD our God will say; and speak to us all that the LORD our God will say . . ." (5:27), God tells Moses:

> "I have heard the words of this people, which they have spoken to you; they have rightly said all that they have spoken. Oh that they had such a mind as this always, to fear me and to keep all my commandments, that it might go well with them, and with their children forever! Go and say to them, 'Return to your tents.' But you, stand here by me, and I will tell you all the commandment and the statutes and the ordinances which you shall teach them, that they may do them in the land which I give them to possess." (5:28–31)

The point is clear: after hearing the voice of God speak the words of the decalogue, the people fear that they cannot hear more and live.

God agrees with this position and commands Moses to teach the people all the commandment, statutes, and ordinances he will tell him. The lawcode is precisely a report of Moses' teaching the people what God had told him. Moses did not in fact die as they thought they would had they heard the words of God which *he* had heard.

The rest of the words of Moses in Deuteronomy, coming before chapter 12 and after chapter 26, comprise what Moses said to prepare the people to hear the word of God contained within the lawcode, and subsequently to spell out for them its implications. 5:22–31 comprises Moses' account of how God commissioned him to speak the central words of the book, the "Mosiac" lawcode of chapters 12–26. 5:28–31 are the authenticating words of God that show the basis for the unique teaching role Moses enjoys in the Book of Deuteronomy. Through them we see why "there has not arisen a prophet since in Israel like Moses, whom the LORD knew face to face" (34:10). These words are most directly explained by what Moses says and does through and in his second address. And within this second address, Deuteronomy 5 contains Moses' account of the vision that authenticates the central role he plays in the book, just as Isaiah 6 does with respect to the rest of that book.

Utterances advancing Israel's unique status are also abundantly present in the second address. The following is representative:

> For you are a people holy (*qdš* = "set apart") to the LORD your God; the LORD your God has chosen you to be a people for his own possession out of all the peoples that are on the face of the earth. (7:6)

What is clear, therefore, about the utterances of the second address is their frequent insistence on the unique statuses of Moses and Israel. But there *are* a few utterances that seem to challenge the main position of the address. A direct challenge to Moses' unique status as teacher of Israel is launched directly at the *source* of Moses' central role in the book, the authenticating utterance of God in 5:28–31. For Moses repeats his account of this divine utterance within the lawcode itself in 18:17–20. This account of the divine commissioning uses Moses' words against himself, as it were, by revealing that *another* "Moses" is part of the package; *his* commission also is to report to the people God's word:

> And the LORD said to me, "They have rightly said all that they have spoken. I will raise up for them a prophet like you from among their brethren; and I will put my words in his mouth, and he shall speak to them all that I command him. And whoever will not give heed to my words which he shall speak in my name, I myself will require it of him." (18:17–18)

A challenge to all the many utterances about Israel's unique status seems to be found in 9:4–5:

> Do not say in your heart, after the LORD your God has thrust the Anakim out before you, "It is because of my righteousness that the LORD has brought me in to possess this land"; *whereas it is because of the wickedness of these nations that the LORD is driving them out before you.* Not because of your righteousness or the uprightness of your heart are you going in to possess their land; *but because of the wickedness of these nations the LORD your God is driving them out from before you,* and that he may confirm the word which the LORD swore to your fathers, to Abraham, to Isaac, and to Jacob. (emphasis added)

This passage, perhaps not as directly contradictory as 18:17–18, vis-a-vis Moses, still casts a shadow on all the many overt statements about God's special treatment of Israel, especially those found in chapters 9 and 10. The special relationship proposed by Moses is to be interpreted against a universal situation in which the ultimate motive for God's giving of the land to Israel is retributive in nature, i.e., to punish for *their* sins the nations dispossessed by Israel. *And what happened to those nations will happen, therefore, to the Israelites also when they disobey God.* It seems, after all, that Israel is no different from the other nations who in the past also have enjoyed God's blessings (for they *do* possess the land which Israel is to take). Israel is simply benefiting from *their* disobedience just as other nations will benefit from Israel's disobedience. And as we shall soon see, the statement about the word sworn to the fathers, and the ideological position it represents, is effectively neutralized by the retributive statements that precede it.

Although 18:17–20 and 9:4–5 are each in its own way a powerful attack on the overtly preponderant message of the second address, it will be hard to take them seriously, and easy to treat them as clumsy additions to the book, unless it can be shown that these two explicit statements coincide exactly with other aspects of the surface composition of the second address. A careful compositional analysis of the phraseological, temporal, and psychological planes of the second address will show in fact that the overt exaltation of Moses and Israel is paradoxically accompanied by a subtle but effective campaign which aims at diminishing their unique roles. We will see how the second address is the central stage in which, as the book develops, one voice progressively gets louder in its portrayal of Moses' and Israel's unique divine election, at the same time as *another* voice, in quiet opposition to the first, is progressively and ever more effectively challenging those statuses. The first voice is a disguised servant of the second.

The Interrelationships between the Surface and
Deep Composition of Moses' Second Address

1. Since the surface planes of the second address seem to result in a point of view that overwhelmingly advances a covenant of retributive justice as the broad context for the depiction of Moses as *the* prophet of an Israel that has been especially chosen by Yahweh, it might be helpful to review how this viewpoint is built up in the second address, and where there are utterances and compositional devices that seem to oppose or alter the predominant position expressed there.

If we begin by examining the broad context of God's retributive justice, which is so predominant in this address that we have not felt it necessary to quote illustrative examples, we shall see that the surface composition of this address does nevertheless contain a number of utterances that do not seem to fit into this broad context. Most of these utterances invoke the oath or covenant which God swore to the fathers, usually in connection with the gift of the land. Consider the following:

> . . . that the LORD may turn from the fierceness of his anger, and show you mercy, and have compassion on you and multiply you, as he swore to your fathers . . . (13:17b)

Here is an utterance that speaks of a God of mercy and compassion rather than of strict retribution. But such an idea is immediately colored by the following verse:

> . . . if you obey the voice of the LORD your God, keeping all his commandments which I command you this day, and doing what is right in the sight of the LORD your God. (13:18)

One way, therefore, of neutralizing the utterance dealing with the idea of an apparently unconditional covenant made with the fathers is to prefix it with, or immediately add to it, an utterance that invokes a necessary condition of obedience. So that when Moses states,

> You shall remember the LORD your God for it is he who gives you power to get wealth; that he may confirm his covenant which he swore to your fathers, as at this day (8:18),

he immediately follows it with:

> And if you forget the LORD your God and go after other gods and serve them and worship them, I solemnly warn you this day that you shall surely perish. (8:19)

Or consider the pattern of preceding an utterance that invokes the promise made to the fathers with an utterance demanding the necessary precondition of obedience:

> All the commandment which I command you this day you shall be careful to do, that you may live and multiply and go in and possess the land which the LORD swore to give to your fathers. (8:1)

Besides the texts just mentioned, we may cite as further examples 6:3, 10–15, 23–24; 7:6–11, 12–13; 10:11–13, 15–17; 11:8–9, 20–21; 12:1; 13:17–18; 26:14–15. This pattern attempts to effect a synthesis of the covenant with the fathers and the covenant at Horeb, and to make the latter a precondition for the former. Obedience thereby becomes a condition of God's apparently unconditional oath to the fathers.

We now see more clearly what our analysis of 4:1–40 and 5:1–5 tentatively indicated: the distinction between the covenant with the fathers and the covenant at Horeb is absolutely basic to the ideological tension within the book. The presence in an utterance in Deuteronomy of a phrase such as "the God of our fathers" or "the covenant made with the fathers" or "the oath which God swore to the fathers" brings with it associations of mercy, grace, and divine election that are at odds with the ultimate viewpoint of the book on the justice of God. Whenever such concepts are brought to mind by these phrases, the basic evaluative stance of the book finds it necessary to neutralize them either by an overt bracketing of them with controlling retributive statements or else by an insinuation that the covenant at Horeb is *somehow* a necessary condition for the fulfillment of the unconditional oath and covenant God swore to the fathers.

This last point brings up the only other major tradition threatening the predominantly retributive nature of the second address: in spite of Israel's disobedience at Horeb, God still gave them the land. Chapters 9 and 10 deal primarily with this topic, and the Deuteronomic voice of retribution succeeds in transforming this merciful act of the LORD into an act of justice by means of two short verses. 9:4–5 effectively neutralizes God's merciful gift of the land by putting it in the wider context of his just punishment of the wicked nations Israel will dispossess. These verses illustrate very well the paradoxical situation in which the Deuteronomist found himself: the oath to the fathers and Israel's disobedience at Horeb were too much a part of his heritage completely to ignore in his account. He therefore had to invoke both ideas within a broader context of retribution that effectively renders powerless the threat they posed to his basic position.

When we recognize the pattern of apparently admitting the unconditional covenant with the fathers, but actually neutralizing its troublesome features in the ways we have just outlined, we see also that the unique status of Israel, so unlike the other nations, is also effectively undermined. No matter how often the second address refers to Israel's special status, as in 7:6, the basic attitude of this address is epitomized in passages such as:

> Like the nations that the LORD makes to perish before you, so shall you perish, because you would not obey the voice of the LORD your God. (8:20)

If the second address consistently and overtly counters any utterance threatening the retributive justice of God, and therefore emphasizes that Israel is ultimately not unique among the other nations, this means that such a strategy is carried out upon the surface composition of this address. We may say, therefore, that the phraseological, psychological, and temporal planes of the address largely concur with its deeper ideological plane, insofar as the conditional nature of God's covenant and Israel's relatively nonunique status are concerned.

When it comes to the question of *Moses'* role as outlined in the second address, it seems that its surface composition almost never concurs with its deep ideological plane. As we described above, the overt viewpoint of the address is one which consistently emphasizes Moses' unique role as God's greatest mouthpiece. It is important now to see how the surface composition in this regard is subtly but effectively undermined by the "ultimate semantic authority" of the book, so that Moses' role in this address even helps to neutralize the voice of the unique election of Israel and the unconditional promise made to the fathers. We must now turn to the lawcode itself.

2. The phraseological composition of the lawcode contained in the second address presents us with the book's most sustained example of the voice that exalts Moses' unique authority. Whereas Moses quoted the ten commandments of the LORD in direct discourse, that is, God was allowed to speak to the Israelites directly, here in the lawcode it is *Moses* who speaks in direct address to the Israelites concerning "the statutes and laws that you shall be careful to observe in the land which the LORD, the God of your fathers, is giving you to occupy as long as you live on earth" (12:1). The practical effect of this compositional device is to raise the authority of the Mosaic voice to a position almost indistinguishable from that of the voice of God. Conversely, in this address the direct voice of God is almost totally silenced. Not that the distinction between God's word and Moses' goes unrecognized here. Rather it seems to be the effect of this most obvious compositional aspect of the lawcode to obliterate the practical importance of the distinction between God's word and Moses'. We hope to see how this device serves the basic ideological stance of the book.

Through Moses' reporting style, we have the promulgation of a lawcode in which a maximum amount of reporting response and commentary (Moses'? the Deuteronomist's?) has been allowed openly to infuse what we may describe as the reported speech of God, insofar as Deuteronomy 5 characterizes the lawcode. What we normally would have expected, and up to this point indeed have found in the book, the Deuteronomist now deliberately avoids. That is, except for parts of the frame-break of 10:6–9, Moses' speech heretofore has been characterized by a reverence for the word of God that always made clear on the surface of the text when he was *reporting* the speech of the LORD and when he was retorting and commenting upon it.[6] This contrast between the subordinate style of Moses' first address and the supremely authoritative promulgation of the lawcode contained in his second address raises for us a central compositional aspect of our analysis of this book. What effect upon the reader's perception of Moses, the hero of this book, does such a shift accomplish? There can be no doubt that the Deuteronomist utilizes this device to manipulate the responses of his intended audience; the nature of this manipulation is crucial here. I want now to attempt to characterize in some detail how and to what degree our perception of Moses is thereby affected. The importance of this topic lies in the intimate connection between the respective roles of the narrator and the hero of this book, and in the compositional means whereby, as we have already seen, the Deuteronomist programs his audience's perception of his narrator by directing their continuing confrontations with the hero of this part of his history.

We can use the conclusions of our analysis of Moses' first address to help us solve the puzzle surrounding the sudden compositional shift embodied in the lawcode. We saw above that the basic compositional structure of Moses' first address mirrors that of the Deuteronomic History. That is, just as the first address neatly divided itself into a Moses who factually reports *God's* words in direct discourse (Deut 1–3), then analyzes and evaluates their significance for the subsequent history of Israel (Deut 4), so also the Deuteronomic History neatly divides itself into a narrator who first factually reports *Moses'* words in direct discourse (Deut), and then himself analyzes and evaluates their significance in the subsequent history of his people (Josh–2 Kgs).

But the strategy of the Deuteronomist does not, of course, end with the first address. If Moses can first report God's words, then interpret their significance for his audience, so also can the Deuteronomic narrator. But Moses' authority and preeminence can be, indeed must be, advanced to accomplish the purposes of the author apparent in the composition of the book. The overall message of Deuteronomy seems to me to be based on the following: as Moses authoritately conveyed and interpreted the word of God, so the narrator authoritatively conveys and interprets the words of Moses; as Moses teaches, so does the narrator. The first stage of this strategy, the first address, is to show Moses first reporting, then commenting on God's words; the second stage, that is, the second address and especially the lawcode, has Moses both reporting and interpreting God's words *at one and the same time and in such a way as to make it impossible to distinguish which parts of the lawcode represent reported speech of God and which represent the reporting speech of Moses.* In the first address, "the explicitness and inviolability of the boundaries between authorial and reported speech reach the utmost limits," to quote Voloshinov's words from another context (1973:120). In the second address, Moses' reporting speech "strives to break down the self-contained compactness of the reported speech, to resolve it, to obliterate its boundaries" (ibid). What the Deuteronomist is gradually obliterating, as his narrator's long report of Moses' various addresses advances, is the distinction between the teaching authority of his hero and that of his narrator. The second address, and the Mosaic lawcode that is central to it and the Book of Deuteronomy itself, is the crucial stage in the Deuteronomist's over-all plan.

The Deuteronomic History, and the Book of Deuteronomy as its panoramic preview, vibrate with the following hermeneutic ratio: as the word of God is to the word of Moses, so the word of Moses is to the word of the Deuteronomic narrator. So that the supreme blurring of the words of God and of Moses in the lawcode serves the same purpose as the other devices of the Deuteronomist we have seen that overtly exalted the unique status of Moses: it contributes toward a subtle but powerful exaltation of the authority of the narrator's words to such an extent that when the narrator is ready to speak in his own voice so as to make the distinction between his words and Moses' practically irrelevant (Josh–2 Kgs), the reader will have been already prepared for this by the hypostasis of the divine-Mosaic words of the lawcode.

3. An example of how the Deuteronomist constitutes his narrator's prophetic authority, whether the latter is busy on the surface of the text exalting Moses' unique authority or denying it, is found in the juxtaposition of two apparently opposed statements within the lawcode, dealing with the activity and authenticity of prophets: 13:1–6 on the one hand and 18:15–22 on the other.

The lawcode begins in chapter 12 with those familiar laws dealing with the centralization of worship, and turns in chapter 13 to the question of how enticers to apostasy are to be treated once Israel inhabits the land. The chapter begins with the admonition:

> Everything that I command you shall be careful to do; you shall not add to it or take from it. (13:1)

Moses immediately details what is to be done in the event that such enticers are prophets or dreamers (*nābî'* or *ḥolēm*). Even if their signs or portents come true, "you shall not listen to the words of that prophet or that dreamer of dreams" (13:4); he "shall be put to death" (13:6). Chapter 18 also deals with the question of prophets:

> For these nations, which you are about to dispossess, give heed to soothsayers and to diviners; but as for you, the LORD your God has not allowed you to do so. The LORD your God will raise up for you a prophet like me from among you, from your brethren—him you shall heed—just as you desired of the LORD your God at Horeb on the day of the assembly . . . (18:14–16)

Then, in order to further authenticate his own words, Moses reports God's words in a manner that is uncharacteristic of the entire lawcode, that is, through direct discourse:

> And the LORD said to me, "They have rightly said all that they have spoken. I will raise up for them a prophet like you from among their brethren; and I will put my words in his mouth, and he shall speak to them all that I command him." (18:17–18)

How will the Israelites recognize a prophet *not* sent by God so that they may put him to death?:

> . . . when a prophet speaks in the name of the LORD, if the word does not come to pass or come true, that is a word which the LORD has not spoken; the prophet has spoken it presumptuously, you need not be afraid of him. (18:22)

The contrast between these two pericopes dealing with words spoken by a prophet in the name of the LORD could not be greater. Both deal ultimately with the status of the very lawcode of which they are a part, and each appears to provide a different explanation of that status. We want therefore to deal with these two pericopes not according to the question of true or false prophecy in general, but in relation to the very prophetic words of Moses of which they are a part in the lawcode. They seem to offer differing if not contradictory instructions concerning whether the lawcode itself is to be accepted as utterly unique or simply fundamental for successive words of the LORD.

13:1–6, with its command in v. 1 not to add or take away anything from the lawcode, cannot be interpreted to show Moses being reported as forever closing off any words of God to Israel subsequent to the lawcode itself. God will again speak as he repeatedly is reported doing throughout the rest of Deuteronomy (e.g., 31:16–21; 32:49–52), and throughout the rest of the Deuteronomic History. But what we do have in 13:1 (as well as in its preceding version in 4:2) appears to be the prohibition of any prophetic speech that blurs the boundaries between God's word and man's interpretation as thoroughly and as authoritatively as Moses is described as doing in the lawcode itself, where direct command of God and Mosaic comment or retort are so interwoven that it is impossible to distinguish *on the surface of the lawcode's text* what belongs to the reporting speech of Moses and what belongs to the reported speech of God. In other words, 13:1, in its present context within the lawcode, forbids subsequent reports of the word of God which synthesize reported speech, retort, and commentary as thoroughly as is the case with the lawcode. What is contained in this prohibition is the promulgation of an *authoritarian dogmatism* (a compositional category described by Voloshinov, 1973:123) that centralizes control over the Mosaic lawcode by forbidding any further authoritative addition to or commentary upon it. The ironic thrust of this verse should not be ignored: this dogmatism expresses itself and provides for self-legitimization through and within prophetic discourse whose surface style is directly contrary to its own authoritarian tyranny. Disregarding its own fundamental synthesis of reporting (Moses') and reported (God's) speech, 13:1 expressly forbids the subordination of the lawcode either to a reporting context that authoritatively reports or comments from without, or to a revisionary process that would, by addition or subtraction, alter it from within. *What Moses could do with God's word, man may not do with Moses' word, which itself has become indistinguishable from God's word.* And it is precisely in this light that 18:14–22 appears so amazingly contradictory to 13:1–6. For we now have to deal with a mandate within the lawcode that provides for a legitimate revisionary process vis-a-vis the lawcode itself.

In relating the lawcode to its context within the second address, we can see very clearly that the divine utterance directly quoted by Moses in 5:28–31 authenticates his central teaching role in Deuteronomy, just as that same utterance, requoted by Moses with necessary modifications in 18:17–20, authenticates the Deuteronomic narrator's teaching role in his history. It will be instructive to set down sections of these two pericopes side by side. They represent Moses twice relating the same incident, and presumably the same utterance of God responding to the people's request for an intermediary to convey God's words to them:

5:23-31	18:16-19
Moses:	*Moses:*

. . . all the heads of your tribes and the elders came to me and said, ". . . Why should we now risk death? for this great fire will devour us. If we hear the voice of the LORD our God again we shall die. . ."

There you said,

"Let us not hear again the voice of the LORD our God, nor see this great fire again or we shall die."

When the LORD heard these words which you spoke to me, he said, "I have heard what this people has said to you: every word they have spoken is right. . .

Then the LORD said to me,

"What they have said is right.

. . . but you yourself stand here beside me, and I will set forth to you all the commandment, the statutes and laws which you shall teach them to observe in the land which I am giving them to occupy."

I shall raise up for them a prophet like you, one of their own race, and I will put my words in his mouth. He shall convey all my commands to them, and if anyone does not listen to the words which he will speak in my name I will require satisfaction from him."

Moses is described therefore as appealing to the same occasion and to the same divine utterance to authenticate both his own prophetic role and that of "a prophet like him." If we ask ourselves what specific laws, commandments, and statutes Moses is empowered by the commission of 5:31 to set forth, we are led by the very clarity of the phraseological composition of the book to answer: the laws and statutes introduced by the words of 12:1; "These are the statutes and laws . . ." and concluded by 26:16; "This day the LORD your God commands you to keep these statutes and laws. . . ." But when we ask what precise words are meant when God says in 18:18, ". . . and I will put my words into his mouth. He shall convey all my commands to them," the answer is not quite so straightforward. Historical critical answers would typically understand 18:14–22 as a later exegesis of an older tradition used anew to provide authentication either for a succession of prophets or else for the coming of a single "eschatological" prophetic mediator (so, e.g., von Rad, 1966:123–4). Thus, 'we are told, the "words" referred to in 18:18 would be those announced by a later anonymous prophet or prophets, truly commissioned by God. We are supposed to find here some kind of an attempt to authenticate the office of prophecy in Israel. My analysis will avoid such examples of historical exegesis not only because of their diachronic implications (I want to ask more elementary literary questions first), but also because they appear to me to be so general in their thrust that specific relationships between 18:14–22 and the rest of Deuteronomy and the Deuteronomic History are unable to be articulated.

There appear to me to be quite specific words which are referred to in 18:18. The words which the prophet like Moses is to speak to the Israelites are precisely twofold: just as Moses first relates the commandments of God in direct discourse (most often in the first address and most pointedly in the second address with the reporting of the decalogue) and then abruptly shifts to a much more authoritative manner of reporting that obliterates, with the exception of a few functionally important instances, the distinction between the divine reported and Mosaic reporting speech (the lawcode of 12-26), so also the prophet like Moses first relates the words of God/Moses in direct discourse (Deut) and then abruptly shifts to a much more authoritative manner of reporting that erases the distinction between the words of God/Moses and his own (Josh–2 Kgs). The "prophet like Moses" is the narrator of the Deuteronomic History, and through him, the Deuteronomist himself. The Deuteronomist uses Moses to explain by a hortatory lawcode the wide-ranging implications of the decalogue; this same author will soon be using the Deuteronomic narrator to explain in an exemplary history the wide-ranging implications of that lawcode.

Using this hypothesis, we can be very precise concerning the words of God referred to in 18:14–22. The very clarity of the phraseological composition of the history allows us to see that these words begin with the narrator's report in Joshua 1:1; "After the death of Moses, the servant of the LORD, the LORD said to Joshua, the son of Nun, his assistant . . ." and end with the final words of 2 Kings 25:30.

An important aspect therefore of the phraseological composition of the Deuteronomic History is highlighted by the following ratio: the decalogue of Deuteronomy 5:6–21 is to the lawcode of 12:2–26:15 as the directly quoted words of Moses in Deuteronomy are to the words of the narrator in Joshua–2 Kings. Concerning the laws and statutes *di-*

rectly quoted by Moses in 5:6–21 we are told that all the Israelites heard God's voice out of the darkness (5:23), and thus Moses' quoting of these laws at this point in the narrative is not described as presenting anything new to his audience. Similarly, we may assume that a great proportion of the Mosaic words found in Deuteronomy are presented as traditions known to most Israelites, not just to that privileged prophet of God who has risen up after Moses. Concerning, however, the laws and statutes reported by Moses in 12–26, we are explicitly told in chapter 5 that only Moses had gone near to listen to all these words of the LORD. His prophetic function is here at one and the same time to declare and to interpret God's word (*maggîd* and *mᵉlammed*). Without him, the Israelites are described as being unwilling and unable either to know or understand God's further word. Similarly, with the beginning of the Book of Joshua, we are presented with a narrator who has taken over the *maggîd* and *mᵉlammed* roles of Moses in such a way that he speaks with as much authority as Moses. The message he proclaims is as authoritative and necessary in relation to the previous book as Moses' lawcode was in relation to the covenantal decalogue that preceded its promulgation.[7]

4. It is precisely at this point that our comparison of the two texts that constitute respectively the prophetic offices of Moses and the Deuteronomic narrator, vis-a-vis the lawcode and Joshua–2 Kings, reveals a difference between what God is quoted by Moses as telling him in 5:23–31 and what God is requoted by Moses as telling him in 18:16–19—a crucial difference that may shed light on the apparent contradiction between 18:15–22 and 13:1–6; that is, the latter seems to forbid any subsequent prophetic activity that would either add to or take away anything from the "further words of God" embodied in the lawcode, while the former seems to sanction it.

Immediately after Moses quotes God's words predicting another prophet like himself, he adds a negative criterion for distinguishing the false from the true prophet: "When the word spoken by the prophet in the name of the LORD is not fulfilled and does not come true, it is not a word spoken by the LORD. The prophet has spoken presumptuously; do not hold him in awe" (18:22). It follows therefore that the people are to hold in awe and recognize the authority of the prophet whose word *does* come true. But when we look at Moses' previous reporting of these words of God in 5:23–31 and its surrounding context, we find not even a hint concerning the possibility that Moses might presume "to utter in my name what I have not commanded him." That there is no consideration of such a situation is entirely appropriate since the Book of Deuteronomy presents its hero's authority as *already* established, whereas we have seen in countless ways and in some detail how the book's primary function is precisely to establish the authority of the Deuteronomic narrator, its "author." It is against the background of these two pericopes that the monumental historiographic work of Joshua–2 Kings is seen in the clearest light. It is the narrator's claim that his monumental work, by the very wealth and accuracy of its historical interpretation, is a true explanation of the various events that shaped Israel's life from their incursion into the land to their exile out of the land. If Moses is depicted in the lawcode as formulating the laws, statutes, and commandments of the LORD in great detail, and only outlining the subsequent history of Israel in general terms (e.g., at the end of his first and second address), the narrator formulates the word of the LORD from another perspective: he puts the laws, statutes, and commandments of the LORD in the background of his own discourse by placing them in the mouth of Moses, and focuses his own discourse on establishing in great detail how the subsequent history of Israel is illuminated by such a background.

The status of the Deuteronomic History as the further words of Moses is directly challenged by 13:1. Not only is this pericope followed by a law relating to apostasy that negates the negative criterion found in 18:21–22, it is also preceded by a commandment forbidding apostasy; 12:29–31. It is as if Moses were depicted as stating in 13:1 that to add to or subtract from these further words of the LORD is tantamount to preaching apostasy since the word of God will have been altered *internally* by adding on spurious laws or withholding genuine ones, or *externally* by presuming to comment on or interpret these sacred and immutable words of the LORD. To alter the word of God is to follow other gods and to entice Israel to follow other gods. *The penalty is death (13:6) even if the (false) prophet offers a sign or a portent that comes true (13:3)*.

The command of 13:1 (as well as of 4:2 of which it is a reiteration) is in fact a hermeneutic anomaly within Deuteronomy. This would not be so were the lawcode formulated as the word of the LORD quoted in direct discourse, so that the "I" of this command referred to the LORD himself.[8] Here in the lawcode, the "I" of the command of 13:1 is the direct word of Moses himself and there is no way one can distinguish between the reporting "I" of Moses and the reported "I" of the LORD. Moreover, there is nothing within the lawcode that enables one to separate the reported words of the LORD from the commenting and responding words of Moses. In such a situation, where statute, commentary, and response are interwoven throughout the entire lawcode by the leveling speech of Moses, *the very words of Moses as interpretation of the further words of the LORD may not be added to or taken away from*. 13:1 is

totally at odds with 18:16–19 since the latter provides for an authoritative revision of the lawcode through the "further words" of the prophet
whom God would raise up after Moses. The hermeneutic dilemma
posed by 13:1 lies in the fact that it both validates and invalidates the
subsequent pericope of 18:14–22. 13:1a commands Israel to "observe
everything I command you." Therefore, the command to listen to and
obey the prophet coming after Moses must be observed. However,
13:1b commands that "you must not add anything to it, nor take anything away from it." Thus, the command to listen to and obey the
prophet coming after Moses must not be observed since this would be
adding to or taking something away from what Moses commands. How
are we to disentangle ourselves from the hermeneutic snare of 13:1 in
which the right hand giveth and the left hand taketh away?

There seem to be two compositional pointers that may set us in the
right direction in interpreting this pair of conflicting pericopes. First,
the word of the LORD expressed in direct discourse in chapter 18 has
the crucial function of authenticating the role of the Deuteronomic
narrator vis-a-vis his history. The "I" of 18:18–20 is directly that of the
LORD. On the other hand, the "I" of 13:1 directly refers to Moses. It
may be therefore that we are listening once more to that dialogue
between two voices that we have been describing in other sections of
Deuteronomy. Both voices are here on the surface of the text, both
voices are in obvious conflict with one another, and it is only by a close
compositional analysis that we can come to some conclusion about the
relative strength of each voice. In 13:1 we undoubtedly hear the voice
that has all along exalted the unique status of Moses as prophet vis-a-vis
Israel. As such, it fits in with the content of the entire lawcode, except
that of 18:14–22. But even here within the phraseological composition
of the two conflicting commands, there is an indication that the voice
represented by 18:14–22 has subordinated the voice found in 13:1 and
throughout most of the lawcode. For, whereas in 13:1 it is only Moses
speaking directly who seems to be exalting his unique role, in 18:18–20
it is (atypically in the lawcode) God who directly denies the unique role
attributed to Moses throughout the greater part of the surface of the
text.

Second, the very *content* of 13:1 is contradicted by the *composition* of
Deuteronomy itself. For if 13:1 forbids anything to be added to or taken
away from a lawcode that is as much commentary and response to
divine legislation as it is divine legislation itself, then the very setting of
this lawcode within the immediate context of the surrounding reported
words of Moses (especially 6:20–25) and within the larger context of
the reporting words of the narrator both in Deuteronomy and in

Joshua–2 Kings effectively neutralizes the command of 13:1 and subordinates the voice for which it stands to another voice that has taken over these words for its own purposes.

What we seem to have in 12:29–13:6 are the words of an argument that threatens, even under the penalty of death, the very existence of the enterprise carried through by the Deuteronomist. Taken at face value, this pericope supports an understanding of Israelite law and religion that is rooted in an attitude toward the divine word which we have called *authoritarian dogmatism*. Taken to its logical conclusion, this voice is the voice of a religious tyranny that allows no room for subsequent revision or revitalization of God's word. However, such a tyrannical voice is devastatingly neutralized in its very proclamation by the varied compositional strategies we have been noting. First, its content is contradicted by the context into which the Deuteronomist has placed the lawcode: Deuteronomy is an interpretation—a putting into perspective—of a lawcode in which is found the command not to interpret it. Second, its content is contradicted by a subsequent portion of the lawcode in such a way that, whereas Moses is described as saying no one may follow him as supreme interpreter of God's word, he is then described as quoting God in direct discourse to the effect that a prophet *will indeed* come after him. Third, and perhaps most importantly, the Deuteronomist has stilled this voice at the same time as he has allowed it to speak *simply by constructing the entire lawcode according to a surface style that directly contradicts this voice's own authoritarian tyranny.* How better to focus on the absurdity of forbidding any ongoing process of interpreting the word of God than by putting such a prohibition within a lawcode whose basic style already inextricably combines word of God with commentary and response to that word?

13:1–6 as representative of other dogmatic utterances like it in Deuteronomy is not just contrary to an isolated pericope following later in the lawcode, it is in fact subjected to a multifaceted compositional attack. This onslaught insures that its readers will ultimately reject its claims as quickly as they are made. The style of the prohibition has been deliberately fashioned to override and submerge its content. To believe that Moses could have spoken as directly as he is characterized as doing in the lawcode of Deuteronomy is, in terms of both style and substance, the means by which the Deuteronomist prepares his audience to accept as authoritative the subsequent books of his history.

The Second Address: A Summary Conclusion

Our discussion of Deuteronomy 5–26 was introduced by a general treatment of its ideological problems and by an illustration of how

surface phenomena of the text, elements on its phraseological, psychological, or temporal planes, may or may not concur with what is happening on its ideological plane. Our analysis of the address itself revealed
that whether its utterances were busy promoting the retributive justice
of God or his great mercy, whether the uniqueness of Moses or Israel
was being defended or attacked, *all* of the utterances were subordinated to a dominant ideological point of view that tended to diminish
the status both of Israel and Moses, within the broad context of God's
retributive justice. Thus, whether the *content* of an utterance advocates
God's consuming justice, as is the case with most of the utterances of
this address dealing with this matter, or rather God's ever gracious
mercy, as in the majority of statements in chapters 9 and 10 which
describe how God decided to give Israel the land in spite of their
disobedience, everything in the utterance serves in one way or another
to bolster the predominantly retributive nature of God's dealings with
Israel. For example, the content of 9:4–5 shows that the subject of
God's mercy is explicitly subordinated to his more basic desire for justice: to punish the nations whom Israel will dispossess. Similarly, when
the phraseological *composition* of the second address is obviously promoting the unique status of Moses, by giving him the authority to teach
God's commandment, laws, and statutes in the form of a direct address
to Israel rather than by reporting God's words in direct discourse as he
did with the decalogue, this phraseological device, although it is an
advance over Moses' first address as an illustration of his authority, still
is at the service of a subtle and complicated ideology. This ultimate
semantic authority diminishes Moses' unique authority either by means
of the reporting frame-breaks of chapters 10 and 27 or else by means of
directly contradictory utterances such as 18:17–21. A commandment as
troubling to it as 13:1 even highlights the basic paradox of the lawcode's
diction: the more exalted Moses' speech is, the less exalted it becomes.
Finally, the hint of a far distant future offering mercy for Israel, which
is found in the *conclusion* to Moses' first address, is swallowed up by the
absolutely merciless conclusion of the second address.

Most of the direct quotations of God in the second address also have
an essential connection with the ideological composition of the book.
That the decalogue is reported in direct discourse in 5:6–21 illustrates
the main distinction of the chapter that whereas God's ten words were
heard by the people, God's further words, chapters 12–26, are known
only through Moses' mediation. This characterizes Moses as a model of
the teacher of God's words that the narrator will become in Joshua–2
Kings. The divine utterance in 5:28–31 authenticates Moses' central
teaching role in the book, just as 18:17–20 authenticates the narrator's

teaching role in the history he presents to us. The divine words directly quoted in chapters 9 and 10 document Israel's immediate idolatrous disobedience at Horeb and God's merciful decision to give them the land in spite of this, and prepare the way for the Deuteronomist's perceptive insight that even in respect of the covenant of Horeb there is an element of unconditionality. Only with the direct divine utterance of 17:16 are we unable to suggest a clear-cut connection with the main ideological stance of the second address.

We see, then, how the overt content, composition, or conclusion of this address of Moses may at points promote or deny God's justice or mercy, diminish or enhance Israel's and Moses' unique roles. But in all cases, the ultimate semantic authority of the book is busy "taking over" these overt positions in the service of a dominating point of view that is ceaselessly a softening, rather than a rejection, of an unconditional covenant between God and Israel, and a diminution, for varying reasons, of the unique status of Israel and of their prophet Moses.

The overriding voice of the Book of Deuteronomy is against an immutable orthodoxy that would petrify the living word of God. If the word of God, expressed by Moses in Moab, is not absolutely immutable, neither is the promise made to our fathers. Here we can see from another angle the inner connection between the themes of the uniqueness of Moses and of Israel and the God of mercy and grace. If the terms of the covenant God made with the Israelites at Horeb are subject to revision at least in the sense of subsequent interpretation, then the same has to be said about the promise God made to our fathers. This promise made to the elect of Israel must not be so unconditionally understood that it provides a rigid guarantee of mercy in the face of widespread disobedience to God's law. On the one hand, whenever the election of Israel and the promise made to our fathers is invoked in the second address, these tendencies toward a comfortable security are generally neutralized by the overriding retributive justice of the covenant made at Horeb. On the other hand, whenever the authoritative status of Moses threatens to overwhelm the second address, this tendency is generally neutralized by the *critical traditionalism* inherent in Moses' style of reporting God's words in the lawcode. These two aspects of the composition of the second address help us see more clearly than in the first address how and why the themes of Moses' and Israel's unique statuses are bound up with the question of the ultimate justice or mercy of God.

Both the dominant voice of retributive justice and the subordinate voice of mercy heard throughout the second address embrace the traditions centering on the promise made to the fathers as well as the covenant made in Horeb. But the voice of mercy wants these two traditions to be understood according to an immutable and authoritarian dogmatism that apparently aimed at preserving the blessings of the elect of God at all costs. Thus, when it is allowed to appeal so often to the promise made to the fathers in the first address, and less often to this theme in the second address, its inclination to focus on the unconditional nature of God's promised blessing can be felt by the reader. When it is allowed to appeal to the conditional covenant at Horeb, its inclination is to focus on the immutable nature of the blessing that follows obedience to the law. Even through the reflecting voice of the Deuteronomist who has taken it over, it can still be heard to proclaim a religion that cuts beneficially both ways: "If you obey God, the covenant at Horeb ensures blessing; if you receive, as you must, the promise made to the fathers, then you must not have disobeyed God, or at least God's mercy has prevailed."

The voice of retributive justice on the other hand rearranges the relationship between these two traditions so that even when the merciful acts of God may not be denied, they are put in the perspective of God's justice. The polemic between these two voices does not involve the denial either of divine election or of God's mercy and justice. Each voice accepts all three traditions. Nor do they disagree about the element of unconditionality emphasized in the promise made to the fathers and the element of conditionality evident in the Mosiac covenant. The issue rather is whether these traditions are to be interpreted so dogmatically that they are absolutely immutable and incapable of varying interpretive emphases from age to age. The creative solution of the dominant voice of the second address of Moses is to admit an element of unconditionality in the Horeb covenant (e.g., chapters 9 and 10 in which Israel is promised the land even though she was disobedient) and to require an element of conditionality in the promise made to the fathers (e.g., by always surrounding such references with the unremitting condition of obedience).

The dominant voice of retribution wins out in the second address because it concentrates on exposing the authoritarian dogmatism implicit in the opposing voice. The ultimate semantic authority of the Book of Deuteronomy, as we have so far discovered it, proclaims an attitude toward the word of God that claims the right to emphasize now one aspect, viz., judgment, now another aspect, viz., mercy, of God's relationship with Israel, *depending on the situation in which they find themselves.* This right recognizes in the word of God a critical traditionalism and a revisionary capability that the opposing voice of the book tends to disallow. Whatever hints there were in the first address of a real ideological dialogue have faded away in the second address. A *monologic* Deuteronomic voice, characterized by a deep sense of critical traditionalism, appears to be in full control as the third address of Moses begins.

The Third Address of Moses (29:1–31:6)

In spite of the brevity of this address, it is still interrupted by an authorial frame-break in 31:1: "So Moses continued to speak these words to all Israel." The interruption here has the same function as the reporting frame-breaks of the first two addresses: the Deuteronomic audience's focal awareness is brought back, for an instant, to "present reality." However, this frame-break is particularly effective since the audience's focal awareness of Moses' words in chapters 29 and 30 is kept exclusively on an exilic disaster and a post-exilic hope that must have been central elements in the present reality of the Deuteronomic audience, either as an imminent probability or an already accomplished fact.

The surface composition of the third address is even more future-oriented than that of the second address. Whereas the bulk of the second address looks to the immediate future encompassed by Israel's history in the land, this third address concentrates on a far distant future that is explicitly exilic. Even though there are only five reported utterances in direct discourse within the address (29:19, 24, 25–28; 30:12, 13), all of them are reports of future speech and two are explicitly placed as spoken in the exile: 29:24 and 25–28. The temporal composition of this address begins where the last address left off. Whereas the words of the second address are explicitly characterized as directed to Moses' audience (11:1–2a) and not to future generations, in the third address Moses explicitly directs his words not just to his contemporaries but also to future generations, especially those of the exile:

> Nor is it with you only that I make this sworn covenant, but with him who is not here with us this day as well as with him who stands here with us this day before the LORD our God. (29:14–15)

> And when all these things come upon you, the blessing and the curse, which I have set before you, and you call them to mind among all the nations where the LORD your God has driven you . . . (30:1)

Besides these temporal aspects, there are a number of phraseological features that typify the third address. In the first two addresses, the periodic manipulation of the Deuteronomic reader back to present reality was accomplished primarily by the subliminal device of interrupting frame-breaks. Here in the third address, in addition to using this device in 31:1, the author also brings his audience back to present reality by the main content of Moses' address (exilic times), and by the words of Moses just quoted (29:14–15 and 30:1). In addition, Moses' utterances in 30:1–10 return to the prediction of God's mercy and grace which he spoke of in 4:29–39. But now there is an even greater emphasis on obedience to the law. Consider the change between descriptions of exilic repentance:

> . . . you will return to the LORD your God and obey his voice. (4:30)

> And you shall again obey the voice of the LORD, *and keep all his commandments which I command you this day.* (30:8; emphasis added)

The ideological composition of the third address is straightforward. As Moses' words begin to diminish in volume, the voice of the Deuteronomic narrator progressively increases its pitch. Just before we reach the traditional "last words of Moses" in the next section, we find that here in the third address it is extremely difficult to distinguish between the voice of Moses and the voice of the narrator. They have merged in respect both of their content and of their explicitly stated audience. In terms of the book's structure, Moses speaks to the exilic community in fulfillment of God's command reported in 5:28–31, just as the narrator is preparing to do, in fulfillment of God's prediction reported in 18:17–20.

As the surface of the text enlarges its description of the grace-filled fate of the exilic people, it also makes more explicit the legal context of God's mercy; thus the additional phraseology of 30:8 in respect of 4:30. We now see that the voice of mercy and hope was softened only temporarily in the central address of the book. The emphasis there was on the immediate future and what Israel had to do to *remain in* the land God was giving them. Here in the third address, emphasis is on the far-distant future of the exile, and on what Israel has to do to *regain* the land. But here, even more strongly than in the first address, obedience to the law and retributive justice are stated as the necessary conditions for the reception of God's grace and mercy.

Consider, finally, the new layer of meaning attached to phrases such as "the land which your fathers possessed" (30:5) and "the land which you are entering to take possession" (30:16). In the preceding addresses, whenever the phrase "your fathers" was used, explicit attention was on the patriarchs; when a phrase such as "the land about to be possessed" was mentioned, a wandering locale such as Moab was presumed to be the location of utterance. In the third address, however, a new dimension is made explicit by these phrases: "your fathers" now refers to those Israelites who had lived in the land from the occupation to the fall of Jerusalem; and the point of departure for "possessing the land" is now perhaps the exilic locale of Babylon.

The Collection of Moses' Final Sayings (31:7–33:29)

The final section of Moses' words acts as a concluding frame in a number of ways. The distinction between the "then" of the hero and the "now" of the narrator, which had begun to dissolve in the last section, now undergoes additional dissolution. That is, up to now the narrator did not interrupt the narrative with too many frame-breaks, so as to maintain the engagement of the reader. At the same time, a small number of frame-breaks had been used, subliminally to impress upon a later audience its "situation of discourse." But the book's "then" and "now" started to become merged in the content of the third address, and this process continues into the final section of the book. In this final section, we find traditional closing formulae that "form natural frames in folklore and literature" (Uspensky, 1973:146). The "last words of Moses" are a signal of his coming death and are a sign of the book's imminent ending.

Working then with this section's frame-breaking *content* is a general breakdown of the construction by which the author had generally maintained the internal point of view of the narrative. The relative reticence of the narrator in the first three addresses now abruptly ends, and we find instead the presence of many reporting utterances interruptingly scattered throughout the last section of Moses' words: 31:7a, 9, 14b–15, 22–23a, 24–25, 30; 32:44–45, 48; 33:1. The narrator's speech forms the final framing statement of the book, 34:1–12.

The final compositional irony of the book is that the Deuteronomist uses the basic device of "reported word of God → account of its precise fulfillment" against Moses himself! 32:48–52 consists of the narrator's report in direct discourse of God's decision to have Moses die in Moab as punishment for his sin in the wilderness of Zin. It is an advance in explicitness concerning *why* God was angry with Moses (cf. earlier 1:37; 3:36; and 4:21–22):

> ". . . because you broke faith with me in the midst of the people
> . . . because you did not revere me as holy in the midst of Israel."
> (32:51)

Then in 34:5 the narrator reports the death of Moses in Moab "according to the word of the LORD." The words of Moses are ended; the words of the narrator now take center stage in the history.

Postscript and Preview

The Book of Deuteronomy, in its ideological and surface composition, offers the reader a bird's-eye view of the entire history of Israel shortly to be recounted in detail in Joshua–2 Kings. This book is the history's opening frame and panoramic synopsis. The *spatial* perspective of Moses' audience and the narrator's audience is similar. The hero of Deuteronomy and his audience are in Moab, that is, outside the land, hoping to possess it with God's power and mercy; the author of Deuteronomy, and *his* audience are apparently in exile, that is, also outside the land, hoping to get in once more with God's mercy and power. The one audience is told under what conditions they will *retain* the land; the other audience under what conditions they will *regain* the land. The temporal perspective of both audiences merges in the phrases, "that day" and "this day." The "that (future) day" of the Book of Deuteronomy becomes the "that (past) day" of Joshua–2 Kings. The "this day" of Moses merges with the "this day" of the narrator. Their separate voices fuse as the book comes to a close.

In the end, all indications of a possible dialogue between opposing and equal ideological positions are now seen to have been merely compositional devices of the author, serving his basic purposes and supporting his basic point of view. The ideological composition of the Book of Deuteronomy is essentially monologic:

> Any intensification of another person's intonation in a particular word or a particular segment of a work is only a game allowed by the author to insure that his own direct or refracted word subsequently seems the more energetic. Every struggle of two voices for possession of and dominance in the word in which they appear is decided in advance—it is a sham struggle; all fully significant authorial interpretations are sooner or later gathered together in a single verbal center and in a single consciousness, and all accents are gathered together in a single voice. (Bakhtin, 1973:168)

Three

THE BOOK OF JOSHUA

Unlike Deuteronomy, the Book of Joshua cannot be segmented into a clear-cut framework simply by delineating the boundaries of reporting and reported speech. Whereas Deuteronomy was predominantly reported *discourse* formulated in extensive speeches with well-defined contours, Joshua and the remaining books of the Deuteronomic History are predominantly *narrative* with the frequent inclusion of numerous reported utterances of those whose exploits are recounted in the text. Between the book's beginning and end, the various shifts of perspective that occur on the phraseological, psychological, spatial-temporal, and ideological planes will help delineate the internal lines of this framework. We will begin our analysis by observing the division of the text according to its obvious thematic content: the occupation of the land (1–12), the apportioning of the land among the tribes (13–21), and subsequent events (22–24). We hope to discover how this superficial division relates to the various shifts of perspective that occur on the surface and deep planes of the book's composition. Our main concern will be to see how the reported speeches of various persons within the story intersect with one another and with the reporting speech that forms the basic narration of the story to constitute the ideological perspective of the entire book.

Preeminence within the reported speech in Joshua belongs to the utterances of Joshua and of God, although there are numerous instances of others' utterances. Most of the book consists of a reporting narrative that is the context for all this reported speech. In this chapter we will continue to be guided by the assumption we held while analyzing the Book of Deuteronomy, namely, that the ultimate ideological stance(s) of the book ought to be looked for both in the reporting narrative of the text as well as in its reported words, especially those of its principal heroes, God and Joshua. Thus, we may expect to find points of view expressed by the reporting speech of the narrator reflected in the reported speech of God and Joshua, and vice versa, on any or all compositional planes of the book. What we will be looking for is a continuation of the main lines of the apparent dialogue that characterized the ideological composition of Deuteronomy. This assumption means in practice that the ideological weight of a particular point of view cannot be determined solely by a consideration of attribution, that is, in such a way as to assign a higher status to a point of view primarily because of the supposed greater status of its speaker. It would be naive to assume, for example, that a point of view expressed in the direct discourse of God should *automatically* predominate over a conflicting point of view of Joshua, or that a particular stance of the narrator's would always "take over" a contrary view expressed, say, by the book's hero, Joshua. Let us now examine chapter 1 as a clear example of why differences in attribution are unable to give us any assistance in determining the ultimate status of a particular expressed point of view. We will then examine the reported and reporting speech of the book in order to see whether the voices of authoritarian dogmatism and critical traditionalism, that is, the main lines of the ideological "dialogue" we found in the Book of Deuteronomy, continue on into the Book of Joshua.

Joshua 1: A Paradigmatic Illustration

The first chapter of Joshua does not at all *begin* the story that the Deuteronomist has to tell his audience; it merely introduces that story by formulating the paradigmatic theme that runs through the entire story as it has been constructed by him. This theme is not new to the history; indeed it is central to the point of view found in Deuteronomy: the people's prosperity in the land which the LORD swore to give to their fathers will result from the diligent observance of "all the law which my servant Moses has given you" (1:7). The Deuteronomist is not so naive as to assume that the complex flow of events which comprises his history can be easily explained by a simplistic application of this paradigm. Rather, by means of a series of reported utterances he offers us a thematic reprise of the Book of Deuteronomy as it applies to the first stage of his long history, the initial occupation of the promised land. He will use the story that follows to interpret this traditional paradigm in a manner that is worthy of the voice of critical traditionalism that was, as we have seen, so much in control of the Book of Deuteronomy.

Chapter 1 does not begin the story because it is nothing but the report of a number of speeches, and contains only the minimum amount of narration necessary to introduce these speeches. In each case of reporting speech (1:1, 10, 12, 16a), the narrator simply introduces the speech of others; God (1:2–9), Joshua (1:11, 13–15), and the people (1:16–18). We have here first a general proposition expressed by means of a speech by God to Joshua, and then a dialogue between Joshua and the people. *Nothing happens except words.* First God and Joshua issue commands, then Joshua and the people accept those commands; Joshua by issuing further commands to the people in obedience to God, and the people by swearing obedience to Joshua. Much of this chapter is a pastiche of Moses' utterances from Deuteronomy, now put into the mouths of God, Joshua, and the people. I will select key sections first of God's speech, then of Joshua's, to illustrate the freedom with which certain points of view are attributed to varying individuals in the Deuteronomic History.

The first part of God's reported speech to Joshua is, with some small additions and changes, almost a literal rendering of a part of Moses' second address preceding the lawcode: Joshua 1:3–5a = Deuteronomy 11:24–25. In Deuteronomy these words are the reported words of Moses to Israel; here in Joshua they are the reported words of God to Joshua. In addition, these words of God in Joshua are described by him as a repetition of the words he spoke to Moses. This indicates that God's words quoted here in Joshua are not meant to be taken as God simply rehashing the speech of Moses to Israel in his own words to Joshua. Rather, it is to be understood that when Moses uttered these words to Israel, he was faithfully relating what God had originally told him. If we assume, as we have all along, that the Book of Joshua belongs to the same literary unity as the Book of Deuteronomy, then we have here a confirmation on the phraseological plane of the book that part at least of Moses' original speech in Deuteronomy 11:24–25 was Moses' reporting of God's words to him, but without any explicit attention to this fact having been drawn in the pericope in Deuteronomy. We have already seen how it is precisely in the second address of Moses that Moses' and God's utterances start to coalesce so completely that one cannot disentangle reported speech from reporting comment and response. If *we* cannot do so, the text here assumes authoritative knowledge that does allow such facility. The narrative is in complete control of the origins of Mosaic speech. A bit further on in this speech we see that 1:5c–7a is very close to Moses' words to Joshua in Deuteronomy 31:7–8 (there are also echoes of Deuteronomy 17:18–20; 29:8):

Josh 1:5c–7a	*Deut 31:7–8*
(5c) I will not fail you or forsake you. (6) Be strong, be resolute; it is you who are to put this people in possession of the land which I swore to give to their fathers. (7) Only be strong and resolute. . .	(8b) He will not fail you or for-sake you. (7) Be strong, be res-olute; for it is you who are to lead this people into the land which the LORD swore to give to their forefathers, and you are to bring them into possession of it. (8c) Do not be discouraged or afraid.

We can see from these two sections of God's speech to Joshua that it accomplishes two purposes. First, it presents the narrator as one who can report God's word directly just as Moses habitually did. Our narrator had already prepared us for his practice of directly quoting God in Joshua–2 Kings by beginning to quote God in direct discourse five times toward the end of the Book of Deuteronomy, as we pointed out in the previous chapter. Thus, the narrator immediately assumes his authoritative role here in Joshua, a role patterned after that of Moses as he is portrayed in Deuteronomy. Second, if the content and context of God's reported utterance exalts now the role of Joshua as the successor of Moses immediately following Moses' death, the phraseological composition of reported and reporting speech in Joshua 1:2–9 impresses upon the reader rather the role of the Deuteronomic narrator as successor to Moses vis-a-vis those readers whom he addresses. By reporting to us these words of God in Joshua 1, the narrator affirms in a new way that part of Moses' second (Deut 11:24–25) and third (Deut 31:7–8) addresses is equivalent to the reported speech of God.

If, as we admitted in the previous chapter, it is impossible to identify by internal means within the lawcode itself which words are intended there to represent the reported speech of God and which the reporting comment and response of Moses, and if we admit that it is useless to attempt to identify which words of the Book of Deuteronomy are actually those of its author as opposed to those presumably uttered by God or even Moses, it is still useful to compare these words of Joshua 1, put in the mouth of God, and those words of Deuteronomy 11 and 31, put in the mouth of Moses. Wherever they appear and in whomsoever's mouth they are placed, they are *authoritative* words whose meaning and context are under the obvious control of the narrator of this work. The Deuteronomist means to emphasize here that the words of Moses and the words of God are one. Moreover, he states without stating it that he is able to distinguish between God's reported and Moses' reporting speech, even in cases such as Deuteronomy 11:24–25 and 31:7–8 that had been presented on the surface of the text as the direct words of Moses rather than of God. By authoritatively commenting on and responding to the words of Moses in such a way as to understand these words now as proceeding directly from the mouth of the LORD, the narrator is once again intent upon increasing the authority of Moses' reported words at the same time as he is exalting his own role as Moses' successor. Whether, therefore, one sees Joshua 1:2–9 as simply God's rehashing of the previous words of Moses or as an indication that what Moses previously taught was indeed the word of God, the intent and effect of the passage is the same; Moses' authority is again emphasized and the authority of Moses' interpreter is thereby enhanced. "Moses' interpreter" means not only Joshua but also the Deuteronomic narrator.

A section of Joshua's command to the transjordanian tribes also portrays the narrator as an authoritative interpreter of Moses' word: Joshua 1:13–15 and Deuteronomy 3:18–20 are almost identical in content, but contain important phraseological differences that help us see the narrator's role more clearly.

Josh 1:12–15: Joshua to transjordanian tribes.	*Deut 3:18–20: Moses to transjordanian tribes.*
(12) To the Reubenites, the Gadites, and the half tribe of Manasseh, Joshua said,	
(13) "Remember the command which Moses the servant of the LORD gave you when he said,	(18a) At that time I gave you this command,
'The LORD your God will grant you security here and will give you this territory.'	"The LORD your God has given you this land to occupy;
(14) Your wives and dependents and your herds may stay east of the Jordan in the territory which Moses has given you,	(19) Only your wives and dependents and your livestock— I know you have much livestock—shall stay in the towns I have given you.
but for yourselves, all the warriors among you must cross over as a fighting force at the head of your kinsmen.	(18b) let all your fighting men be drafted and cross at the head of their fellow Israelites.
You must help them, (15) until the LORD grants them security	(20) This you shall do until the LORD gives your kinsmen security

like you and they too take possession of the land the LORD your God is giving them.

You may then return to the land which is your own possession, the territory which Moses the servant of the LORD has given you east of the Jordan."

as he has given it to you, and until they too occupy the land which the LORD your God is giving them on the other side of the Jordan; Then you may return to the possession which I have given you, every man to his own."

Joshua's quotation of Moses' command is a direct reference to Deuteronomy 3:18–20 in which we do not have a direct command of Moses but rather Moses' reporting of his previous command to the east Jordan tribes. As such, Joshua 1:12–15 is the Deuteronomic narrator reporting Joshua reporting Moses, just as Deuteronomy 3:18–20 is the Deuteronomic narrator reporting Moses reporting Moses. In the account of Moses' command in Deuteronomy 3, Moses prefaces the actual command with a statement of God's gift of the East Jordan land to the two and a half tribes Moses is addressing; then he issues the command itself. It is remarkable here that it is the LORD who gives the two and a half tribes the land in the command's preface (18) but in the command itself, Moses refers to "the towns *I* have given you" (19) and commands them to return to the possession "which *I* have given you" (20). Between the historical prologue and the command itself, the identity of the land-giver shifts twice from the LORD to Moses:

1. "the LORD" has given you the (east Jordan) land (18)
2. "I" (Moses?) have given you the (east Jordan) towns (19)
3. "the LORD" gives them the (west Jordan) land (20)
4. "I" (Moses?) have given you the (east Jordan) possession (20).

When Joshua is described in Joshua 1 as quoting this previous command of Moses, he quotes directly only what was Moses' preface to his command. Joshua then gives the rest of Moses' command in the form of his own direct command. Even though he shifts some of the content around, Joshua still retains the same sequence with regard to the identity of the land-giver, changing the "I" of Moses' direct command to the appropriate "Moses" of his own formulation of the command:

1. "the LORD" gives you the (east Jordan) land (13)
2. "Moses" has given you the (east Jordan) land (14)
3. "the LORD" gives them the (west Jordan) land (15)
4. "Moses" has given you the (east Jordan) land (15).

Notice that the Deuteronomy 3 formulation is ambiguous: does the "I" of vv. 19 and 20 refer to Moses or to God? Or are we to assume, for example, since Moses never refers to west Jordanian land "which *I* am giving you," that the important distinction here is between the land east of the Jordan, which can be referred to as given to Israel by God *or* by Moses, and the land west of the Jordan, which can only be referred to as given by the LORD? When we turn to the Book of Joshua's reformulation of this Mosaic command, even though Joshua has retained the content of the command and the exact alternation between "the LORD" and "I", he has removed the ambiguity about the identity of "I" by placing "Moses" in its place.

In this speech of Joshua, as in God's speech above, we see the reappearance of the authoritative word of Moses in a different context. What Moses originally quoted himself as saying in Deuteronomy 3, Joshua is now quoted as saying in Joshua 1. Once again we see the authorial voice emphasizing a particular theme by placing it in the mouth of now one, now another, authoritative personage in his story. Whereas God's speech centered attention on the intimate connection between prosperity in the land and observance of the law, Joshua's command to the transjordanian tribes emphasizes for some reason the distinction between the promised land which only the LORD can be said to have given Israel and the gift of the land east of the Jordan, which may be attributed either to the LORD or to Moses as its donor.

The response of the people (1:16–18; are these the words of the whole community or just of the transjordanian tribes?) to Joshua's commands is to pledge their obedience to Joshua. We should keep in mind here that the success of Israel's occupation of the promised land is a foregone conclusion since Deuteronomy 9–10 had already answered the question of how an undeserving and disobedient Israel could still receive the land. What is still to be discovered is how the complicated nature of Joshua's and the people's response to God's commands is related to the *certainty* of God's gift of the land.

Finally, notice how often the theme of *promise* repeats itself in the eighteen verses of chapter 1:

"the land which I am giving them" (2)
"I have given it to you as I promised Moses" (3)
"all this shall be your land" (4)
"the land which I swore to give to their fathers" (6)
"the country which the LORD your God is giving you
    to possess" (11)
"the LORD your God will give you this territory" (13)
"the territory which Moses has given you" (14)
"the land which the LORD your God is giving them" (15)
"the territory which Moses has given you" (15)

The exact nature of the fulfillment of that promise is somehow dependent on observance of the law, as exemplified in vv. 7–9 and 16–18. Chapters 2 through 24 of Joshua explore the nature and extent of God's fulfilled promise in relation to the occupation of the land and in relation to Israel's observance of the law. The fact that the book describes that fulfillment as considerably less than the promise outlined in chapter 1 is central to the ideological position of the Deuteronomist vis-a-vis the occupation of the land.

The First Section of Joshua (1–12): How Joshua and Israel Fulfilled the Commands of the LORD

We have just seen how Joshua 1 is an exercise in shift of attribution: what Moses once said in Deuteronomy, God and Joshua now say in Joshua. What they all say constitutes the command and promise of God. Chapters 2–12 comprise the Deuteronomist's formulation of how Joshua and the Israelites fulfill that command. We shall now see in surprising fashion how the entire first section of Joshua is a polemic response to a simplisitc characterization of Joshua's and Israel's fulfillment of God's commands.

Reported Speech of God and Joshua in 1–12

1. Did Joshua actually fulfill all the commands laid on Moses by the LORD? By examining first the direct discourse of God, we will begin to see how each corpus of reported speech in this first section shapes and defines what "the LORD's commands" means, thereby predetermining what constitutes fulfillment of that command. Here in Joshua 1–12, God is quoted in direct discourse in 1:2–9; 3:7b–8; 4:2–3, 16; 5:2b, 9b; 6:2b–5; 7:10b–15; 8:1b–2, 18b; 10:8b; 11:6b. As one would expect, the bulk of God's direct utterances either prophesies the future (3:7b; 6:2b; 10:8b; 11:6b) or simply issues commands (3:8; 4:2–3, 16; 5:2b; 6:3–5; 7:10b, 13–15; 8:2a, 2c, 18b). However, we have three divine utterances which constitute an *interpretation* and/or *application* of an existing authoritative "word," either of God or of Moses or of Joshua.

The first instance of this interpretive word of God concerns the circumcision of the Israelites at Gilgal. In 5:2b the LORD commands:

> "Make knives of flint, seat yourself, and make Israel a circumcised people again."

After this command is obeyed, we are then told that God said to Joshua:

"Today I have rolled away from you the reproaches of the Egyptians." (5:9b)

At this point we need not attempt to explain the significance of the LORD's allusion; we shall do so below at the appropriate place. What is directly relevant and immediately obvious, even without considering the specific intent of God's allusion, is that God is quoted in v. 9b as revealing the intent of his command in 2b to circumcise the Israelites. A second kind of divine interpretive word is found in 7:11–12. Here, after the Israelites' initial defeat at the hands of the army of Ai, God tells Joshua:

> Israel has sinned; they have broken the covenant which I laid upon them, by taking forbidden things for themselves. They have stolen them, and concealed it by mingling them with their own possessions. That is why the Israelites cannot stand against their enemies; they are put to flight because they have brought themselves under the ban. (7:11–12)

Israel's temporary defeat at Ai, God explains, is caused by (Achan's) taking of forbidden things at Jericho, an action that is in direct conflict with Joshua's command of 6:17–19. Moreover, what Achan did was contrary to the oath of obedience quoted in 1:16–17 and deserving of death. We have here an instance where God's direct word (7:11–12), by interpreting an event in Israel's history, interprets and applies an authoritative command of Joshua. God's direct word interprets an authoritative word in a third way in 8:2:

> Deal with Ai and her king as you dealt with Jericho and her king; *but you may keep for yourselves the cattle and any other spoil that you may take.*

Here a Mosaic command is interpreted and applied precisely by its temporary inapplicability in a particular instance, that is by *epiekeia*. God's words here are in direct conflict with the Mosaic rules for holy war found in Deuteronomy 20:15–18 where the rules for nearby cities command that "you may not leave any creature alive" (Deut 20:16). This particular application of the Mosaic law is actually a decision to refrain from applying the law in its full rigor, and is all the more to be emphasized because it immediately follows upon the stoning of Achan for having taken forbidden things at Jericho. Achan has just been executed for the private, unauthorized taking of spoil that all the Israelites are now permitted to take at Ai! We shall see that this contrast is an important part of the overall composition of this section of Joshua.

Through an examination of the direct utterances of God in Joshua 1–12, we can tentatively conclude that the word of the LORD is not static or unchangeable. God himself is described in his direct utterances as interpreting and applying his own words (either issued directly by him, or through Moses' or Joshua's mediation) in a threefold manner: he interprets them directly as in chapter 5, he interprets them indirectly by interpreting the events that follow inexorably upon actions seen to be contrary to those commands as in chapter 7 , and he interprets his own commands by temporary suspension of them as in chapter 8. This characterization of the word of the LORD as open to further understanding, interpretation, and application is not a haphazard feature of the divine utterances. We shall now turn to the direct discourse of Joshua to see that it too portrays the law of God in a dynamic and changeable light.

2. In this first section, Joshua is directly quoted in 1:11, 13–15; 3:5b, 6b, 9b–13; 4:5b–7, 21b–24; 5:13c, 14d; 6:6b, 7b, 10b, 16b–19, 26b; 7:7–9, 19b, 25b; 8:4–8; 9:22b–23; 10:12b, 18b–19, 22b, 24b, 25b. Just as God's (1:2–9) and the people's (1:16–18) utterances authenticate Joshua's role as successor to Moses, so too Joshua's first utterance in the Book of Joshua (1:11, 13–15) is a report of his authoritative commands to the people. If we look closely at the direct words of Joshua reported in Joshua 2–12, we shall be able to make some interesting comparisons with the direct words of God discussed above. As was the case with the reported speech of God, most of these direct words of Joshua either simply issue commands or prophesy the future. In addition, Joshua asks questions (5:13c, 14d; 9:22b) and implores the LORD in behalf of his people (7:7–9). There are, however, four classes of Joshua's utterances which understand, interpret, or apply authoritative words of God, Moses, or Joshua himself.

By the very fact that Joshua *reiterates in his own words* the directly reported commands of God, he thereby understands, interprets, and applies them in a distinctive way that emphasizes and sanctions a kind of authoritative and critical stance toward the word of God. This mode of interpretation occurs four times. In 3:9b–13 Joshua reiterates God's command of 3:7b–8. Similarly, 4:5b reiterates 4:2–3; while 6:6b, 7b, 10b, 16b reiterate 6:2b–5, and 8:4–8 reiterates 8:1b–2. It is obvious here that all of these reiterations are *reformulations* that *interpret*. These interpretations can involve phraseological expansion (3:9b–13) or compression (4:5b) of the already reported word of God, and it can be the case that an expansion involves a substantive issue. For example, Joshua's command in 6:7b to place the soldiers from the two and a half tribes in front of the Ark while encircling Jericho has no reflex in the preceding word of God, and one may therefore presume that this small detail has a direct bearing on the overall conception of the narrative. As one would expect, this first mode of interpretation (reiteration) has no counterpart in the direct utterances of God studied above. However, the next three modes of Joshua's interpretive words do find an echo in the reported words of God in Joshua 1–12. As we have seen, God interprets authoritative commands by articulating their intent, or by interpreting events that reveal disobedience to these commands, or by *epiekeia,* that is, by refraining, in a specific instance, from applying the full rigor of the law. These modes of interpretation are precisely mirrored in Joshua's own utterances.

Just as God expressed the divine intent of the circumcision of the Israelites at Gilgal (5:9b), so too Joshua twice explains the significance of God's command to set down the stones from the Jordan "in the camp where you spend the night" (4:3):

> These stones are to stand as a memorial among you; and in days to come, when your children ask you what these stones mean, you shall tell them how the waters of the Jordan were cut off before the Ark of the Covenant of the LORD when it crossed the Jordan. Thus these stones will always be a reminder to the Israelites. (4:6–7)

Joshua repeats this interpretation in 4:21–24 with important additions and changes, but the mode of interpretation is the same as before: to explain why God gave such a command in the first place. A second mode of interpretation used by Joshua is similar to God's procedure in Joshua 7 of interpreting an authoritative command by explaining that a specific event, the intital defeat of Israel by the army of Ai, is caused by disobedience to that command. Joshua's words to Achan are a direct reflex of the divine words of 7:10–15:

> What trouble have you brought on us! Now the LORD will bring trouble on you. (7:25)

The final mode of interpretation used by Joshua is precisely that used by the LORD: *epiekeia.* Just as the LORD refrained from applying the full rigor of the law of Deuteronomy 20:15–18 in the specific instance of allowing the Israelites to keep "cattle and any other spoil" from Ai, so also Joshua is reported as suspending this same law with respect to Rahab of Jericho:

This city shall be under solemn ban: everything in it belongs to the
LORD. No one is to be spared *except the prostitute Rahab and everyone
who is with her in the house,* because she hid the men whom we sent.
(6:17; emphasis added)

The Reporting Speech of Joshua 2–12: The Story of the Occupation
In our examination of the reported speech of God and Joshua, there
has emerged a similar hermeneutic pattern of interpretation with respect to the authoritative words of God, Moses, and Joshua. The three
specific ways in which both God's and Joshua's words interpret what
may generically be termed the law of God force us to recall the words
of Moses in Deuteronomy 13:1:

See that you observe everything that I command you: you must not
add anything to it, nor take anything away from it.

In the previous chapter, we singled out this statement as representative
of the voice of an *authoritarian dogmatism* at odds with, and completely
subordinated to, the dominant ideological stance of the Book of
Deuteronomy. This ultimate semantic authority of the book we characterized as a voice of *critical traditionalism,* primarily because its attitude
toward the Mosaic law and the promise made to the fathers recognizes
the constant need for revision and varying interpretations of the traditions that formed the core of its message. As we now begin to examine
the narrative proper of 2–12, we shall see how these two voices of
unequal weight find expression in the recounting of Israel's occupation
of the land. Even though Deuteronomy 9–10 had made the success of
the occupation a foregone conclusion, a consistent perspective on the
justice and mercy of God and on the unique status of Israel and their
prophetic leader, now Joshua, is what weaves together the various episodes that form the fabric of this section.

Any attempt to construct an adequate compositional framework of a
narrative ought to provide insight concerning both the very selection of
episodes included in the story itself as well the particular perspectives
according to which each episode is presented. What is it about these
particular exploits and their treatment that ties them together into a
unified literary whole? To answer that they all took place in the course
of the occupation is to provide no answer at all. For the choice of
materials is obviously highly selective and the particular vision that
infuses each story is equally narrow. What guides the selective vision
constituting the very narrative? How is it specifically connected with
what literarily precedes it, that is, the Book of Deuteronomy, and with
its subsequent literary context, the rest of the Book of Joshua? As we

begin to answer such questions, we are again led to affirm our assumption that basic points of view discovered in the reported speech of God and Joshua are likely to be found in the reporting speech of the narrative on any or all of its compositional planes. As we attempted to show in the preceding section, a key issue in the reported speech of God and Joshua concerned the understanding, interpretation, and application of "the law which my servant Moses has given you" (1:7). This line of investigation leads us to expect that the Deuteronomist's own description and interpretation of the events that comprised the occupation of the land will be *his* attempt to declare and teach what this "law of Moses" as the word of God means. There are a number of instances within the history itself which offer microscopic models for this particular way of approaching the narrative. When a question arises as to the meaning of something, be it of the Mosaic precepts, statutes and laws (Deut 6:20), or of the wrath of the LORD (Deut 29:24), or of a particular command of the LORD (concerning the stones of Josh 4:6, 21), *the answer is given in the form of a narrative.* Thus, the short story of Deuteronomy 6:21–25 is a narrative that gives the significance of the Mosaic lawcode; the short story of Deuteronomy 29:25–28 is a narrative that interprets the misfortunes recounted in the previous verses; and the short stories of Joshua 4:7 and 4:22–24 are narratives that interpret God's command to set up a memorial or sign at Gilgal. These three instances involve Moses or Joshua "interpreting" either the Mosaic lawcode itself, or a particular command of the LORD, or the wrath of the LORD, by constructing a narrative.

We begin our analysis of the occupation, therefore, by assuming that we have a series of events narrated in such a way as to highlight a number of *cruces interpretationis* with respect to the word of God in general and the "book of the law" in particular.

The Spying of Jericho and Encounter with Rahab (2:1–24)

Neither God nor Joshua speak directly in chapter 2, and yet the story therein is an extended dialogue between them on the justice and mercy of God, on the Mosaic law and the promise made to the fathers, and on the unique status of Israel. The narrative contains a number of interesting shifts in point of view on the surface that intersect in a complex way to serve the ideological thrust of the narrative. Consider first the implications of Joshua's decision to send spies into Jericho. Immediately after the Israelites admonish Joshua to be strong and resolute (1:18), thus echoing the LORD's words (1:6, 7, 9), Joshua sends two spies out to reconnoiter the country. We are immediately reminded of Deuteronomy 1 in which Moses recalls his words to Israel at Kadesh–Barnea:

> Go forward and occupy the land in fulfillment of the promise which
> the LORD, the God of your fathers made you; do not be discour-
> aged or afraid. (Deut 1:21)

Instead, the people timidly requested spies to reconnoiter the land. As
Moses pointed out then, the spies' reports discouraged the Israelites,
they muttered treason, and God punishes them by forbidding their
generation to enter the land. In the first chapter of Joshua, we had God
telling Joshua what Moses had told the Israelites:

> Now it is time for you to cross the Jordan. . to the land which I am
> giving you. . . .Do not be fearful or dismayed. (1:2, 9)

In response, Joshua timidly sends out spies to reconnoiter the country,
and we are immediately alerted that Joshua may not be as strong and
resolute as God and the people had encouraged him to be. The spy
incident in Deuteronomy discouraged and disheartened the Israelites,
but here in Joshua the spies exultantly return with the news that the
inhabitants are panic-stricken at Israel's approach. Nevertheless, we
sense immediately that this new generation of Israelites under Joshua is
no more confident of God's promise to give them the land than their
predecessors were. They seem to need eyewitness proof before they will
carry out the crossing of the Jordan.

Then consider the extended dialogue between Rahab and the two
spies. Central here is Rahab's insistence that the spies take an oath to
spare all in her household once the attack on Jericho takes place. In
turn, the spies make explicit more than once that their oath will be
binding only so long as Rahab honors her promise not to betray them.
Note that the promise made to Rahab by the spies is in direct disobedience to the Mosaic rules for holy war in Deuteronomy 20:15–18 (see
also Deut 7:1–5). We have already seen in our discussion of the direct
speech of Joshua that when the city was about to be taken Joshua
proclaimed the ban according to which nothing living was to be spared,
but he explicitly exempted Rahab and everyone in her household (6:17)
in accordance with the spies' promise to Rahab here in chapter 2. How
could the spies take such an oath and how could Joshua sanction it,
especially since Achan is later stoned to death (7:25) for defying the ban
in the very attack on Jericho? How does one determine what "defying
the ban" means?

We see, therefore, that this episode raises two basic hermeneutic
questions for the Israelites concerning the word of God. First, how does
one interpret and apply God's command to put complete trust in him
while taking over the land; how does an Israelite comport himself so as

not to be discouraged and afraid? Second, how does one interpret the Mosaic rules for holy war? Both questions are directly related to the fact that, in spite of Israel's apparent timidity, a timidity that had previously helped to condemn a whole generation of Israelites to die outside of the land, and in spite of Israel's apparent defiance of the ban, a defiance which would subsequently bring death to Achan and his household—in spite of all this—Israel miraculously invades and conquers Jericho. We see that there is at the heart of this story of Rahab and the spies a fundamental consideration of the status of Israel vis-a-vis their God, seen against the background of their successful occupation of a land that had belonged to others.

If we look at the psychological and spatial-temporal composition of this episode, it will become obvious that this story involves a continuation of the basic themes so central to the Book of Deuteronomy. We begin to hear once more the main voice of that book as it attempts to counter an authoritarian dogmatism by using the narrative traditions of Israel to illustrate the sometimes unconditional aspect of the covenant at Horeb and the sometimes conditional aspect of the promise made to the fathers. We will be led to see in the Rahab incident how just as Israel receives a land of which they are explicitly described as not deserving, so also certain inhabitants of the land, here represented by Rahab and her household, avoid a punishment of which they, as part of their community, have been explicitly described as deserving. In other words, we have an extended meditation on Deuteronomy 9:4–5.

The shift in perspective between chapters 1 and 2 could not be more complete. On the psychological plane, what first strikes us is that the narrator portrays Rahab as adopting the point of view of the invaders: she recounts the mighty acts of God, the terror they inspired in the inhabitants of the land, and even utters a typical Israelite profession of faith:

> for the LORD your God is God in heaven above and on earth below.
> (2:11)

If she describes her compatriots as panic-stricken, it is still obvious that she has complete power over the lives of the timid Israelites. Whereas we would have expected the Israelites' *first* crossing of the Jordan to have resulted in the inhabitants of Jericho concealing themselves among the stalks of flax on every rooftop in utter fear, the reverse is the case. It is in Rahab's hands whether Israel will so easily conquer Jericho. The psychological perspective of this episode is turned upside-down. Whereas it is the non-Israelite, Rahab, who acknowledges that "the

LORD has given this land to [Israel]" (2:9), it is the Israelite spies who reveal that they do not deserve the land given them by the LORD since they allow themselves to be pressured into taking an oath that apparently defies the ban. Seen from the point of view of those whose land is about to be possessed, the occupation is not the conquest of the unrighteous by the righteous, but simply the fulfillment of a promise made by a God who is "God in heaven above and on earth below" (2:9).

We have with the Rahab episode the first hint in the Deuteronomic History of a perspective that will play as great a role in the book of Judges as it does here in the Book of Joshua. When Moses in Deuteronomy 9:4–5 explained to the Israelites that they were to occupy the land not because of their own righteousness but because of the nations' wickedness, he expressed this theme from the point of view of the Israelites. We now find this same theme in Joshua 2 expressed from the point of view of the dispossessed nations. Rahab is the typological representation of those nations discussed in the second part of Joshua and in the opening chapters of the Book of Judges who are not conquered and dispossessed by the Israelites. That some inhabitants of Jericho at the very beginning of the occupation escape destruction (Josh 2 and 6), that some nations remain in possession of their land during Joshua's lifetime (13:1–6), and that some nations remain unconquered by the Israelites in the succeeding generations after Joshua's death (Judg 1 and 2) all involve the very same explanation as that of Deuteronomy 9:4–5. But the formulation found here in Joshua 2 is expressed with a shift into the point of view of the non-Israelite: it is not because of Rahab's merit that she and her household will continue to occupy the land, but because of the wickedness and lack of faith of Israel.

Why the two spies went to the house of a prostitute named Rahab and thus effect her salvation is no more able to be explained than why God chose Israel to occupy the land. Once it is seen that *the story of Rahab is really the story of Israel told from the point of view of a non-Israelite*, then the larger themes of the justice and mercy of God vis-a-vis Israel can be recognized as central to the very story itself and to its position as the initial episode in the Deuteronomist's account of the occupation of the land.

The story involves also a *spatial* shift into the land even before Israel ceremonially crosses over in chapter 3. The dialogue between Rahab and the spies, taking place in the land at a time prior to the actual crossing, is meant to outline and color the subsequent account of the crossing of Israel in 3:1–5:1. In this same sense, the Rahab story is a *temporal* preview of the significance of the Israelite occupation. The narrative of Joshua 2 performs the same function for the rest of the book that the schematic cyclical philosophy of history found in Judges 2:6–3:6 will perform for the rest of that book: we have a preview of the ideological point of view of the entire book, a point of view that produces a subtle and complex picture of Israel's relationship to God and to the nations whose land they have come to possess.

How can this episode be a narrative treatment of the theme of God's mercy and justice when nothing is explicitly said therein about the merit or integrity of either Israel or the Canaanite prostitute? The answer lies not only in my initial remarks about how the literary context of this episode invests the actions of Joshua and the spies with an aura of timidity, faithlessness, and apparent wickedness, but also in the very psychological composition of the story itself which shifts the narrative from the previous point of view of Israel to the point of view of the dispossessed Canaanites. This shift in perspective allows us to see that the situation of the Canaanites vis-a-vis the justice and mercy of God is amazingly close to that of the Israelites. Rahab is allowed to settle permanently in the midst of Israel for exactly the same reasons that Israel is allowed to settle permanently in her homeland. Rahab, as representative of the dispossessed nations, is in a situation similar to Israel's. Once again we begin to hear how the uniqueness of Israel vis-a-vis their God is tempered by the prevailing voice of the Deuteronomic History. We can see how this is accomplished through the phraseological composition of the Rahab story.

Rahab's first words to the Israelite spies contain a confession of faith in the LORD (2:11). The spies respond by taking an oath promising to deal honestly and faithfully (*ḥesed we'ᵉmet*) by Rahab (2:14). They point out, however, that this oath or "token of good faith" (*'ôt 'ᵉmet*) is binding only so long as she follows their instructions (2:14, 17, 20). Now this relationship of an oath of salvation that establishes an obligation of obedience is exactly the relationship between Israel and the LORD described in great detail in Deuteronomy and summarized in the opening speech of God to Joshua in 1:2–9. If therefore Rahab stands in this story not only for her own nation but also in the place of Israel, it is now clear that the two Israelite spies stand in the place of God. When Rahab agrees to the spies' conditions, "It shall be as you say" (2:21), she is thereby described as accepting a binding relationship with Israel (God) that *from her point of view* is seen as justice. On the other hand, given the legal background of Deuteronomy 20:15–18 and 7:1–5, the oath she forces the spies to take must be seen *from their point of view* as a transgression of the Mosaic law at worst, or at best as a merciful decision—because of Rahab's prior confession of faith in the LORD—not to apply the full rigor of the law in her case. That the two spies are meant to stand for God in this episode is clear if we recall that when God decides in Deuteronomy 9–10 to allow Israel to occupy the land in spite of their disobedience, the reason given is not only because of the wickedness of the other nations but also because of the promise he made to the fathers (Deut 9:5). The complicated relationships in Deuteronomy 9:4–5 between God, Israel, and the other nations are once more affirmed in Joshua 2 with the spies taking the place of God, Rahab taking the place of Israel, and Israel taking the place of the other nations. Rahab's descendants will continue to dwell in the land not because of their own merit or integrity but because of the "wickedness" of Israel and the promise made to their ancestress by the Israelite spies.

In addition, Rahab's reference to "what you did to Sihon and Og, the two Amorite kings beyond the Jordan" (2:10), recalls Moses' account of the transjordanian passage of the Israelites in Deuteronomy 2 and 3. There, as we pointed out in the last chapter, the narrator's frame-breaks (e.g., Deut 2:10–12), as well as Moses' reporting of God's direct words (e.g., Deut 2:9), represent a complicated picture of God's mercy and justice toward Moab and Ammon and the other nations living there, complicated even further by the promise made to the Israelites. The story here in Joshua 2 reviews this whole question from another perspective: the LORD will deal with all the nations *in* the promised land in the same way as he dealt with those nations living *outside* the promised land, in respect of the complications that arise because of promises made both to Israel and to other nations. In all cases, there is to be mercy and *ḥesed*, but these divine actions are intimately bound up with the question of retributive justice. Neither Rahab nor Israel deserve God's beneficent acts toward them, but once he has entered into a promissory and legal relationship with them, obedience to his commands are as necessary inside the land as it was necessary outside it in Trans-Jordan. Thus, what God did to Sihon and Og was an act of justice from the point of view of these Amorite kings, but an act of mercy from the point of view of Israel: Og and Sihon deserved to be defeated but Israel did not deserve the victory they were allowed to achieve.

The underlying ideological position of the Rahab story as a preview of the entire Book of Joshua is that some nations (represented by Rahab) will be spared a punishment they deserve, just as Israel (also represented by Rahab) obtains a land they do not deserve. Similarly, it will be necessary for God (represented by the two Israelite spies) to fulfill his word and apply his law in a manner that at times may appear to violate that word, but actually establishes mercy and equity, that is, what the spies of Joshua 2 call *ḥesed we 'ᵉmet* (2:14). There is therefore a nonconcurrence of the phraseological and psychological composition of this chapter with its ideological composition. The surface of the story presents a viewpoint largely external to the theological concerns of the human heroes of the story, Joshua and the Israelites. The deep composition utilizes this "estranged" point of view to present a basic ideology that intimately concerned these theological questions. The surface point of view of Joshua 2—that is, the occupation as viewed by a non-Israelite—is carried out to the very end of the chapter. For the two spies recross the Jordan, return to Joshua and relate to him their experiences, the significance of which they give by concluding their account and the chapter with a rephrasing of Rahab's words of 2:9–11:

> The LORD has put the whole country into our hands, and now all its people are panic-stricken at our approach. (2:24)

The authority of these words derives, strangely enough, from their having been uttered not by God, nor by Joshua, but by a non-Israelite and a prostitute at that.

The Crossing of the Jordan (3:1–5:1)

1. Joshua 3 now shifts back to the Israelite point of view and narrates the crossing of the Jordan from this perspective. The chapter begins with the Israelites about to cross the Jordan and ends with the words, "and all Israel passed over on dry ground until the whole nation had crossed the river" (3:17). Joshua 4 then combines the two accounts of the crossing of the Jordan (that of chapter 2 and that of chapter 3) in a typical Deuteronomic explanation of the twofold significance of these crossings as memorialized by the twelve stones from the Jordan set up in Gilgal at God's command.

The need for a competent literary analysis to precede historical critical considerations of biblical material such as this is exemplified by the unintelligibility of typical commentaries on these two chapters. For example, the obvious erudition and good sense of a scholar like J. A. Soggin (1972) do not keep his analysis of 3:1–5:1 from approaching depths of historical critical obfuscation that are an embarassment to the hermeneutic aims one should expect of biblical commentaries. Whatever may be the historical genesis of the "obvious" chronological discrepancies of 3:2 and 4:19, as they look back to 1:11 and forward to 5:11 respectively, and however obvious it is that in chapter 4 there is evidence of two parallel "recensions" sharing the theme of twelve stones, the reader of this text, be he a contemporary of the

Deuteronomist or of Soggin, seeks to determine what the text *in its present form* is saying to him. And contrary to the often unvoiced claim of the modern scholar, his ancient counterpart was no less capable of recognizing and dealing with textual and chronological discrepancies. If it is true, as this analysis has been attempting to show throughout, that the Deuteronomic History is fundamentally a brilliant exercise in the hermeneutics of the word of God, then it is important to let the text provide the foundation for what are crucial problems of interpretation and what are not. However much the chronological indications of 3:2 and 4:19 may actually raise "historical" problems, they do not seem to set up a problem in the narrative since they do not appear to play a key role in the issues and themes that are central to the story. A preliminary reading of the episode should look for indications from the text concerning what is important to the story being told; there is simply nothing in the text at this point either to warrant investing such hermeneutic energy in the problem of these chronological discrepancies, or to justify basing one's interpretation of this episode upon such a perspective. Discrepancy or not, the chronological datum of 3:1, for example, serves no apparent function in the text other than to allow the reporting context to indicate that the authoritative words of Joshua in 1:11 are about to be fulfilled. There *are* other chronological discrepancies that do seem to affect the story as a whole, and we will deal with them in great detail in a moment.

2. Joshua 3:1–5:1 is the first occurrence of an especially important framing device in the book: the *liturgical narrative*. Because the special world of the ritual can be so clearly demarcated as to its beginning and its end, the liturgical narrative is especially appropriate as an important framing device of the Book of Joshua. If Joshua 1 constitutes the introductory statement of the problem or theme of the entire book, and if Joshua 2 provides us with an important indication of how that theme is going to be understood and interpreted in the book, then Joshua 3:1–5:1 provides us with a highly stylized and detailed narrative of the initial stage of the occupation, the crossing of the Jordan and its significance. Between this first ritual story and the concluding ritual of Joshua 24, the Deuteronomist will liturgically frame his narrative at key points. We will therefore devote an inordinate amount of space to an analysis of Joshua 3:1–5:1. The liturgical nature of this passage and the compositional point of view of this book will be heuristically emphasized in the process.

It is not difficult to see why, from a literary and semiotic perspective, the ritual drama has been chosen as an important framing device of the Book of Joshua. As Uspensky points out:

> In many instances, it seems to be psychologically necessary to mark out the boundaries between the world of everyday experience and a world that has special semantic significance. . . . The borders between the conventional (imaginary) world of the performance and the ordinary world remain inviolate. (1973:138)

The world of the cultic performance has special semantic significance here in the Book of Joshua, we would maintain, not because of any proposed contrast between the world of the ritual narrative as "imaginary" and that of the noncultic narrative as "real"—as narrative, neither type is more or less imaginary than its counterpart—but rather because of the immense potentiality for stylization that a cultic narrative allows its author. As such, the ritualized narrative permits an author to clearly demarcate a special question or answer, a thematic problem or its solution. The "ordinary world" of Joshua has its outer frame in 1:1–2:24 on the one hand and 24:29–33 on the other. Within this outer frame there is added a contiguous liturgical frame that is formed by 3:1–5:1 at its beginning and 24:1–28 at its end. In between these two extremes, that is, within 5:2–23:16, the story alternates between the world of ordinary narrative and that of ritually stylized narrative.

Although we are emphasizing the *syntactics* of compositional structure (in Uspensky's understanding of this term) in our analysis of the Deuteronomic History, it is important to remind ourselves that these syntactic shifts have semantic repercussions. The alternation between cultic and noncultic narrative in this book is particularly impressive in this regard. By describing the same or similar events, now ritually, now nonritually, the author presents us with mutually complementary points of view of his main topic, the various stages in the occupation of the land, and their implications for an adequate understanding of how the word of God is to be interpreted. This semantic function of syntactic shifts in point of view is well expressed by Uspensky:

> Often the same reality (the same event) may be described from different points of view, each of which distorts reality in its own way. These different points of view may be mutually complementary, and when they are brought together they offer the reader a more nearly adequate image of the described reality. (1973:128)

That this alternation between narrative styles is an important framing device of the book is also seen by the ease with which most of the ritual episodes can be isolated in the text. Besides 3:1–5:1, we have obvious cultic narratives in the capture of Jericho (6:1–27), the ceremony of Mount Ebal (8:30–35), the major portion of the account of the division of the land among the tribes (13–21), and the covenant ceremony at

Shechem (24:1–28). We will devote special attention to the first cultic narrative to illustrate how powerfully these cultic performances can affect and effect the ideological perspectives of the book. The ritual nature of 3:1–5:1 allows the Deuteronomist to construct a highly intricate and amazingly precise compositional structure. The programed and stylized aspects of a *cultic procession* provide the narrator with a vast array of literary devices that interconnect the various surface points of view of the story to a degree that approaches geometric precision.

The Temporal Composition of 3:1–5:1

1. The proper sequencing of incidents that are narrated in 3:1–5:1 has exercised the patience of many an exegete over the centuries. Certainly the failure of historical critics to come to any satisfactory solution to the hermeneutic problems of this passage is partially the result of inattention to the highly complex nature of the *literary* interconnections that make up its unity. A key feature of this complexity is a frequent and often puzzling shift in temporal point of view. For one thing, Joshua commands the Israelites in 3:12 to chose twelve men from the tribes of Israel, yet it is not until 4:2–3 that God commands him to do so. Then, after the text tells us twice that the whole nation had finished crossing the river (in 3:7–4:1), one is surprised by 4:10–11 which states that the people hurried across and finally finished crossing. We read once more in 4:19–20 that the people came up out of the Jordan and, to confuse things further, they camp in Gilgal and set up twelve stones, although much earlier in the beginning of this chapter (4:1–8) the twelve men had set down the stones from the Jordan in the Israelite camp. And once more in 4:21–24 we have an account of "what these stones mean," supplementing the first explanation of 4:6–7. Finally, the narrative in 4:11 describes how the Ark of the LORD and the priests with it cross the river; but further on in 4:15–18 we find an account of God's and Joshua's command to the priests to cross the river, whereupon the narrative asserts that they obey and come up from the river-bed.

No wonder the commentaries are filled with a vast network of historical reconstructions of this narrative. Bakhtin's warning is never more clearly illustrated than with these historical critical attempts to remove the temporal "confusion" of Joshua 3–4: "Without such a preliminary orientation [a synchronic literary investigation] historical investigations degenerate into a disconnected series of chance comparisons" (1973:230, n.4). The following is an attempt to use preliminary literary analysis to remove many of the interpretive problems that have troubled exegetes and fragmented our understanding of 3:1–5:1.

If we attempt simply to understand the temporal sequence of narrated actions that go to make up the story of these two chapters, we might begin with the following chain of representative events:

1. journey from Shittim to the Jordan
2. procession to the river bank
3. the priests carrying the Ark enter the river
4. the waters pile up
5. the people enter the river
6. the priests stop in the middle of the river
7. the people cross over
8. Joshua has twelve stones set up at Gilgal
9. Joshua has twelve more stones set up in the middle of the Jordan
10. the priests carrying the Ark come up out of the Jordan
11. the waters of the Jordan return to their place.

Using this scheme, we might visualize chapter 3 as the first *episode* in the story, an episode that progresses without difficulty from event 1 ("all the Israelites set out from Shittim and came to the Jordan"[3:1]) to event 7 inclusive ("and all Israel passed over on dry ground until the whole nation had crossed the river"[3:17]). Then a second episode is narrated in 4:1–8 which represents an account of those happenings connected with event 8, beginning with God's command to choose twelve men (4:2) and ending with their setting down of the twelve stones in the Israelite camp (4:8).

These first two episodes comprise a narrative that relates events 1 to 8 in an absolutely straightforward fashion, with one exception: in 3:12 Joshua commands the Israelites to "choose twelve men from the tribes of Israel, one man from each tribe," yet we are not told until 4:2–3 that God commanded Joshua to institute such a selection. 3:11–12 seems to be a prefiguring connective which anticipates episode 2 and thus provides a literary link between the two episodes. (This kind of device will be used again before the end of the story.) Thus, in the middle of the first episode, we are given a hint about the central event of the second episode. Since the command in 3:11–12 to choose twelve men while the Ark is stationed in the river has no apparent connection with what immediately precedes or follows it, and since there is no reason given here *why* the twelve men are to be chosen, these two verses tantalizingly set the reader up to anticipate something that in fact will soon follow in 4:1–8.

A third episode comprises the material narrated in 4:9–14. Everything related in these verses takes place between event 5 (the people enter the river), and event 10 inclusive (the priests come up out of the Jordan). Event 5 is referred to when we are told in 4:12 that the two and a half tribes cross over at the head of the Israelites, and event 10 is mentioned in 4:11 "then the Ark of the LORD crossed. . . . " The temporal limits of this third episode extend both before and beyond those of the second episode. 4:9–14 may be seen therefore as another temporal shift in composition that retraces certain events that occur within the time limits established for the first two episodes, and anticipates an event that will be narrated in the next episode. Just as 3:12 in the first episode is an anticipation of the central event of the second episode and enters into it in a prefigurative way, so also, 4:11 in the third episode is a literary foreshadowing of the central event of the fourth episode, that is, the priests carrying the Ark come out of the Jordan.

4:15–18 comprises the fourth episode of the story and narrates the final two events of our scheme—the priests come up and the waters recede. We see immediately that episodes 1 and 2 are related to each other in exactly the same manner as episodes 3 and 4 are related; that is, the events of one episode follow immediately upon those in the preceding episode, in the middle of which is found a verse prefiguring the following episode. In addition, we have seen that there is a temporal shift between episodes 2 and 3, since episode 3 narrates events that extend backwards into the time period represented in the first two episodes.

Finally, there is a fifth episode, 4:19–5:1, recounting the same event as that of the second episode, 8. Joshua sets up twelve stones at Gilgal. It may help to visualize all these temporal shifts in the following way:

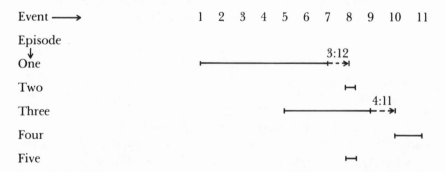

If it is the case that the narrative of 3:1–5:1 shifts back and forth in its temporal perspective, there are at least two obvious functions for such changes. First, given a specific time frame, events that were either not mentioned at all or simply referred to in passing may subsequently be highlighted for the sake of the ideological position of the narrative. Thus Joshua's seeing to it that the two and a half tribes cross over at the head of the Israelites is recounted in 4:12, long after its natural place. Such a temporal shift signals the reader that this narrated fact is to receive special emphasis. Thus also 3:12 and 4:11 are literary signals to the reader that two events in the narrative, the setting up of the twelve stones and the coming up of the priests, are to be highlighted in a special way in the text. Second, a temporal shift in perspective allows the narrative to present the same event or events from different surface points of view. Thus, as we shall see, the temporal shift by which 4:15–24 "replays" the same events as 4:1–8 allows the narrative to display these events from different spatial and psychological points of view. In the same way, the well-known temporal shift of 2:17–21 contributes to the psychological thrust of the chapter, as described in the preceding section.

2. Besides these extended shifts in temporal sequencing of our story, there are two instances of temporal shift in point of view that are directly reflected on the phraseological level of the text. These involve a shift, in two places, from the perfective form of the verbs that are predominant in the reporting speech of the narrative to an imperfective verbal form, that is, to the participle. The two imperfective forms effect a momentary change in the predominant temporal point of view of the narrator that signals their important function in the text.

At the end of the first episode, we read:

> And all Israel was crossing (ʿobᵉrîm) on dry ground until the whole nation had finished crossing (ʿad tammû laᶜᵃbor) the river. (3:17)

Why the sudden shift to a narratologically rare participial form, and then immediately back to the usual perfective form of the narrative verb? Uspensky provides us with the beginning of an answer:

> The form of the imperfective aspect is opposed to the form of the perfective aspect mainly in terms of the observer's position in relation to the action. . . . The imperfective form gives the effect of extended time; it invites us to place ourselves, as it were, in a synchronic relationship to the action, and to become witnesses to it. . . . In other words, the opposition of these two aspectual forms, on the plane of poetics, emerges as the opposition of the synchronic and the retrospective positions of the author. (1973:75)

This alternation between two authorial points of view expressed by the narrator in the very last verse of the first episode is a framing device in the narrative by which we are instructed about the completion or fulfillment of this episode's main theme (the retrospective position of the perfective verb form) and about the inner essence, as it were, of this theme (the synchronic position of the imperfective verb form). Retrospectively, what Joshua 3 is all about came to fruition: the whole nation did indeed cross the river (*tammû laᶜᵃbor*). Synchronically, however, what the narrative in Joshua 3 is all about is mobility, change, transition, the *very-crossing-of-the-river* itself; "And all Israel was crossing over (*ᶜobᵉrîm*)." Thus the text emphasizes the centrality of movement by the use of the participial form of *ᶜābar*.

When we come to Joshua 4, the focus shifts from movement to the absence of movement, from change to immobility. This change of image is indicated by the following:

> And the priests carrying the Ark were standing (*ᶜomᵉdîm*) in the middle of the Jordan until every command which the LORD had told Joshua to give to the people was fulfilled (*ᶜad tom*). (4:10)

What the narrative of chapter 4 up to this point has been emphasizing is, therefore, the immobility of the Ark and the priests, just as chapter 3 focused upon the mobility of the people. What chapter 4 is about so far is the setting up of the twelve stones, and the narrative's shift into the synchronic point of view emphasizes how crucial the Ark's stationary position was to the actual accomplishment of the setting up of the memorial stones. More than this: the very mobility of the people, the very possibility of the people crossing the river, is dependent upon the continued immobility of the priests and the Ark they are carrying. There is a complementary relationship expressed therefore by these two synchronic shifts: the Ark's immobility is *for the sake of* the people's mobility; the people's mobility is *on account of* the Ark's immobility.

We find a confirmation of the synchronic message of the reporting speech of 4:10 in the reported speech of Joshua:

> Look, while the Ark of the Covenant, the LORD of all the earth, is crossing (*ᶜobēr*) before you in the Jordan [that is, while it is still stationed in the middle of the river], choose twelve men from the tribes of Israel. . . . (3:11–12)

We have already seen how 3:11–12 is precisely the literary prefiguring in the first episode of the main topic of the second episode, the setting up of the stones. Thus, even in the verses that prefigure the account of the setting up of the stones, the emphasis is given, by the synchronic point of view of the participle, *ᶜobēr*, to the immobility of the Ark and its priests. Paradoxically, the very crossing of the people (*ᶜobᵉrîm:* 3:17) signifies change and motion, while the very crossing of the Ark and its priests (*ᶜobēr:* 3:11) signifies immobility, lack of motion, spatial stability.

There are no other temporal shifts in Joshua 3–4 between the synchronic and retrospective positions of the narrator, and it is difficult to avoid the conclusion that the account of liturgical procession that begins in 3:1 and ends in 4:24 is composed in such a way on the temporal plane in order to emphasize the spatial stability of some of its participants, that is, the Ark and its priests, and the spatial mobility of other participants, the people. In addition, the narration of this procession by means of five interlocking temporal episodes that shift back and forth over various longer or shorter segments of the time frame within which the procession from Shittim to Gilgal takes place indicates the temporal freedom with which the narrator himself can shift from one time frame to another to serve his own ideological purposes.

The Spatial Composition of 3:1–5:1

We can introduce our description of the shifts apparent in the *narrator's* spatial position throughout 3:1–5:1 by examining the spatial shifts apparent in the ways *characters* express themselves in the story. We will use the reported speech of episode 2, 4:1–8, for this purpose.

When God commands Joshua to choose twelve men who will carry the twelve stones from the Jordan to the Israelite camp, he says:

> Command them saying, "Carry the stones out from here, from the middle of the Jordan, where the feet of the priests stand firm, and take them across with you and set them down in the camp where you spend the night." (4:3)

How must we visualize the respective spatial positions of God and Joshua while this command is being given? God is quoted as speaking *from his location at the Ark in the middle of the Jordan or else from some other location;* the text does not give us enough information to decide. But what *is* clear is that the LORD commands Joshua to give orders to the twelve men in words that indicate that he (Joshua) is to speak them while in the middle of the Jordan after he and they have left their positions on the west side of the river ("When the whole nation had finished crossing the Jordan, the LORD said to Joshua . . ." 4:1). The LORD, wherever he is conceived of while speaking to Joshua, issues his command to Joshua in words that suppose that Joshua and the twelve men will be together with the priests when Joshua commands the men to carry the stones to the camp. This is clear from the threefold indication, "from here," "from the middle of the Jordan," and "where the priests' feet stand firm." In addition, the phrase, "take them across with you" to the camp, indicates that at the moment of the command Joshua and the men are already in the dry bed of the Jordan.

Then in v. 4 we are told that Joshua obeys God, summons the twelve men, and says to them:

> Cross over in front of the Ark of the LORD (*ᶜibᵉrû lipnê 'ᵃron YHWH*) your God to the middle of the Jordan . . . (4:5)

Clearly there is a shift in spatial perspective between these words of Joshua and the words God commanded him to say in 4:3. Here in 4:5, Joshua and the men he commands must both be on land, on the western side of the Jordan. They are not in the middle of the Jordan because Joshua commands them to cross over the Jordan from where they presently are after having crossed the Jordan with all the people, as 4:1 had indicated. Thus, although the narrative makes perfectly clear that Joshua fulfilled God's command to him to order twelve men to carry stones to the Israelite camp, he is reported as doing so from a spatial position different from that implied in the words God puts in his mouth in 4:3. In other words, God is reported speaking in 4:2–3 as a whole *as if* Joshua were in the middle of the Jordan (where he is not), and Joshua is reported speaking in 4:5–7 as a whole from somewhere on the land west of the river (where he and the people at that moment actually are, after originally crossing the river in the solemn procession described in chapter 3).

Then in 4:8 the twelve Israelites are reported as obeying Joshua's command. But the narrator has omitted any reference to the men's journey from their position somewhere west of the Jordan, and picks up the action only after they reach the middle of the Jordan:

> The Israelites did as Joshua had commanded: they lifted up twelve stones from the middle of the Jordan . . . and carried them across (*wayyaᶜᵃbirûm*) with them to the camp and set them down there. (4:8)

Here the narrative has switched back from Joshua's spatial position in 4:5–7 to the spatial position implied in God's command of 4:2–3. The narrator could have indicated that the twelve men, for example, "did as Joshua had commanded: they lifted up twelve stones and *brought them back to the camp (hebî'ûm 'el hammālôn)*," just as the kind Ephraimite of Judges 19:21 brought back the Levite to his house (*waybî'ehû lᵉbêtô*). The fact that *ᶜābar* is used in 4:8 indicates direction away from the Ark, the position from which the narrator speaks in this verse.

In other words, God's words of 4:3 indicate either his own position or

Joshua's visualized position in the middle of the Jordan, Joshua's words of 4:4 indicate his and his men's actual position somewhere west of the Jordan, and the narrator's words in 4:8 indicate his and the twelve men's position in the middle of the Jordan.

We are now able to discuss the shifts that occur in the narrator's spatial position at crucial points in the story, as indicated by his reporting speech in Joshua 3–4. The consistency of the phraseology of these two chapters allows us to conclude that *episodes 1 to 3 (3:1–4:14) are narrated from a vantage point outside of the promised land, whereas episodes 4 and 5 (4:15–5:1) are narrated from a vantage point inside of the promised land.* We want to emphasize here that we are dealing now with the narrative portions, that is, the reporting speech of Joshua 3–4; as we have just seen with the reported speech of Joshua in 4:5, and the words God had put in his mouth in 4:3, the spatial position of a character may also shift depending on where he is conceived of as located when speaking.

The evidence for this major spatial shift of the *narrator* consists primarily in a consistent change of terminology after episode 3. Up to this point both priests and people are described as crossing over (*ʿābar*) the river. This indicates a movement conceived of as having a point of departure that, in practical terms of the story, is somewhere between Shittim and the middle of the Jordan where the Ark is. The procession in episodes 1 to 3 is a movement either with or away from the narrator toward the promised land. On the other hand, the narration (again, we are referring to the *reporting* speech of the narrator, not the *reported* speech of various characters in the story) in episodes 4 and 5 (4:15–5:1) *never* refers to the crossing of the river, but to the coming out or up from the Jordan (*ʿālāh mittôk* or *min hayyardēn*). This indicates a shift in the narrator's spatial point of view as if the narrator in 3:1–4:14 took his narrating position from the point of view of the Israelites entering the land, but then in 4:15–5:1 takes his perspective from the point of view of a non-Israelite watching the progress of this miraculous procession as it begins to touch upon what he conceives of as his own territory. What is, up to 4:14, a solemn procession becomes in 4:15–5:1 a terrifying and awesome threat. Both priests and people "cross over" in 4:11; yet in the episode which this verse anticipates, both priests (in 4:16, 17, 18) and people (in 4:19) "come up out of" the Jordan. Let us now see how this spatial shift is mirrored in the psychological composition of this story.

The Psychological Composition of 3:1–5:1
   Uspensky writes:

> In those cases where the authorial point of view relies on an indi-
> vidual consciousness (or perception) [as opposed to an "objective"
> description] we will speak about the psychological point of view.
> (1973:81)

Uspensky goes on to explain that the psychological consciousness of
characters in a narrative may be expressed either from the point of
view of an outside observer who describes only the behavior which is
visible to an onlooker (*external* psychological viewpoint) or from the
point of view of the character himself or of an omniscient observer who
is permitted to penetrate the consciousness of that person (*internal* psychological viewpoint).

It is obvious that the Deuteronomic narrator is able to penetrate the
psychological consciousness of all his characters, and very often he narrates his story from these internal points of view. The question we want
to pose now is whose internal psychological point of view is expressed
by the narrative of 3:1–5:1? The preceding spatial and temporal analyses of this passage have presented us with relevant information in this
regard. The temporal shifts from retrospective to synchronic points of
view and then back again in 3:17 and 4:10 emphasized the mobility of
the people and the immobility of the priests and Ark in the ritual
procession across the Jordan. In both cases the inner consciousness of
Israel is directly addressed. Coupled with this temporal aspect is the
spatial perspective of 3:1–4:14 that aligns itself with the Israelite procession and describes the events leading up to the first mention of the
priests having crossed the river (4:11), always from the Israelite
perspective of entering the land from outside. On the other hand, our
spatial analysis pinpointed a shift into the point of view of an inhabitant
of the land now being penetrated by the Israelite procession; this shift
occurs in 4:15ff and obviously involves a psychological shift as well. We
shall now examine other evidence in the narrative that supports our
previous conclusions.

Notice first the strange location of the narrator's announcement that
the prediction of God in 3:7 to exalt Joshua like Moses in the eyes of all
Israel is now fulfilled:

> That day the LORD made Joshua stand very high in the eyes of all
> Israel, and the people revered him as they had revered Moses all
> his life. (4:14)

This notice occurs at the end of episode 3, even before the full account
of the Ark and the priests coming out of the Jordan in 4:15–18. A more
logical location would have been later, after the waters have receded.
What is clear, at least, is that 4:14 is the observation of an omniscient
observer who has penetrated the psychological consciousness of "all

Israel." In other words, the account of everything up to 4:14 is described on the surface of the text according to its effect upon the inner consciousness of *Israel*.

If we look, however, at the last verse of our story, we see that the narrator once again has penetrated the consciousness of characters in his story:

> When all the Amorite kings to the west of Jordan and all the Canaanite kings by the sea-coast heard that the LORD had dried up the waters before the advance of the Israelites until they had crossed, their courage melted away and there was no more spirit left in them for fear of the Israelites. (5:1)

This time, however, the narrator reveals the inner consciousness of the invaded inhabitants of the land, and this verse turns out to be the logical conclusion of episodes 4 and 5 which, from a spatial point of view, were narrated from the perspective of the inhabitants of the land being invaded by the Israelites. (One should note here that the use of *ᶜābar* in this verse does not belong to the reporting words of the narrator but rather to the message he reports in indirect discourse.)

We now see that the liturgical performance of the crossing of the Jordan is narrated first from the spatial and psychological point of view of participants in the procession (3:1–4:14) and then from the spatial and psychological point of view of those who witnessed this miraculous event from afar: the non-Israelites whose land was being invaded (4:15–5:1).

We can now focus upon the double account of the setting up of the stones, and Joshua's explanation of their significance (4:1–8 and 4:15–5:1) to see a confirmation of this interpretation. The stones set up at Gilgal were external signs, memorials of some type, whose significance is somehow twofold. They testified to a miraculous crossing that was to have a profound effect on both invaders and invaded. The question, "What do these stones mean?" could be answered in two ways when later generations sought out their meaning. On one hand, they testify to the impact of the miraculous crossing upon the inner consciousness of the Israelites themselves; this is the psychological point of view of the first account of 4:1–8. Joshua's first answer describes the cutting off of the Jordan's waters and concludes:

> Thus these stones will be a reminder *to the Israelites*. (4:7; emphasis added)

On the other hand, Joshua's answer in 4:21–24 indicates another function of these stones. Instead of a reference to the stones being a reminder to Israel, we have:

Thus *all people on earth will know how strong is the hand of the* LORD; and
thus *they* will stand in awe of the LORD your God forever. (4:24;
emphasis added)

In both episodes, the question is to be asked *by* Israelites, and its answer
has significance primarily *for* Israelites; but that significance is expressed first from a psychological perspective that is internal to Israel in
4:1–8, and then from a perspective internal to non-Israelites in 4:15–
5:1.

The Phraseological Composition of 3:1–5:1

The phraseological composition of a narrative affects the mutual
relations and influences of reported and reporting speech. Our story
heightens its ritualistic nature as a cultic performance by extremely
precise patterns of phraseological composition, especially in episode 1.
The phraseological pattern of 3:1–5:1 illustrates the basic "promise/
fulfillment" structure of the entire Deuteronomic History with an as-
tounding display of variations on this structural theme. It is on this
plane that the stylized nature of the liturgical performance is best seen.

We have already encountered the pattern in the Book of
Deuteronomy: both Moses and the narrator report the predictive word
of God and then state that this word was fulfilled in such and such a
way. This basic form of the pattern is found in the present story; God is
reported as predicting:

Today I will begin to make you stand high in the eyes of all Israel
. . . (3:7)

and further on in the story, the reporting narrative tells us:

That day the LORD made Joshua stand very high in the eyes of all
Israel . . . (4:14)

A variation of this pattern is one in which a command, rather than a
prediction, given by God, is fulfilled. This can be understood in two
ways. First, since God commands Joshua to command the people, when
Joshua is reported directly commanding the people, *his* command can
be seen as the fulfillment of *God's* command. Thus, the report of
Joshua's commands in direct discourse in 3:9–13 and 4:5–7, and the
report of his command in an indirect way in 4:17 are to be seen as the
fulfillment of God's commands to him in 3:7–8; 4:2–3; and 4:16 respectively. Second, when the reporting speech of the narrator indicates that
what God commanded through Joshua actually took place, this report
can be seen as the fulfillment of God's command. Thus, the reports of

3:14–17; 4:8; and 4:18 respectively, are a second type of fulfillment of God's three commands to Joshua just mentioned. Another variation on this theme occurs when some statement in the text *prefigures* what is subsequently found in the reporting speech of the narrative. Thus, the statement, "where they encamped before crossing the river" (3:1b), foreshadows the entire account of the crossing in 3:2–17. Similarly, as we have already indicated, the command of Joshua in 3:12 to choose twelve men is not immediately followed up in the story, but actually prefigures the accounts of the setting up of the twelve stones found in the second (4:1–8) and fifth (4:19–5:1) episodes of the story. So also the statement in 4:11, ". . . then the Ark of the LORD crossed," is a literary prefiguring of the following episode (4:15–18).

We may say, therefore, that these variations involve the narrative fulfillment of prescriptive, predictive, or prefigurative statements in the text. Put another way, all the variations we have so far discussed are repetitive structures of the type "anticipation/confirmation." If we search for an adjective that is more in conformity with the nature of this story as a liturgical performance, we might see the story as the working out of an *antiphonal pattern* that brilliantly mirrors the ritual nature of the events described.

The intricacy of this pattern is best seen in the first episode, in which the combination of four anticipatory and realized statements is repeated four times. In each of these four instances, there are four statements or phrases: the first anticipates the second; the second confirms the first and anticipates the third; the third confirms the second and anticipates the fourth; and the fourth confirms the third.

The first instance involves the *command* concerning precedence in the procession: first the Ark carried by the priests, then the people:

1. (Reported Speech) Anticipation: "You [the people] are to follow it [the Ark] . . . . Keep some distance behind, about a thousand yards." (3:4)

2. Confirmation/Anticipation: (Reported Speech) "You [the priests] shall lift up the Ark of the Covenant and pass in front of the people." (3:6a)

3. Confirmation/Anticipation: (Reporting Speech) So they lifted up the Ark of the Covenant and went in front of the people. (3:6b)

4. Confirmation (Reporting Speech): So the people set out from their tents to cross the Jordan with the priests in front of them carrying the Ark of the Covenant. (3:14)

The second instance involves the *prediction* of the drying up of the Jordan:

1. (Reported Speech) Anticipation: ". . . for tomorrow the LORD will do a great miracle among you." (3:5)

2. Confirmation/Anticipation: "By this [miraculous event] you shall
   (Reported Speech)   know that the living God is among you
                                   . . . the waters coming down from up-
                                   stream will stand piled up like a bank."
                                   (3:10, 15)

3. Confirmation/Anticipation: . . . the water coming down from up-
   (Reporting Speech)   stream was brought to a standstill; it
                                   piled up like a bank for a long way
                                   back. . . . The waters coming down to
                                   the Sea of the Arabah, the Dead Sea,
                                   were completely cut off. (3:16)

4. Confirmation (Reporting Speech):   . . . on the dry bed . . . [twice] (3:17)

The third instance involves the *command* to the priests to enter the Jordan and station themselves in the middle of the river bed:

1. (Reported Speech) Anticipation: "Tell them [the priests] that . . . they are to take their stand in the river." (3:8)

2. Confirmation/Anticipation: "When the soles of the feet of the priests
   (Reported Speech)   come to rest [or settle: $k^en o^a h$] in the
                                   waters of the Jordan . . ." (3:13)

3. Confirmation/Anticipation: When the priests reached the Jordan
   (Reporting Speech)   and the feet of the priests carrying the
                                   Ark were dipped into the edge of the
                                   waters . . . (3:15)

4. Confirmation (Reporting Speech):   The priests carrying the Ark of the
                                   Covenant of the LORD stood firm . . .
                                   in the middle of the Jordan. (3:17)

The fourth instance involves the *prefigurative* statements of the reporting speech of the narrator concerning the crossing of the river by the people:

1.	Anticipation:	. . . where they encamped before cross-ing the river. (3:1)
2.	Confirmation/Anticipation:	So the people set out from their tents to cross the Jordan. (3:14)
3.	Confirmation/Anticipation:	And the people crossed over opposite Jericho. (3:16)
4.	Confirmation:	And all Israel was passing over . . . until the whole nation had crossed the river. (3:17)

Combining all of this with aspects of our temporal analysis, we can see that there are two types of anticipation/confirmation patterns in this narrative. The first is *intraepisodal* and is best represented by the repetitive structure of the first episode as we have just outlined it. Other examples would be found in the contents of 4:2–4, 5–7, and 8 in the second episode, and in the interrelationships of 4:16, 17, and 18 in the fourth episode. The second type of anticipation/confirmation scheme is *interepisodal:* we have already seen how 3:11–12 and 4:11 anticipate subsequent *episodes* which may be viewed as these verses' literary realization.

The Interrelationships between the Various
Compositional Planes of 3:1–5:1

Our analysis of the temporal composition of 3:1–5:1 did not resolve all of the temporal ambiguities of this story. Yet a surprising number of these temporal shifts were seen to have interesting connections with the spatial, psychological, and phraseological points of view discovered in the text. 3:11–12 and 4:11 were temporal shifts connected with the basic phraseological device of anticipation/confirmation so intricately worked out in the story. The gaze backwards and forwards of episode 3 (4:9–14) allows the story at this point to summarize the account of the crossing from the psychological viewpoint of Israel in the same way as the gaze forwards and backwards in time of episodes 4 and 5 allows a comprehensive statement of the psychological perspective of non-Israelites vis-a-vis the crossing and setting up of the twelve stones.

Our spatial, psychological, and phraseological analyses offered a number of important instances where the various surface planes of the story concur. The most striking example in this regard is the concurrence of the psychological and spatial shifts between episodes 1 to 3 on the one hand, and 4 to 5 on the other: 3:1–4:14 is narrated from a spatial and psychological point of view that is internal to Israel, whereas

4:15–5:1 is narrated from a spatial and psychological point of view that is external to Israel.

What has all of this to do with the ideological perspective of this story? Our temporal analysis uncovered a shift away from the normal retrospective stance to a momentary synchronic perspective in 3:17 and 4:10, and led us to the tentative conclusion that the account in 3:1–4:14, spatially and psychologically internal to Israel, emphasized on the one hand the mobility of the people and on the other hand the stability of the Ark and the priests. Each facet of the crossing plays a complementary role with regard to the possibility of the crossing to signify anything whatsoever. The twelve stones whose very essence is to be a vehicle for the significance of the crossing could not have been set up had the people not actually *moved* into the vacuum created by the miraculous drying up of the Jordan. Yet the people could not have actually finished crossing the Jordan had the Ark and its priests not *remained stationary* in the middle of the Jordan. There would be no significance at all, that is, no memorial stones at Gilgal, without the combined interaction of change and stability, mobility and immobility.

The procession enters the Jordan with the Ark first and the people last; the procession crosses over into the promised land with the people first and the Ark last. Israel enters the Jordan led by the Ark of the LORD of all the earth and emerges led by an armed force from the two and a half tribes of Reuben, Gad, and Manasseh.

The Ark does not leave the Jordan "until every command which the LORD had told Joshua to give to the people was fulfilled" (4:10). *The stability of the Ark symbolizes the exact fulfillment of the word of the LORD.* Words echo out of the Book of Deuteronomy:

> See to it that you observe everything I command you: you must not
> add anything to it, nor take anything away from it. (Deut 13:1)

But then we wonder about the twelve stones Joshua sets up in the middle of the Jordan (4:9). There is no trace of a command from the LORD to do so. Has not Joshua added to the commands of the LORD? In Deuteronomy, the predominant voice of critical traditionalism neutralized a voice of dogmatic immobility inherent in 13:1 by all kinds of compositional devices. This same powerful voice neutralizes once again the one-sided view of Israel's religion as unchanging allegiance to an unchanging law, by complementing an unswerving loyalty to God's commands with the image of change and mobility. It is the essence of the people to cross over, to adapt, to change their position. It is somehow impossible to keep the Ark stationary, that is, to fulfill the LORD's command without adding to it or taking away from it. Every interpretation of God's word is an adding to it or a taking away from it. The stones Joshua additionally erects in the Jordan are, therefore, a testament to the necessity of change and mobility in the understanding, interpretation, and application of God's word. Joshua fulfilled every command of the LORD—and then some. The people have to pass the Ark and the priests by. Only then can the Ark once more take its place at the head of the procession into the promised land. The meaning of the twelve stones set up at Gilgal refers to the meaning of the crossing itself; the meaning of the twelve stones set up by Joshua in the middle of the Jordan refers to the meaning of meaning itself, the very *possibility* of interpreting the Mosaic law and the word of God. The first set-up is particular, the second universal.

The ideological stance of 3:1–4:14 retraces the same hermeneutic territory as the Rahab story in chapter 2, only now from Israel's viewpoint rather than that of a non-Israelite. If the two spies improvise, and promise not to apply the full rigor of the ban when they take Jericho, Joshua now also improvises when he sets up the twelve additional stones in the Jordan. The success of the crossing is matched by the adaptability of Joshua's decisions. The twelve stones in the Jordan are a memorial to the complementarity of Israel's religion embodied in the mobility of the people and the stability of the Ark. And the concluding verse of this section, "That day the LORD made Joshua stand very high" (4:14), is the Deuteronomist's explicit appreciation of the interpretive role of Joshua as leader of Israel. Like Moses, Joshua does not just *declare* God's word, he *teaches* it.

The narrative now shifts back to a spatial and psychological presentation of the crossing that is internal to the nations soon to be dispossessed. But this shift on the surface planes of the text still serves an ideological position that is internal to *Israel*'s self-consciousness. 4:15–5:1, like 2:1–24, once more asks Israel to understand themselves from the point of view of the other nations. They are to stand outside themselves to see themselves better. The confession of faith that is here the significance of the twelve stones at Gilgal,

> Thus all people on earth will know how strong is the hand of the LORD; and thus they will stand in awe of the LORD your God forever (4:24),

is a repetition of, a confirmation of, Rahab's confession of faith in 2:9–11. It served the same function and the spies take it back with them to Joshua and repeat it in 2:24. Similarly, the narrative now concludes the present story with the repetition of 5:1.

There are no echoes here of the theme of God's justice and mercy vis-a-vis Israel and the nations, as there was in the Rahab story. The issues are here confined to those hermeneutic problems involved in the fulfillment of God's word. As we now come to the events of 5:2–15, the question of God's justice and mercy, raised in Joshua 2, will once more be raised. In this way, Joshua 2 and 5 can be seen to bracket the liturgical account of the crossing itself with a meditation on its legal implications.

Circumcision and Passover at Gilgal; Encounter with the Lord's Commander (5:2–15)

Once in the land, Joshua is commanded by God to circumcise the Israelites; he immediately does so, and the reporting speech of the narrator introduces the significance of this divine command with the words, "This is why Joshua circumcised them . . ." (5:4). What follows in 5:4–9 is an extended meditation on key passages in Deuteronomy, with specific literary allusions that illuminate the ideological reason for including this episode precisely at this point in the history of the occupation. Together with Joshua 2, this chapter deals primarily with the theme of God's mercy and forgiveness in allowing Israel to occupy the land.

Joshua 5:4–7 recalls the Israelites' disobedience at Sinai and Kadesh-Barnea, and God's threat to destroy them (Deut 1:19–35; 9:12–23). Moses in Deuteronomy 9:26–29 had pleaded with God to remember the fathers and overlook the stubbornness, wickedness, and sin of Israel. He had argued that Israel was God's people and should not be destroyed,

> otherwise the people in the land out of which thou didst lead us will say, "It is because the Lord was not able to bring them into the land which he promised them, and because he hated them, that he has led them out to kill them in the wilderness." (Deut 9:28)

Moses argues that, if God *does* completely blot out Israel, as he had threatened in Deuteronomy 9:13–14, he would incur the smug reproaches of the Egyptians who will interpret this punishment of Israel as both a proof of God's inability to fulfill what he had promised (to bring Israel into the land) and also a sign of God's hatred of Israel. The successful result of Moses' intercessory supplication is then recounted:

> . . . Once again the Lord listened to me; he consented not to destroy you. The Lord said to me, "Set out now at the head of the people so that they may enter and occupy the land which I swore to give to their forefathers." (Deut 10:10–11)

But the Book of Joshua describes how the second generation of Israelites has no more trust in the LORD than the first generation had. The Rahab incident shows how Joshua timidly sends out spies to reconnoiter Jericho. They return, puffed up with confidence not because of God's words but because of the admission of Rahab that the inhabitants of the land are terrified at Israel's coming.

In spite of all this, God effects the miracle of the crossing, the second generation of Israelites is allowed to be circumcised, and we are told:

> The LORD then said to Joshua, "Today I have rolled away from you the reproaches of the Egyptians." (5:9)

Far from being an enigmatic and unclear allusion, these reported words of the LORD to Joshua show that the account of the occupation, begun in Joshua 2 and proceeding on through the miraculous crossing and the immediate circumcision of the Israelites, is the Deuteronomist's understanding, interpretation, and application of Moses' account of Israel's disobedience and distrust in Deuteronomy 1–2 and 9–10. More specifically, Joshua 5:9 is a direct literary allusion to Deuteronomy 9:28. God's words here in Joshua respond to Moses' main argument for divine mercy in Deuteronomy 9:28. God's decision in Deuteronomy 10:10–11 to allow a second generation of Israelites to enter the land in spite of the first generation's disobedience and lack of faith did indeed remove the reproaches of "the people in the land out of which thou didst lead us" (Deut 9:28). God's earlier command to cut two more tablets of stone and his decision to give Israel the land (Deut 10) in spite of their disobedience and lack of faith, as described in Deuteronomy 1–2, 9, are functionally equivalent to God's command to "once more make Israel a circumcised people" (Josh 5) in spite of their lack of faith, as described in Joshua 2.

The account of the first Passover in the land and the Israelites' first consumption of the spring harvest is an implicit reference to the liturgy commanded in Deuteronomy 26:1–11 for the bringing of the first fruits to "the place which the LORD your God will choose as a dwelling for his name." There the Israelite is commanded to say to the priest, "I declare this day to the LORD your God that I have entered the land which the LORD swore to our forefathers to give us" (Deut 26:3). Here at Gilgal *for the first and only time,* these words can be stated with full literal as well as liturgical truth by each Israelite who has just indeed "entered the land which the LORD swore to our forefathers to give us."

The so-called "fragmentary" story of the appearance of the commander of the army of the LORD in 5:13–15 is in actuality the Deuteronomist's final and complete statement of the meaning of the initial stage of the occupation, the crossing of Israel, in the light of God's legal and promissory relations with both Israel and the nations who are to be dispossessed. By alternating his account of the crossing with episodes that are now external (2; 4:15–5:1), now internal (3:1–4:14), to Israel's psychological and spatial point of view, the Deuteronomist has been able to spell out brilliantly the relationships between God's mercy and justice as they are complicated by his varied relationships with Israel and the other nations.

Joshua's question to the LORD's commander is precisely the question that the Deuteronomist has been attempting to answer with his history of Israel's exploits:

> Are you [God] for us or for our enemies? (5:13)

Seeking to see the occupation of the land now from Israel's viewpoint, now from their enemies' viewpoint, the narrative provides no simple answer. The situation is much more complex than the familiar answer of an authoritarian dogmatism would have it: "God is on our side; we have the promise made to our fathers, and the law given to Moses!" The commander's answer is not so clear-cut;

> I am here as captain of the army of the LORD. (5:14)

It is not insignificant that Rahab, the non-Israelite, fearfully professes faith in Israel's God as "God in heaven above and on earth below" (2:11), that the significance of the twelve stones at Gilgal help "all people on earth" to know how strong is the hand of the LORD (4:24), and that the Ark of the Covenant belongs to him who is "lord of all the earth" (3:11, 13). Since the LORD's justice and mercy will provide now for Israel's, now for another nation's, victory or defeat, the only certainty is that expressed by the command given to one who has left Gilgal but not yet reached Jericho (5:13):

> Take off your sandals; the place where you are standing is holy.
> (5:15)

The holy place upon which Joshua stands is between the certain possession of the place from which he proceeds, Gilgal, and his as yet unrealized destination, Jericho. But Joshua, like Moses before him and the Deuteronomist after him, also travels between the certain possession of the word of God and an as yet unrealized destination, the *meaning* of that word. There is only one thing certain about the determined effort to get from God's word to its "correct" interpretation: the itinerary of such a journey proceeds upon holy ground.

The Capture of Jericho and Ai (6:1–8:29)

We come upon another liturgical narrative in the story of the miraculous taking of Jericho (6), followed by a "realistic" account of the initial setback and final victory at Ai (7–8). From a compositional point of view, we might profitably analyze chapter 6 with as much detail as we did the liturgical narrative of the crossing of the Jordan, except that limitations of space will not permit this. We intend, therefore, to analyze these two stories together in a synthetic way, since they are already uniquely combined in the text by the narrative thread that stitches together most of the stories in this first section of the book. More specifically, both stories have to do with the correct interpretation and application of the Mosaic law on the ban. The Jericho story completes the question about the ban begun in Joshua 2 with the spies' promise not to kill Rahab and her household, and answers that question in a definitive manner. The Ai account then raises two further case studies concerning Moses' legislation on the ban. By the end of chapter 8, the narrative has already illustrated three different ways in which both Joshua and God "observe all that is written in the book of the law" (1:8) with respect to the ban.

Joshua's last command before Jericho falls (6:16–19) accomplishes two things. First, it sanctions the spies' decision not to apply the full rigor of the Mosaic law on *ḥerem*, the "ban," in the case of Rahab and her household "because she hid the men whom we sent" (6:17). Second, it foreshadows the second case study on the ban, to be discussed in Joshua 7:

> "And you must beware of coveting anything that is forbidden under the ban; you must take none of it for yourselves; this would put the Israelite camp itself under the ban and bring trouble on it." (6:18)

With regard to the Rahab question, the narrative reports Joshua sanctioning the spies' promise to Rahab as an acceptable application of the Mosaic legislation of Deuteronomy 20:15–18. Although it would appear that Moses' command is clear-cut and admits of no exception:

> In the cities of those nations whose land the LORD your God is giving you as a patrimony, you shall not leave any creature alive (*lo' t^eḥayyeh kol n^ešāmāh*)." (Deut 20:16)

Joshua makes an exception of Rahab and her household for aiding the Israelites. What appeared to be the disobedience of Israelites in Joshua 2 now turns out to be legitimate mercy toward non-Israelites in Joshua 6. More than this, the mercy that allows Rahab to continue to live in the land is not very different from the mercy that allows Israel to occupy the land in the first place. Neither party *deserves* the land. Possession of it by one party depends to a certain extent upon the wickedness of the other party, and both parties benefit from a merciful application of the law of God. What Moses accomplished for Israel in Deuteronomy 9–10, Joshua accomplishes for Rahab here in Joshua 6. As Joshua 4:14 finds much of its significance not only in the miraculous crossing of the Jordan (we recall that the story is still in progress when the narrator tells us that "that day the LORD made Joshua stand very high in the eyes of all Israel") but also in Joshua's establishment of an *additional* set of memorial stones (4:9), so 6:27 ("Thus the LORD was with Joshua and his fame spread throughout the country") draws its significance not only from the miraculous defeat of Jericho but also from his *exceptional* interpretation of what is under the ban. That Rahab was not killed is a significant decision for Israelite and non-Israelite alike.

The initial setback at Ai (7) is ascribed not only to Achan's surreptitious taking of forbidden booty from Jericho (a mantle, silver, and gold) but to Joshua's once again sending spies to explore Ai. Had the Israelites relied more on God's words than on the spies' overconfident recommendation (7:3), they might not have had to suffer this initial defeat. But the burden still lies with Achan's sin. He is discovered by Joshua's following of God's procedure (7:13–15), he confesses, and is stoned to death (7:16–26). Joshua's interpretation of what is forbidden under the ban at Jericho (6:18–19) is thus sanctioned by God in chapter 7. Here we have the second example of the narrative's case-history on the interpretation of the legislation on the ban.

Immediately after Achan is executed, God applies the law of the ban in a third case:

> . . . but you may keep for yourselves the cattle and any other spoil
> that you may take . . . (8:2)

The Israelites follow God's words, as 8:27 states. The contrast between the situation at Jericho and that at Ai could not be greater. Achan is executed for doing at Jericho what every Israelite is given permission to do at Ai. More than this: they may even keep the *cattle*, living things that are directly forbidden by the legislation now temporarily relaxed by the LORD. There seems to be no doubt at all that the narrative is intent upon outlining some of the possible hermeneutic situations that could arise in the continual understanding, interpretation, and application of divine commands. The Deuteronomist chooses the law of the ban to exemplify what is involved when a law is to be interpreted. Using the traditional stories connected with the occupation of the land, the Deuteronomist weaves a narrative that is also a hermeneutic meditation on the word of God. The critical traditionalism that sparked the Book of Deuteronomy now pushes forward the story of Israel's conquest of the land. The sacred ground being progressively occupied is also the book of the law.

The Ceremony on Mount Ebal (8:30–35)

After Israel's two great victories at Jericho and Ai, the narrative recounts Joshua's fulfillment of the commands of Moses concerning a ceremony to be performed at Mount Ebal and Mount Gerazim. Reference is made to the Book of Deuteronomy: "according to what is written in the book of the law" (8:31), "according to everything written in the book of the law" (8:34). The commands in Deuteronomy which Moses gave concerning this ceremony bracket the lawcode itself: Deuteronomy 11:29–30; 27–28. One particular command of Moses is singled out:

> . . . to fulfill the command of Moses the servant of the LORD that the blessing should be pronounced first. (8:33)

This is apparently a reference to the sequence followed in Deuteronomy, where Moses mentioned the blessing of the people first and then the cursing of the people (Deut 11:29; 27:12), and where, if we disregard the Levite curses of Deuteronomy 27: 14–26, the list of blessings precedes the list of curses in Deuteronomy 28. Since our account in Joshua ends with the assertion that Moses read aloud to the people every single word of Moses' commands (8:35), there can be no doubt that this account emphasizes the accuracy and completeness with which Joshua fulfills the commands of Moses concerning the ceremony on Mount Ebal.

Yet, we miss perhaps the most important feature of this narrative if we fail to recognize that, like the preceding narratives in Joshua 2; 3:1–5:1; and 6:1–8:29, Joshua's understanding, interpretation, and application of Moses' commands are significantly different from the words of Moses, all of which, we are told, Joshua read to the people that day. For example, Moses commands half the tribes to stand *on* Mount Ebal and half to stand *on* Mount Gerazim. Yet our account of

Joshua's fulfillment of this command has him placing the Israelites on either side of the Ark, half of them standing *toward* Mount Gerazim and half *toward* Mount Ebal. Now even if we might reconcile these varying formulations, as seems possible, by assuming that those who are said to be facing Mount Gerazim are actually standing *on* Mount Ebal (and vice versa), the fulfillment text in Joshua mentions the participation of "native and alien alike" (8:33, 35), whereas the book of the law focuses only on the twelve Israelite tribes. This "addition" of Joshua's, that is, the including of "native (*'ezrāḥ*) and alien (*gēr*) alike" in the ceremony, does not *contradict* Moses' commands; it simply fills out and applies those commands in the circumstances in which Joshua finds himself and in the context of the literary composition of the book. Moreover, do just the male Israelites participate in the ceremony? No, for we are referred a second time to "the whole congregation of Israel, including the women and dependents, and the aliens (*haggēr*) resident in their company" (8:35).

We see, therefore, that the concluding verse of this story states the hermeneutic problem in a deliberately expressive way, focusing first on the very law itself which is in need of interpretation,

> There was not a single word of all that Moses had commanded which Joshua did not read aloud before the whole congregation of Israel . . . (8:35a),

and then on the very interpretation that this law, like every law, demands:

> . . . including the women and dependents and aliens resident in their company. (8:35b)

In this way the present account in 8:30–35 continues the hermeneutic reflections discovered in the preceding narratives of Joshua. The promise God made to the fathers, and the covenant first entered into at Sinai, have legal repercussions for friend and foe alike. In the description from Deuteronomy, six Israelite tribes stand for the blessing and six stand for the curse; in the confirming account of Joshua, Israelite and non-Israelite alike stand for both the blessing and the curse. This addition helps to answer the question previously posed by Joshua to the commander of the LORD's army:

> Are you for us or against us? (5:13)

*The Gibeonite Covenant and the Conquest of the Amorite Kings
and All of Southern Palestine (9:1–10:43)*

1. Why does the story of Israel's covenant with the Gibeonites occur at
this precise spot in the narrative? Its connection with what immediately
follows in 10:1–27 is clear from 9:1–2. These verses describe how the
various nations of the land band together to fight the Israelites. Thus
the present account of the Gibeonite covenant gives the background for
the forthcoming decision, in chapter 10, of the five Amorite kings to
attack the traitorous city of Gibeon. The literary connection of the
Gibeonite story with what immediately *precedes* is clear from our discussion of the Ebal ceremony, in which emphasis was given to the addition
of "aliens resident in your company" (8:33, 35). In the liturgical context
of the Mount Ebal ceremony, whose participants include not only the
Israelites who have just crossed over into the land but also "aliens"
resident in their midst such as Rahab and her household, *the very categories of "native (ʾezrāḥ) and "alien" (gēr) are dramatically reversed: the native is
now the alien and the alien has become a native.* This juxtaposition and
reversal of categories of those who inhabit the holy place upon which
they stand (5:15) was easily seen as a continuation of the sequential
alternation of internal and external points of view apparent in the
surface composition of 2; 3:1–4:14, 15–5:1, 2–15; and 6:1–8:29; except
that in 8:30–35 the two points of view were synthesized in the surface
composition of this cultic narrative. The story ended in 8:35 with
Joshua reading aloud all of Moses' commands to the whole congregation of Israel "including the women and dependants and the aliens
resident in their company." Joshua 9 now focuses upon a story which
explains how one such group of aliens became resident in Israel's company. We shall see how the purpose of this expansion upon the theme
of "aliens within Israel's midst" is exactly the same as the purpose that
lay behind the Rahab story of Joshua 2. The same themes of God's
mercy and justice, seen in the light of God's promises to the fathers and
the Mosaic covenant, and complicated by his relations to other nations,
motivate the entire story. More than this, Joshua 9:3–27 has a direct
literary connection with Deuteronomy 29:1–21 which, together with
Deuteronomy 9–10, provides the basis for yet another interpretation of
the Mosaic legislation having to do with the fate of those who live under
the ban (Deut 20:10–18; 7:1–5). That the Gibeonite story is a deliberate
literary allusion to Deuteronomy 29, or vice versa—the direction of
influence is not meaningful from a compositional point of view—means
that the community of Israelites and Gibeonites that results from the
treaty they enter into in Joshua 9 is, in a sense, already present before
Moses during his third address in Deuteronomy.

We can synopsize the beginning of Moses' third address to Israel as follows: 1) Even though you were disobedient, God led you forty years in the wilderness and gave you victory over Sihon and Og. You shall therefore keep the covenant that you may prosper (29:1–9); 2) God is ready to make this covenant with you and with future generations, as he has promised you and as he swore to your fathers (29:10–15); 3) But do not think that because God is mercifully entering into this covenant with you he will not be willing to destroy you according to the terms of this covenant (29:16–21).

We have already discussed the compositional implications of the use of imperfective verbal forms in a narrative. They often signal a *synchronic* point of view that is meant to put the reader into the very story itself and emphasize what is really happening. In Deuteronomy 29 Moses speaks to his audience in terms that signify the permanent, ongoing nature of what he is describing to his audience:

> you are taking your place (*niṣṣābîm*) . . . (9)
> the covenant which God is making (*kōrēt*) . . . (11)
> I am making this covenant (*kōrēt*) (13)
> with those of you who are standing (*ʿōmēd*) here today . . . (14)

In addition, the narrative complements the synchronic nature of this congregational gathering by having Moses state explicitly that the congregation he is addressing is multigenerational:

> It is not with you alone that I am making this covenant and this oath; [I am making it] not only with all those who stand here with us today before the LORD our God but also with those who are not here with us today. (14–15)

But who precisely was in the audience standing before the LORD listening to Moses? The various categories of Moses' listeners are enumerated:

> You all stand here today . . . tribal chiefs, elders and officers, all the men of Israel, with your dependants, your wives, the aliens who live in your camp—all of them from those who chop wood to those who draw water . . . (10–11)

And what is the history of this assembly? Moses quotes God referring to his providential guidance in the wilderness:

> Your clothes did not wear out on you, nor did your sandals wear out and fall off your feet; you ate no bread and drank no wine or

strong drink, in order that you might learn that I am the LORD your God." (5–6)

Moses even reminds them of past victories:

You came to this place where Sihon king of Heshbon and Og king of Bashan came to attack us, and we defeated them. (7)

Joshua 9:3–27 is a brilliant narrative meditation upon these words of Deuteronomy 29 through its portrayal of the covenantal relationship between the LORD and the Israelites in terms of the covenantal relationship between Israel and the Gibeonites. It effects this connection by a number of literary allusions. The Gibeonites, whose clothing, shoes, and provisions should have been new but are displayed as old and worn out, are meant to remind us of the Israelites themselves, whose clothes and sandals should have been old but, as God has pointed out, were good as new; the Gibeonites, who eat dry and moldy bread when they could have eaten fresh bread, now meet those who had needed no bread at all to survive in the desert; the Gibeonites replaced new wineskins with old wineskins, and the next step is Israel's no wineskins at all (Deut 29:5–6). In addition, the Gibeonites now remind Israel of her victory over Og and Sihon just as Moses had reminded them of this in Deuteronomy 29:7. And when the Gibeonites request, "We are your slaves; please grant us this treaty" (Josh 9:11, 6, 8), they know that the terms of the Mosaic covenant preclude them by right from entering into a treaty with Israel; they even say so in 9:24. Similarly, when Moses told the Israelites, "but to this day the LORD has not given you a mind to learn, or eyes to see, or ears to hear" (Deut 29:4), he referred to the lack of faith, mistrust, and disobedience of Israel already discussed in Deuteronomy 9–10, which by right had caused God to exclaim, "Let me be, and I will destroy them and blot out their name from under heaven" (Deut 9:14). Both Gibeon and Israel realize that they have no right to the covenant they in fact enter into with Israel and God respectively. They know that strict interpretation of the Mosaic covenant would stipulate death for them both.

But the ruse of the Gibeonites works and Israel is persuaded to spare their lives, "so that the oath which we swore to them may bring no harm upon us" (9:20). Because of a solemn promise, an oath made to Gibeon, the strict terms of the Mosaic covenant will not be fulfilled. Similarly, in spite of Israel's disobedience (Deut 29:4) strictly requiring their obliteration, God will in fact enter into a covenant with them:

> The covenant is to constitute you his people this day, and he will be
> your God, as he promised you and as he swore to your forefathers,
> Abraham, Isaac, and Jacob. (Deut 29:13)

But why will God do this? Moses has already explained this to us in
Deuteronomy 9. The words of Israel's leaders about the Gibeonites just
quoted (9:20) could just as easily have been reported from God's mouth
according to the argument of Moses in Deuteronomy 9:27–28 where he
prayed for forgiveness lest the Egyptians reproach God for impotency
and diabolical destruction of his own people. In both cases, that is,
Moses' words in Deuteronomy 9:27–28 and Israel's words in Joshua
9:20, a solemn promise once sworn may not be taken back without
harm to the one who uttered it. Nevertheless, the trickery of the
Gibeonites has a price, just as had the disobedience of the Israelites.
The Gibeonites are forever to be the source of slaves for Israel—this is
Joshua's curse upon them. Similarly, the first generation of Israelites
had to die off before Israel was allowed to enter the land. Something
short of the full benefit of the covenant, but not quite total annihilation,
is the decision of God in Deuteronomy 9–10 and of Joshua in Joshua 9.

In all these ways, therefore, the Gibeonite story plays out once more
the main lines of the story of Israel's covenant with the LORD in the
Book of Deuteronomy. Gibeon is saved from destruction because of a
previous promise just as Israel was. Thus we find the drawers of water
and the hewers of wood already present, and actually mentioned, in the
congregation of Deuteronomy 29:10–11 because Gibeon is already present there in the Israelite congregation. Israel *is* Gibeon writ large.
When Israel's descendants would ask their fathers what these Gibeonite
slaves signify, they are to be told how Israel themselves were once cut
off from destruction because a solemn promise had been made to their
fathers by God. These drawers of water and hewers of wood from
Gibeon shall always be a reminder to the Israelites.

Deuteronomy 29 as a literary foreshadowing of Joshua 9, and
Deuteronomy 9–10 as its theological background, are the bases, therefore, for the present application of the law of *herem* especially as found
in Deuteronomy 7:1–5 where treaties with the occupied cities are expressly forbidden. As God once mercifully dealt with the deceitful Israelites, so Joshua now does with the Gibeonites, who are an accurate
personification of the relationship between God and Israel as described
in the Book of Deuteronomy. We continue to see that each of the legal
cases that the Book of Joshua spells out for us is not only about the
interpretation and application of a specific Mosaic law, the law of the

ban, but also about the reciprocal relations of Israel and her neighbors vis-a-vis the justice and mercy of the LORD. When Joshua warns the Israelites,

> And you must beware of coveting anything that is forbidden under the ban; you must take none of it for yourselves; this would put the Israelite camp under the ban. . . (6:18),

it is now clear that the Deuteronomic History is a reminder to Israel that they were once under the ban, yet were saved because of God's promise to the fathers. They were God's merciful booty in the occupation of the land following the exodus; perhaps they will once again be God's merciful booty in the reoccupation of the land following the exile.

2. The account in 10:1–27 describes the attack of Gibeon by five Amorite kings, and Israel's subsequent defeat of them. The contrast between Gibeon, who had made peace with Israel, on the one hand, and Jerusalem, Hebron, Jarmuth, Lachish, and Debir on the other hand, who now oppose the occupation of the land by the Israelites, is a cisjordanian reflection of Israel's transjordanian experiences as recounted in Deuteronomy 2–3. The five Amorite kings of the Cis-Jordan are a functional counterpart in Joshua 10 of the two Amorite kings of the Trans-Jordan, Og and Sihon, in Deuteronomy 2:26–3:6. Similarly, the Gibeonites of Joshua 9 are a cisjordanian reflection of the friendly Moabites and Ammonites of Deuteronomy 2:9, 19. And just as both the words of Moses and the narrative frame-breaks of Deuteronomy 2–3 served the ideological purpose of countering a dogmatic view of the absolutely unique status of Israel through an insistence on the gift of the land to Moab and Ammon, so also here in Joshua 9–10 the account of Israel's relations with Gibeon underscores the similarity of the position of Gibeon and Israel by its depiction of Gibeon's plight in terms of promises made to Israel.

In fact this has been the main ideological perspective of the Book of Joshua up to this point, as the text has kept alternating between stories narrated from perspectives internal and external to Israel's psychological point of view. In the present case, since Gibeon "stands for" Israel in Joshua 9 vis-a-vis his right to live in the land, the attack by the five Amorite kings, and Israel's subsequent steps to save him from destruction, function as a narrative explanation, begun from a non-Israelite point of view that quickly shifts to Israel's perspective in 10:8, of God's protection of Israel in the face of their enemies. The Gibeonites' message to Joshua, "We are your slaves, do not abandon us, come quickly to our relief (*wᵉhôšîᶜāh lānû*)" (10:6), demands an answer that was in fact

given by Moses when he outlined the rules for warfare in Deuteronomy
20:4:

> Do not lose heart or be afraid or give way to panic in face of your
> enemy; for the LORD your God will go with you to fight your enemy
> for you and give you victory (*l^ehôšîᶜ 'etkem*).

The defense of Gibeon quickly dissolves into a defense of Israel when
God says to Joshua, "Do not be afraid of them. I have delivered them
into your hands" (10:8). Joshua then reiterates the Mosaic exhortation
to the Israelites after the Amorites are defeated and as the five
Amorite kings lay cowering at the feet of Israel:

> Do not be fearful or dismayed; be strong and resolute; for the LORD
> will do this to every enemy you fight against. (10:25)

From the point of view of the stories we have already encountered in
Joshua, the execution scene in Joshua 10 is similar to that portrayed in
Joshua 7: Achan the Israelite dies under the ban just as the five non-
Israelite kings die under the ban. Conversely, Rahab of Jericho (Josh 2,
6), the cattle of Ai (Josh 8), and the inhabitants of Gibeon (Josh 9) are
non-Israelites who escape the ban just as the second generation Israelites, descended from those who worshiped an idol at Sinai, also escape
the ban.

Without having space to examine all the various surface points of
view of Joshua 10, we will simply draw attention to its *temporal* composition. It has been said that the Israelites' return to Gilgal as stated in
10:16 is absurd historically speaking, since they then would have been
moving in a direction away from Makkedah and the other cities to the
south reported conquered by Israel in 10:28–39. However, from a
literary point of view, if we recall the temporal shifting back and forth
that has already occurred in Joshua 2, and especially in 3:1–5:1, there
does not seem to be anything unexpected here. The description of the
events that occur in a particular time-frame by means of a sequence of
"episodes" that often overlap one another is one of the ways the
Deuteronomic narrative is able to give a "more nearly adequate image
of the described reality" (Uspensky, 1973:128).

We might understand the events narrated in chapter 10 as having
taken place during one, or at the most two, miraculously long days. The
story consists of five episodes. The first episode (10:1–11) stretches
from Adonizedek's hearing of the success of Israel's battles (10:1) to the
killing at Makkedah of those Amorites (but not their kings) who had
fled the battle of Gibeon (10:10). The second episode (10:12–15)

backtracks and reports Joshua's miraculous staying of the sun and moon at the beginning of the day's battles until all the cities mentioned in this chapter were captured and the Israelites return to Gilgal (10:15). The third episode (10:16–27) returns again to the fleeing of the kings after their rout at Gibeon, and ends with sunset of that miraculously long day when the bodies of the five kings are taken down from the trees and buried. The next episode (10:28–39) backtracks again to the point after which all those Amorites who had fled the battle were killed, soldiers and kings alike, and describes the miraculous conquests of Makkedah and the other cities. In this episode, the remark in 10:32 that "they took [Lachish] on the second day" is difficult to reconcile with the reconstruction we are proposing. In any case, the fifth episode (10:40–43) again recapitulates most of the time period of the chapter's events, from the battle of Gibeon to the Israelites' return to Gilgal, and emphasizes once again that Joshua took all these kings and their lands "at one time (*pa‘am ’eḥat*)" (10:42). That 10:28–43 is concerned with the full application of the law of the ban, in contrast to Joshua 9, which details a relaxation of that law, is seen not only in the summary statement of 10:40 but also in the individual references to the law of *ḥerem* in vv. 28, 30, 32, 33, 35, 37, and 39.

The Conquest of the North and General Summary (11:1–12:24)

Just as the preceding section contrasts two applications of the law of *ḥerem* in which the law is first relaxed (Josh 9) and then applied in its full rigor (Josh 10), so this section contrasts the full application of the ban on Hazor and its sister cities, "as Moses the servant of the LORD had commanded" (11:11–12), with a relaxed application of the ban on other, northern cities, "whose cattle and other spoil [the Israelites] took" (11:14). It is to be especially noted that in both cases, that is, when cattle are destroyed in Hazor and when they are kept as booty in the cities on mounds, the text explicitly interprets these practices as fulfilling Moses' command "not to leave anything alive that breathes" (Josh 11:11, 14). If therefore "the slaying of all living things" in one case means humans and animals alike, and in another case means just the human inhabitants of a city, and if in both cases the law of Moses on the ban is expressly judged to have been fulfilled, then the concluding verse of this section means to state that there are ways and there are ways to fulfill Moses' commands:

> Not one of the commands laid on Moses by the LORD did [Joshua] leave unfulfilled. (11:15)

Joshua 11:16–12:24 summarizes Joshua's victories in the south and north (11:16–19), and gives a list of the conquered kings (12:1–24) together with a footnote on the fate of the Anakim (11:21–22), the tone of which reminds us of the learned, almost pedantic, frame-breaks of Deuteronomy 2–3. The significance of these achievements, as a summary of all the exploits recounted in 2:1–11:15, is given both in 11:20, which states that it was the LORD's purpose to exterminate all these kingdoms under the ban, and in 11:23, which states that Joshua took the whole country and fulfilled all the commands the LORD had laid on Moses.

The Ideological Perspective of 2–12

When the Deuteronomic narrator quotes God commanding Joshua to

> observe all the law which my servant Moses has given you (1:7),

and when this same narrator concludes that

> Joshua fulfilled all the commands which the LORD laid on Moses
> (11:23),

it is clear that the exploits narrated between these two statements are intended to explain precisely how it could be said in truth that Joshua fulfilled all these divine commands, given the complicated picture of the authoritative decisions Joshua made in the course of the occupation. While the surface drama of 2–12 details the course of the occupation itself, the deep drama of this first section of Joshua concerns itself with the varied ways in which Joshua had to understand, interpret, and apply God's commands, especially illustrated in the Mosaic legislation on the ban. Taking to heart God's words to Joshua, "This book of the law must be ever on your lips" (1:18), the Deuteronomist keeps it ever before his pen, so that his account of the occupation is nothing but a continual meditation upon the meaning of the book of the law, and even upon the meaning of interpretation itself. What binds together the various exploits chosen to be narrated in 2–12, and the very manner of presenting them, is their hermeneutic potential concerning the complicated relationship between the LORD and Israel as it is based upon the Mosaic lawcode.

From the start of our investigation, we saw that basic ideological points of view could not be presumed to be confined to the words and actions of the authoritative personages in the story, God and Joshua, nor were we surprised to find reflexes of a subordinated ideology upon their lips. Rather, an examination of the phraseological plane of 2–12 showed that both the reported speech of authoritative individuals and the reporting speech of the Deuteronomic narrator were found to be conveyors of the ultimate semantic authority, or basic ideological point of view, of the book. Just as the very words of God and Joshua were shown to be *interpretations* of previous authoritative utterances in a consistent variety of different ways, so the narrator himself did in fact mirror in his reporting speech these same modes of interpretation, as our initial assumption had led us to expect.

When we then turned to an initial compositional reading of 2–12, the phraseological, psychological, and spatial-temporal planes of the individual stories contained therein helped us to discover the voice of critical traditionalism in as full control of the ideological plane of this book as it was in the Book of Deuteronomy. By means of the basic framing function of the liturgical narrative, we encountered the alternation between "realistic" and "cultic" recitations of the various events constituting the occupation. Similarly, we found a consistent alternation between accounts narrated from psychological and spatial points of view external to Israel and those narrated from perspectives internal to their consciousness and experience. Temporal shifts in perspective within the same story also helped to vary the perspective of the narrative. In all these cases of shift in point of view, we saw evidence of a sophisticated, even brilliant, ideological stance with respect to the understanding, interpretation, and application of the word of God as concretized in the book of the law. The valuable distortions brought about by these constant shifts in perspective offer the reader a much more adequate image of the occupation of the land as the fulfillment of God's word than the flat, universalized, and pat evaluations of the voice of authoritarian dogmatism, the reflexes of whose simplistic ideology can be still heard in the categorical assertions of, say, 4:10b (". . . until every command which the LORD had told Joshua to give to the people was fulfilled. . ."); 8:35; 10:14, 40; and 11:23. As he had done in the Book of Deuteronomy, the Deuteronomist "takes over" these traditional statements of Israel's religion and subjects them to a critical evaluation that does not so much reject them as subordinate them to a vibrant, revisionary hermeneutics of the word of God.

We chose the cultic account of the crossing of the Jordan in 3:1–5:1 to illustrate in detail the complicated compositional technique utilized by the Deuteronomist to declare and teach the word of God according to the critical traditionalism that is his basic ideological stance. Yet, in *all* the stories within 2–12, we have attempted to show how the Deuteronomic History, contrary to the prevalent view of scholars, is not representative of an orthodox retribution theory carried to its most mechanistic extreme, but rather a subtle and often powerful exposition of the complicated nature of God's justice and mercy, and of a remarkably universalistic stance concerning the unique role both of Moses vis-a-vis other prophetic interpreters and of Israel vis-a-vis other nations subordinated to "the LORD of all the earth" (3:11, 13).

Throughout 2–12, certain characters enjoy a functional equivalency with reference to Israel's relationship to the LORD in general, and to the application of the Mosaic legislation on the ban in particular. Thus Rahab functions in the stories of Joshua 2 and 6 in a way similar to how the cattle and booty function in 8:1–29 and 11:14, the aliens resident in Israel's midst in 8:30–35, and the Gibeonites in 9 and 10. Those things excepted from the ban represent Israel themselves who, although they should have been destroyed by the LORD (Deut 9:13–14) for idolatry and lack of faith, were still preserved and given the land. The Deuteronomist's choice of the law of *ḥerem* as the uniting theme of his meditation on the laws of Moses is appropriate for his larger hermeneutic purposes since the rationale for the ban is precisely avoidance of the very idolatry that by rights should have caused Israel to forfeit the land in the first place:

> so that they may not teach you to imitate all the abominable things that they have done for their gods and so cause you to sin against the LORD your God. (Deut 20:18)

By Israel's sin of idolatry at Sinai, they were in effect put under the ban. That they continued to exist, that they escaped the ban, made them functionally equivalent to all those exempted from the ban in 2–12. Each time they fulfilled the ban, either in its full rigor or by a special relaxation, Israel in effect confessed their own past sins and the present mercy of God.

Joshua 2–12 was an examination of the complexities of what 11:23 meant when it stated that Joshua fulfilled "all the commands which the LORD had laid on Moses." Joshua 13–21 will now examine a similarly complex picture that illustrates what this same verse means when it states that "Joshua took the whole country." 2–12 was a meditation on what the commands of the LORD mean; 13–21 is a meditation on how the word of the LORD is fulfilled.

The Second Section of Joshua (13–21):
How God Fulfilled the Promises He Made to the Fathers

The LORD's giving of the whole land to Israel, as opposed to his giving of only part of it, is dependant upon the Israelites' keeping of all the commandments that Moses laid down (Deut 19:8–9). 13–21 now seeks to emphasize the *difference* between the land actually taken possession of during Joshua's lifetime and that larger territory promised Israel by God. That there is a discrepancy between these two poles once again points to a serious ideological problem even though there is no direct reference to such in 13–21.

This section does not end as it began. There is a deliberate and obvious contrast between God's opening words,

> much of the land remains to be occupied (*lᵉristāh*) (13:1)

and the section's closing assertions:

1. Thus the LORD gave Israel all the land which he had sworn to give to their forefathers; and they occupied it and settled in it (*wayyirāšûnāh*)

2. The LORD gave them security on every side according to everything he had sworn to their fathers;

    of all their enemies not a man could withstand them; the LORD delivered all their enemies into their hands.

3. Not a word of the LORD's good promises to the house of Israel went unfulfilled; they all came true. (21:41–43)

Since the entire section is built upon the premise that the allocation of land is to proceed even before its total occupation (13:1, 6–7) and in spite of Joshua's long labors (11:17), the repetitively exaggerated claims with which this section ends could not be put into greater relief. The very nature of 21:42 and 43 as repetitions of 21:41, and the repetitions within each of the verses themselves, are intended to leave no doubt at all about the authorial irony that envelops the sweeping claims of these concluding verses. It is not that the authoritarian dogmatism, whose shrill voice is here being mocked, claimed that *in a certain sense* Israel received the land, e.g., in the sense that they had a right to it; rather, what is ironically represented by these inflated claims are assertions that Israel at some point in their past in fact controlled and possessed all the lands claimed for them in their traditions, that they in fact had had security on every side, that in their initial occupation of the land none of their enemies in fact could withstand their onslaught, and that not one of God's promised blessings (*haddābār haṭṭôb:* 21:43) had failed to come true. What is being opposed here is not the claim that all of God's word had been fulfilled in the sense that Israel's mixed success was dependent upon their half-hearted obedience. Rather what is exposed to ridicule is any sweeping and grossly unrealistic assertion, such as 21:43, that all of God's promised blessings had in fact come upon Israel in spite of their acknowledged violations of the covenant in the very beginning.

The geographic detail with which 14–21 delineates the tribal allotments of land west of the Jordan is, from the beginning of the section, clearly understood to be *an ideal not an achieved reality*. It is this feature of its detailed contents that leads one to conclude that its geographic formulations are meant to function within the center of the Book of Joshua in precisely the same way as the legal formulations of the Mosaic lawcode function in the center of the Book of Deuteronomy. The Mosaic lawcode of Deuteronomy 12–26 "maps out the territory" that constitutes the commands God gave to Moses just as Joshua's allocation of land in 14–21 "promulgates the legal limits" of the promised land God gave to Israel. This similarity between the central sections of Deuteronomy and Joshua confirms what our compositional analysis of Joshua 1–12 had led us to conclude: the account of their progressive conquest of the land was at the same time an account of Israel's progressive conquest of the meaning of the Mosaic lawcode. The story of Israel's military exercises is also a story of their exercises in legal and theological interpretation. Their maneuvers are seen to be at once strategic and hermeneutic.

Let us examine in some detail the composition of this second section to see how the ultimate semantic authority of the book establishes its predominant perspectives. We shall discover how extensively 13–21 constitutes a critique of the overly sweeping claims of 21:41–43 in precisely the same way as all of 2–12 constitutes a critique of the overly sweeping claims of 11:15. The account of how God fulfilled his promise to give Israel the land (13–21) is as complicated as the story of how Joshua fulfilled God's commands in the initial phase of taking over that land (2–12).

The Phraseological Composition of 13–21

1. Most of this section is the reporting speech of the narrator. God speaks only in 13:1, 6–7 and 20:1–6. Joshua's words are directly quoted only in 17:15, 17–18 and 18:3–7, 8. The only other directly reported speech is that of Caleb in 14:6–12 and 15:18, of Achsah in 15:19, of Zelophehad's daughters in 17:4, of the Josephites in 17:14–16, and of the Levites in 21:2. The paucity of reported speech in this section leads me to suspect that whenever someone's words *are* directly quoted, they perform an especially important function in the text. The most important reported speech is God's in 13:1, 6–7, which commands Joshua to begin the allotment of land to the nine and a half tribes. Every other reported speech in this section involves an important facet of the interpretation and application of this initial command of the LORD.

The ground rules governing the narrative's content are clear and are synopsized in 14:1–5. Two and a half tribes had already been allocated land by Moses, as reported by the narrator in 13:8–33. This left nine and a half tribes to be given land, as commanded by God in 13:6–7. After the allocation of territory to Judah is recounted in 15:1–63, eight and a half tribes remain to be accounted for. The allocation of land to the one and a half Joseph tribes is dispensed with in 16:1–17:18. The remaining seven tribes are dealt with in 18:1–19:48. Within these seven tribes, the special case of the Levites is treated in 21:1–40.

One function of the reported words in this section is to depict distinctive applications of the allotment of land to the nine and a half tribes. Thus, the dialogue between Joshua (17:15, 17–18) and the Joseph tribes (17:14, 16) explains how these one and a half tribes request and receive two lots instead of one as their patrimony. Similarly, the words of the heads of the Levites (21:2) apply the Mosaic legislation of Deuteronomy 13:14, 33 and 18:7, so that while the Levites receive no allotment of territory they do receive forty-two cities scattered throughout the lands of the other tribes.

A second important function of the reported speech in 13–21 is to help specify how the words of the LORD in 13:1 (". . . and much of the land remains to be occupied"), are verified in specific cases. Thus, the dialogue between Joshua and the Joseph tribes in Joshua 17 and the reported words of Joshua to "the seven remaining tribes" in Joshua 18 corroborate God's words of 13:1 with respect to these tribes' territory. Similarly, Caleb's words to Joshua about Anakim and their cities, "Perhaps the LORD will be with me and I shall dispossess them as he promised" (14:12), make the same point. A particularly important example of this second function is found in the words of God found in 20:1–6. Here God commands Joshua to appoint cities of refuge in accordance with the words he spoke to Moses. The text here directly refers both to Deuteronomy 4:41–43, which stipulates three such cities in the territory east of the Jordan, and to Deuteronomy 19:1–13, which commands the initial establishment of three cities of refuge, but then adds,

> if the LORD your God extends your boundries, as he swore to your forefathers and gives you the whole land which he promised to them, because you keep all the commandments that I am laying down today and carry them out by loving the LORD your God and by conforming to his ways for all time, *then you shall add three more cities of refuge to these three.* (Deut 19:8–9; emphasis added)

It is to be noted that God's words to Joshua in 20:1–6 do not specify how many cities Joshua is to appoint. However, the reporting speech of the narrator goes on to record the establishment of three transjordanian cities in 20:8. This action fulfills the Mosaic legislation of Deuteronomy 4:41–43. However, the establishment of only three cisjordanian cities of refuge in 20:7, while fulfilling the legislation of Deuteronomy 19:1–7, reaffirms the LORD's words of 13:1, since according to the legislation of Deuteronomy 19:8–9 a total of *six* cities of refuge were to be appointed if and when Israel possessed the whole land. We thus see that the words of God in 20:1–6 set the scene for the narrator's corroborative application in 20:7–9 of God's words of 13:1.

The remaining reported speech in this second section carries out a third important function in interpreting God's command of 13:6–7. These instances of reported speech concern special allocations of land that affect the entire community of Israel, indeed specify who is to be included with "the entire congregation of Israel (*kol qᵉhal yiśrā 'ēl*)." Just as in the first section of Joshua, 8:30–35 interpreted and applied the Mosaic legislation of Deuteronomy 27:4–13 by specifying "the whole congregation of Israel, including the women and dependants and the aliens resident in their company" (8:35), and just as Joshua 2, 6, and 9–10 gave illustrations of how these women, dependants, and aliens came to be a part of Israel's congregation, so here in the second section of the book key reported utterances illustrate under what circumstances certain women, dependants, and aliens were allocated land originally promised by God not to them but to the tribes of Israel. In this way the reported speech of Caleb in 14:6–12 and 15:18, and that of Achsah in 15:19, relate how certain "aliens" or non-Israelites, viz., the Kenizzites Caleb and Othniel, receive allotments of land. Similarly, the words of Zelophehad's daughters in 17:4 testify how these women and dependants in Israel also have a right to the land, as "the LORD commanded Moses to allow us to inherit on the same footing as our kinsmen."

We see, therefore, how all the reported speech of this second section understands, interprets, and applies both the legislation from the Book of Deuteronomy and the words of God to Joshua in 13:1, 6–7. It is already obvious that Joshua continues to concern itself not simply with a "straightforward" account of the occupation of the land but with a narrative application of the commands of the LORD, especially concretized in the book of the law that "must be ever on your lips" (1:8). We shall now see how the reporting words of the narrator fill out this hermeneutic picture.

2. The first thing to notice about the reporting speech of the narrator in this section is that it often supports the LORD's words of 13:1 and thereby "speaks with a different voice" from that with which it concludes this section in 21:43. In this way it mirrors one of the key functions of the very speech it reports. Just as the reported speech that is found in the words of Caleb in 14:12, in the dialogue between Joshua and the Joseph tribes in 17:14–18, and in the words of Joshua in 18:3–7, 8, all give examples of land yet to be occupied, so too will the narrator give numerous examples of the truth of God's words reported in 13:1. First on the list is his sweeping summary in 13:2–5. Then we find Jerusalem described as a divided city:

> At Jerusalem, the men of Judah were unable to drive out the Jebusites who lived there, and to this day Jebusites and men of Judah live together in Jerusalem. (15:63)

We are also told that the Manassites did not drive out the Canaanites who dwelt in Gezer (16:10), nor were they able to occupy a number of other Canaanite cities that belonged to them: Beth-shean, Ibleam, Dor, En-dor, Taanach, and Megiddo (17:11–13). Further, the narrator tells us in 18:2 what is repeated in the reported speech of Joshua in 18:3–7, 8: the remarkable fact that seven of the twelve tribes had not yet taken possession of their land! In addition, we have already shown above how the narrator's account of the establishment of only three cities of refuge in the land west of the Jordan (20:7) is an implicit assertion, given the Mosaic legislation of Deuteronomy 19:8–9, that not all of the land promised by God had been occupied. Finally, we can mention the narrator's account of Dan's loss of his southern territory in 19:47, and of Moses' distribution of cisjordanian land in which the unconquered land of the Geshurites and the Maacathites is mentioned (13:13).

By means of the combined weight of both the reported and reporting speech about "all the land that remained to be occupied" (13:1, 2–5, 13; 14:12; 15:63; 16:10; 17:11–13, 14–18; 18:2, 3–7, 8; 19:47; 20:7), we see a clear shift in point of view on the phraseological level between the detailed account of the allocation of land in 13:1–21:40 and the concluding verses of this section, 21:41–43. The compositional importance of this shift is not difficult to understand:

> Irony occurs when we speak from one point of view, but make an evaluation from another point of view; thus for irony the nonconcurrence of point of view on the different levels is a necessary requirement. (Uspensky, 1973:103)

Because of the opening statement of the LORD in 13:1, and the repeated corroboration of this by the utterances of Joshua, Caleb, and representatives of the Joseph tribes, because of the numerous state-

ments of the narrator about the ineffectiveness of the Israelites against
many of the peoples of the land—statements which flesh out the narrator's sweeping summary of unoccupied land in 13:2–5—because of
the effect that all of this has on the reader as he simultaneously assumes
this perspective and joins with the narrator, the point of view expressed
by the narrator in 21:41–43, which in spite of its brevity with respect to
what precedes it is equally sweeping and repetitive, produces a situation
of authorial irony well described by Uspensky:

> In this instance the positions of the author and the reader diverge,
> because the author has deliberately taken on a role which is by no
> means his own. (1973:125)

There is absolutely no way that the reader can extricate himself from
the overwhelmingly negative reaction produced by the reading of
21:41–43; everything that the narrator has previously placed before his
eyes causes him to recoil from the ideological position underlying the
phraseology of these concluding verses of the second section of Joshua:

> Irony is thus a special case of authorial pretense, in opposition to
> the reader's "natural" position as defined by the author. (1973:126)

We have no clearer example in Joshua of the explicit formulation of
an ideological point of view which must be immediately and categorically denied by the reader if he chooses to continue to read and accept
the basic ideological position of the text before him. The author of this
work, through the narrator who is totally under his control, has carefully planned the nonconcurrence, at this point, between two ideological positions expressly stated on the surface of the text, and between the
positions of author and reader: if one is to understand and accept the
ideology that controls all of 13:1–21:40, the ideology that supports the
phraseology of 21:41–43 must be categorically rejected. Just as the
entire Mosaic lawcode is compositionally constructed in such a way that
it ceases to have any effective meaning for the reader if Deuteronomy
13:1 is literally accepted by him, so also the basic point of view of the
Book of Joshua ceases to have meaning for the reader if the evaluation
expressed in 21:41–43 is literally rather than ironically construed. The
Book of Joshua is scarcely intelligible if 21:41–43 is not read in an ironic
sense.

The voice of critical traditionalism is here in clear opposition to, and
in complete control of, the voice of authoritarian dogmatism. The author does not silence this opposing voice; rather he allows it even to use
the mouths of authoritative characters in his story, such as Moses and

Joshua. He subdues a voice even as he allows it to speak; he does so by a complicated compositional technique.

3. Most of the text of 13–21 is concerned with a detailed delineation of tribal territories and their boundaries narrated in such a way that a formal analysis of its spatial and psychological composition yields little result. However, this section is affected by the spatial and psychological composition of the preceding section, and we would like to discuss some of these reverberations.

Because we are concerned here with a land only incompletely possessed by Israel in spite of the fact that God had stated categorically,

> every place where you set foot is yours. I have given it to you (*nᵉtatîw lākem*). . . . From the desert and the Lebanon to the great river, the river Euphrates, and across all the Hittite country westwards to the Great Sea, all this shall be your land (1:3–4),

the spatial and psychological perspectives of the preceding section merge here in an interesting way. From a semantic point of view, the spatial contrast between *all* the land which God *has given* Israel and that land which Israel *still* must go in to possess, that is, between the ideal and the real, matches the legal contrast between "*all* the law which my servant Moses has given Israel" (1:7) and that law which Israel still must go in to possess, as it meditates on it night and day (1:8). Thus, the story of the occupation of the land is at the same time, and in a deeper sense, the story of the occupation of the law. This is why, we believe, the story of the progressive occupation of the law and the land, as it developed in 1–12, centered so often on incidents narrated from a spatial and psychological viewpoint *external* to Israel. The gradual incorporation of elements external to Israel and their subsequent legal existence within Israel was a constant compositional theme of 1–12 that served to remind Israel of their initial disobedience to God's word. Rahab and Gibeon are *types* of the Israel depicted in the Deuteronomic History because they mercifully escaped God's justice as had Israel. What was brought inside Israel became an embodied reference to how much of the outside had been within them from the beginning.

So also the spatial contrast between the *given* and the *possessed* land is represented by means of the incorporation of the *alien*, the Kenizzites and the dependent women of Zelophehad, into the *native* by means of the "Israelite" allotment of land to native and alien alike. (Never mind, as we have said, that the crossing of the Jordan had turned these categories upside down so that the invaded native had become thereby an alien in his own land, and that the incoming alien started to call himself a native, an *'ezrah*.) The fact that the Israelites could not conquer the

Jebusites of Jerusalem and the Canaanites of a number of cities of the hill-country and the north is directly related, in the story, to Israel's inability to secure a large part of the Mosaic law within their own borders. And what Joshua does in 13–21, as he did in 1–12, is to make a place within the land and the law for *typical* outsiders. We shall see that a particular version of the theme of the typical outsider, the role of the transjordanian tribes, reaches its climax at the beginning of the third section of the book in Joshua 22. To the non-Israelite Kenizzites, the Israelite Levites (whose constant companions in Deuteronomy are aliens, orphans, widows, slaves, and children), and the daughters of Zelophehad, that is, to those who are all in their own way the "outsiders" of section 2, Israel is reported to have exceptionally allocated land within their borders so that these elements might be a constant *internal* reminder of Israel's own deficiencies, just as the powerful Jebusites and Canaanites were a constant *external* reminder of them.

The characters change between the sections, but the function of Rahab and Zelophehad's daughters, Caleb and Gibeon, remains the same. What is psychologically and spatially external to Israel's consciousness and possession was brought inward, within their midst, so that a multidimensional view was achieved of what the inside and outside of Israel really signified. Paradoxically, this incorporation of external elements acts in the Deuteronomic History as a powerful strategy complementing the rationale given in Deuteronomy 20:18 for the law of *ḥerem*, i.e., the avoidance of idolatry. To avoid the contagion of idolatry, one therefore either destroyed the pagan idolator (*ḥerem*), kept him outside Israel in both a tribal and territorial sense, or else sought to bring him within Israel's midst territorially or cultically.

The Third Section of Joshua (22–24)

The Status of the Transjordanian Tribes (22)
1. The Book of Joshua's constant theme of the outsider in Israel now reaches its climax with a story about how the two and a half tribes, as they are returning to their transjordanian lands, built an altar in Canaan at Geliloth "in addition to the altar of the LORD our God which stands in front of his Tabernacle" (23:29). If the first two sections examined the role of the outsider in Israel by considering the status before the law of those elements within their midst who lived *in* Israel but were not fully *of* Israel, this section continues the examination by clarifying the status before the law of those elements within their midst who were in some sense *of* Israel, but did not live *in* Israel. First the outsiders inside the land, then the insiders outside the land.

The story is ingenious. The plot revolves around a decision by the two and a half transjordanian tribes to build a memorial altar in Canaan as a witness forestalling any future cisjordanian Israelites from claiming that since the former lived outside Canaan they should have no share in the LORD. After the altar is built, it precipitates a cisjordanian delegation going to the builders and suggesting that, whereas the transjordanian land perhaps is unclean, the two and a half tribes should cross over to "the LORD's own land" (22:19). By the building of an additional altar, the two and a half tribes bring about what they had intended thereby to avoid. The story is clearly about the status of the transjordanian land inhabited by the tribes of Reuben, Gad, and half-Manasseh, and about these tribes' full inclusion within the community of Israel.

When the captain of the LORD's army had said to Joshua, immediately after the crossing, "Take off your sandals; the place upon which you are standing (*ʿōmēd*) is holy" (5:15), could this evaluation be applied to *all* the land possessed by the twelve tribes of Israel, or just to the "LORD's own land" west of the Jordan? Is the land possessed by the two and a half tribes truly unclean, as the Israelite delegation implied in 22:19? What is the correct assessment of Israel living outside Israel? It goes without saying that the answer to these questions was as relevant to the Deuteronomist's audience as it appears to be to Joshua's earlier audience. Another way of expressing the central problem of this story is to ask, "Who belongs to Israel? Who belongs to the 'whole community of Israel?' Is it just those tribes whose land was west of the Jordan, or does it include the two and a half tribes whose land was east of the Jordan?" In spite of the overwhelming evidence for the full complement of the twelve tribes of Israel found everywhere throughout the Deuteronomic History and the Bible itself, Joshua 22 testifies that the inclusion of the two and a half transjordanian tribes as full-fledged members of the community of Israel was a serious issue.

2. As Uspensky has illustrated (1973:25–32), one of the surest ways of determining the phraseological composition of a text is to examine the manner in which an author, narrator, or character *names* those he talks to or about. One way then to get at the question of membership within the community of Israel is to inquire how various elements in the story are designated. In other words, besides the proper names of the Israelite tribes, how are they *named* in this story both individually and collectively? Joshua calls the nine and a half cisjordanian tribes "brothers" of the transjordanian tribes (22:3, 4). Phinehas and the ten tribal leaders refer to "the entire community of the LORD" (22:16), "the entire community of Israel" (22:18, 20), "each of the [ten] tribes of Israel" (22:14), and "Israelites (*bᵉnê yiśrāʾēl*)" (22:31, 32, 33 bis). The two and a half

transjordanian tribes talk about "Israel (*yiśrā'ēl*)" (22:22), or about "our sons" and "your sons" (22:24, 25, 27). Finally, the reporting speech of the narrator refers to "the entire community of Israelites (*kol ᶜᵃdat bᵉnê yiśrā'ēl*)" (22:12), "Israelites (*bᵉnê yiśrā'ēl*)" (22:12, 31, 32, 33 bis), "the clans of Israel" (22:21, 30), and simply "the community" (22:30).

There are a number of interesting features of this terminological inventory. For one thing, whenever "the entire community of the LORD/of Israel" is used, that is, by the narrator in 12:12 and by Phinehas and the ten tribal leaders in 22:16, 18, 20, *the two tribes of Reuben and Gad are obviously excluded from membership according to the context*. Thus, those delegated to speak to the alleged culprits in behalf of "the entire community" include, besides Phinehas, representatives from each of the ten tribes whose inherited land is west of the Jordan, that is, from each of the tribes except Reuben and Gad. When the "entire community" assembles at Shiloh to deal with the problem at hand (22:12), it is clear that Gadites and Reubenites are not present since they *are* the problem and it is *to them* that the delegation is finally sent. (The transjordanian half-tribe of Manasseh is sometimes named, sometimes not, when the transjordanian tribes are spoken to or about in this story; it is clear from this that since half of their brethren *did* have land west of the Jordan, their plight was not so dire as that of the other two tribes, Reuben and Gad, who had *no* land west of the Jordan.) Moreover, it is significant that after the explanation of the transjordanian tribes is reported as acceptable to the delegation from Shiloh in 22:30, there is no reference again in the story to "all Israel" or "the entire community"; so that when the narrator describes the delegation's return trip and their reception back at Shiloh, those whose interests they represent and who live west of the Jordan are referred to three times only as "Israelites (*bᵉnê yiśrā'ēl*)" (22:32, 33 bis). They are no longer referred to as "the entire community of God/Israel."

In other words, both reporting and reported speech begin the story by referring to the western tribes as "all Israel" or "the entire community of Israel/the LORD," but by 22:30 both reported and reporting speech uses only "*bᵉnê yiśrā'ēl*" or "the community" when referring to all or part of the twelve tribes. The story begins as if the ten cisjordanian tribes constituted the entire community of Israel, but shifts its point of view before the end of the story.

The compositional importance of this shift in terminology can not be overestimated, since the story's subject matter centers around the fear of the transjordanian tribes that some day their "brothers" across the Jordan might say to them:

What have you to do with the LORD, the God of Israel? The LORD put the Jordan as a boundary between our sons and your sons. You have no share in the LORD, you men of Reuben and Gad. (22:24–25)

It was because of this fear that the additional nonsacrificial altar was built, and it was because of this altar that the delegation from the west traveled across the river to adjudicate the action of their eastern brothers. We see here how a specific interpretation and application of the Mosaic legislation about the legality of sacrifice only at the altar located "in the place the LORD your God will choose," legislation that is so often expressed in the book of the law, becomes the vehicle for the Deuteronomist's depiction of Israel's identity. The decision of the Israelite community's delegation reported in the words of Phinehas (22:31) and those of the narrator (22:32–33) was not just a decision that acquited the transjordanian tribes of the charge of violating the law of Moses by building an altar "in addition to the altar of the LORD our God which stands in front of his Tabernacle" (22:29). This decision asserts also the right of the transjordanian tribes to be considered full-fledged members of the community of Israel. Surely this is the deeper meaning of Phinehas's remarks to the two and a half tribes, "thus you have preserved Israel from punishment at [the LORD's] hand" (22:31). Another decision would not only have dismantled the altar named "Witness," it would also have dismembered the community called Israel.

3. Another indication that membership in the community of Israel is at stake here comes from the spatial level of the text and concerns the terminology used in the story to indicate passage across the Jordan. We saw in great detail in the liturgical drama of 3:1–4:15 how the verb "to cross over (ʿābar)" (the Jordan) was used precisely to indicate Israel's passage from promise to fulfillment. As soon as "all the nation had finished crossing the Jordan" (4:1), God's promise to the fathers began to be fulfilled. This use of ʿābar in 3:1–4:14 indicated the spatial and psychological point of view of Israel themselves as to the significance of the passage itself: the Israelite is *par excellence* "the Hebrew (haʿibrî)" from his brother's point of view, as Deuteronomy 15:12 brings out. In contrast to this, the terminology used by the narrator in 4:15–5:1 expressed the spatial and psychological point of view of the non-Israelite, him whose land was now in the process of being occupied. Thus the priests and the people after 4:14 were described only as "coming out of or up from the Jordan." "To cross the Jordan" therefore meant quite concretely "to enter into the LORD's possession."

When we look at the precise terminology of Joshua 22, we find that it is absolutely consistent with the evidence amassed in our analysis of 3:1–5:1. When Joshua twice tells Reuben, Gad, and half-Manasseh to return home on the other side of the Jordan (22:4, 8), when the narrator tells us these tribes turned to go home (22:9), when he tells us that they arrived at Gilead (22:15), and when he reports that the Israelite delegation left Trans-Jordan and reported back to the Israelites in Canaan (22:32), although in all of these cases the crossing of the Jordan was indicated or actually accomplished, the verb "to cross (over) (*ʿābar*)" is never used. The reason for this is that "the crossing over" had already taken place. By the solemn procession of 3:1–4:14, Israel had begun to take possession of the land. Although the story refers five times to actions which necessarily imply going from one side of the Jordan to the other, it never uses the verb *ʿābar* in these cases.

Only once does the story refer to the passing from one side of the Jordan to the other as a "crossing over (*ʿābar*)" and it is precisely where the verb is to be expected, if our compositional analysis is correct. When the Israelite delegation speaks to their brothers in Gilead, they tell them,

> If the land you have taken is unclean, then cross over (*ʿibʿrû*) to the LORD's own land, where the Tabernacle of the LORD now rests, and take a share of it with us. (22:19)

This action, therefore, would be tantamount to admitting that the land of the two and a half tribes is not "Israel," that the two and a half tribes have not yet "crossed over," that they are not "Israel" in the full sense, and that they have not yet entered into the LORD's possession.

One less important aspect of the spatial composition of the story can be mentioned here. In contrast to the verb, *ʿābar*, the preposition, *ʿēber*, "beyond or across" is used in various ways according to the point of view of the speaker. Thus, when Joshua tells Reuben, Gad, and half-Manasseh to go home, his reported speech reflects his own spatial position west of the Jordan, so that his use of "*bʿʿēber* the Jordan" indicates "east of the Jordan." On the other hand, when the narrator in 22:7 indicates that Moses had given to half of the tribe of Manasseh land "*mēʿʿēber* the Jordan," he clearly takes the point of view of Moses, speaking in Trans-Jordan, and the phrase now means, "west of the Jordan," as the added *yāmmāh* of 22:7 indicates. This preposition, therefore, helps us determine various shifts in the spatial composition of the text.
4. The temporal perspective of the *reporting speech* of the narrator remains in the retrospective past throughout the story until the end, where we read:

. . . and the Israelites thought no more of attacking Reuben and Gad and ravaging the land in which they were living (*'ªšer yošᵉbîm bāh*). (22:33)

The imperfective form of *yāšab* here indicates a shift to the synchronic point of view on the part of the narrator, and is compositionally important. That the land of Reuben and Gad is described as "the land in which they were living," rather than an equally possible formulation such as "the land in which they lived (*'ªšer yāšᵉbû bāh*)," points to the story's emphasis on solving the question of *what it means* to the identity of these two tribes and the land they live in that it is west of the Jordan. By the shift to the synchronic viewpoint here, the narrator's perspective now concurs with the *spatial* point of view of the story outlined above. The narrator's indication that the two tribes were continuing to live in this land east of the Jordan is an implicit narrational response to the Israelite delegation's smug invitation to them in 22:19 to "cross over . . . and take a share of [the LORD's own land] with us." There is no need to cross over; that part of Israel that lives outside of Israel continues to remain inside.

On the other hand, the temporal composition of the *reported speech* in the story continually shifts between the past, the present, and the future. The temporal indicators of these shifts are especially numerous. The frequent indication of the retrospective past within the speech of the various characters in the story is accomplished as usual by perfective verb forms such as Joshua's first words in 22:2, "You have observed. . . ." The frequent shift to the synchronic present of the speaker is seen in the unusual number of times variations of *hayyôm*, "today," are found in the story (22:3, 16 bis, 17, 18, 19, 22, 29, 31). We find shifts to the future especially with the use of *māḥār*, "tomorrow, in the future."

In the reported speech of Joshua (22:2–5, 8), the shift from retrospective to synchronic perspective (the two and a half tribes have been perfectly obedient *ᶜad hayyôm hazzeh*, "up to this very day") introduces the legal subject of this story: having always up to that point been obedient, did the two and a half tribes sin by building an additional altar at Geliloth by the Jordan? Within the reported speech of Phinehas and the Israelite delegation (22:16–20, 31b), the synchronic perspective brought about by *hayyôm* is used in 22:16 bis, 18 to indicate the initial affirmative answer to the question we have just raised, while *hayyôm* in 22:31 indicates a final not-guilty verdict. The synchronic use of *hayyôm* in 22:17 indicates the continuing impurity of Israel from generation to generation, based upon the *hayyôm/māḥār* principle stated in 22:19: if you sin against God today, tomorrow he will be angry with all Israel. But since the allegedly sinful building of the altar has already taken place, the *māḥār* of 22:19 is contextually equivalent to the *hayyôm* of the speaker. When we look at the temporal indicators of the speech of the Reubenites, Gadites, and the half-tribe of Manasseh (22:22–29), we find the same situation: all uses of *māḥār* fade into a continually present *hayyôm*. First, the retributive principle enunciated by Phinehas in 22:19 is actually restated in 22:22 with *hayyôm* replacing *māḥār:* "if *today* you sin, *tomorrow* God will be angry with us" now becomes, "if we had sinned (yesterday), you could not save us today." Second, all the other uses of *māḥār* in 22:22–29 are made equivalent to *hayyôm* either by placing *māḥār* within a past speech embedded in the present speech of the two and a half tribes (22:24, 28), or else by having *māḥār* refer to a future situation that is already realized by the present confrontation between east and west (22:27).

The repetitive use of *hayyôm* and the curious equivalency in this story of *māḥār* and *hayyôm* indicate that the issues at stake here are of a continually abiding nature. What was true yesterday about these issues is true today and will continue to be true tomorrow. The synchronic perspective of this story, emphasized so often by the repeated use of *hayyôm* and *māḥār* indicates the enduring significance of this story on the ideological level.

Finally, the words of 22:27 synthesize the spatial and temporal perspectives of this story about a disputed altar. That altar, like the story about it, is to be

a witness between us and you   = West and East : today
and between our descendants after us = West and East : tomorrow

5. We are now in a position to see why the transjordanian tribes have occupied an unusually prominent position in the Book of Joshua. They were given special attention in the opening chapter (1:12–18), cross over the Jordan at the head of the entire procession (4:12–13), and go in front of the Ark of the LORD in the procession around Jericho's walls (6:7). Moses' prior allotment of land to them is narrated in detail in chapter 13, and reference to this special situation of theirs is repeated (14:3; 18:7). Now Joshua 22 gives us additional evidence for their typological status within the Book of Joshua itself. Intent upon emphasizing the continuing unworthiness of Israel and her lack of right to the land she is herein described as occupying, the Deuteronomist has chosen the two and a half eastern tribes of Israel to dramatize these themes. Like the other "aliens"—Rahab, the Gibeonites, Caleb, the Levites and dependants in the Book of Joshua, all of them representative versions of the same typology—the transjordanian tribes are a permanent representation of the obedience to God's law that never quite makes it. As Phinehas testifies to these "outcasts,"

> We know this day . . . that you have saved the people of Israel from the hand of the LORD. (22:31)

Joshua's Farewell Speech (23:1–16)

This speech signals the death of Joshua soon to be recounted in 24:29. Joshua tells Israel that the process of driving out the peoples of the land is not completed. These peoples are "outsiders" within the borders of Israel, commerce with whom can ultimately destroy Israel. The role of these outsiders will become a central theme of the Book of Judges. Here in Joshua 23 these nations point to the discrepancy between the ideal and the real present within Israel's traditions, already described in section 2 of Joshua. The "ideal" is represented by universalistic formulations such as 23:9 ("to this day not a man of them has withstood you") and 23:14:

> You know in your heart of hearts that nothing that the LORD your God has promised you has failed to come true, every word of it.

But instead of putting these comforting but unrealistic assertions into critical perspective by the harsh facts of the history that precedes them, as he did in 12–21, the Deuteronomic narrator now neutralizes these soporific claims with the harsh prophecy of a future that awaits Israel (23:11–13, 15–16). The palpable feeling of security meant to be engendered by the sweeping assertions so dear to the heart of an authoritarian dogmatism is utterly destroyed by an appeal first to the just narrated past (13–21) and then to the predictable future (23:11–13, 15–16).

The Covenant at Shechem and Joshua's Death (24:1–33)

The liturgical narrative of 24:1–28 is the final framing story of the book. Two things are remarkable about it: first, the content and composition of the LORD's words in 24:2–14, and second, the content and composition of the dialogue between Joshua and Israel in 24:15–24. As to content, the focus of God's account of his mighty acts is on mercy, and contains absolutely nothing of a retributive nature at all, whereas Joshua's didactic interpretation of the divine words he has taken over concentrates on their retributive "implications." The compositional re-

lationship between these two sections of Joshua 24 sets in relief once
again the retributive emphasis of the dominant voice of critical
traditionalism versus a voice that, by concentrating on the comforting
aspects of God's mercy, would allow an Israelite to ignore all too easily
his covenantal responsibilities.

1. The historical critical conclusions of von Rad's important discovery
of the absence of reference to law in "historical credos" such as 24:2–13
have unfortunately obscured their compositional importance within the
larger literary context of the text. It *is* crucial, as von Rad recognized,
that 24:2–13 makes no explicit reference to the Mosaic covenant, nor to
any retributive aspect flowing from it. It is even more crucial, however,
to recognize the retributive nature of Joshua's interpretation and application of these divine words as recounted in the liturgical dialogue that
follows them. The divine mercy of 24:13 that recalls how God allowed
Israel to *attain* the land (in spite of Israel's disobedience which implicitly
hovers in, around, and under God's account here) is not allowed to overpower the minatory words of 24:19–20 that testify how certain it is that
Israel will not *retain* the land if they forsake the LORD and worship
foreign gods:

> . . . although he once brought you prosperity, he will make an end
> of you.

Here as elsewhere, God's mercy is never denied, it is simply put into a
situational perspective that is meant to correct and neutralize what the
ultimate semantic authority of the book sees as an overdependence on,
and an overemphasis of, God's mighty acts on behalf of Israel. This
Deuteronomic perspective has been exemplified in diverse ways
throughout our compositional analysis of Joshua, and its final chapter is
a fitting conclusion to the book.

What is important in the phraseological composition of 24:2–13 is
that we have here in the directly reported words of the LORD a narrative of Israel's exploits told in the first person: God's autobiographical
account of the significance of his previous relations with Israel. If we
recall on the one hand that the other occurrences of these short
explanatory speeches (Deut 6, 26; Josh 4 [twice]) are already a narrative answer to the question, "What does this or that mean?" and on the
other hand that nowhere else in the Deuteronomic text already analyzed do God's direct words perform this important explanatory function, we can see clearly the compositional implications of this reported
speech of God. Because we have encountered these narrative explanations many times before this, it is easy to see here that God's words are
already a *selective* understanding, interpretation, and application of the

many events that theoretically could have made up an account of Israel's past relationship with God. The special nature of *this* interpretation, glossing over as it does not only the Mosaic covenant but also Israel's numerous past violations of that covenant, is that this is the only example of *God's direct narrative explanation of the significant aspects of his past dealings with Israel.* And *God's* explanation, in contradistinction to Moses' countless rehearsals of the events that preceded his speeches at Moab as well as Joshua's and the Deuteronomic narrator's many narrative explanations in the Book of Joshua, *gives no special status to law and covenant in the depiction of Israel's essential relationship to God.* Rather, what God emphasizes here is the unmerited nature of Israel's blessings, culminating in the gift of the land (24:13).

But the narrative of Joshua 24 depicts Joshua immediately commenting upon and retorting these divine words in 24:14ff. Even apart from the specific characterization which Joshua gives to God's words here, the very fact that Joshua's last act, as it were, is to determine the significance for Israel of God's words allows us to hear once more the voice of the author as he reinforces his ideological message upon the reader. That it is Joshua, not God, who is depicted as telling Israel that they ought to, although they do not have to (24:15), enter into solemn covenant with the LORD in order to faithfully apply the direct word of God he has just reported is compositionally important here because Joshua's interpretation *so obviously goes beyond what the words of God say.* How can Joshua possibly get from the LORD's concluding words of unmerited blessing in 24:12–13 to his interpretive warning of merited doom in 24:19–20? Whether the reader agrees or not with Joshua's particular interpretation of God's words, it is obvious that he is depicted as immediately interpreting these words in 24:14ff, as his opening word, "Now therefore ($w^{ec}att\bar{a}h$)," attests. (See on this rhetorical term of the Deuteronomic History, Weinfeld, 1972:175–176.) And as a practical application of the direct word of God, Joshua's interpretation accomplishes here what it has been continually depicted as doing throughout the book: it proclaims its own abiding necessity whenever the word of God is to be observed.

Not only Joshua but the people are depicted as interpreting and applying God's word (24:16–18). They further synopsize what is already God's synopsis of his mighty acts, and delimit even more than Joshua the options open to them. Joshua stated in 24:15 that they were free to worship other gods if they so chose; they state in 24:16–18 that this is almost unthinkable. Joshua then transforms God's words of mercy into a prophecy of doom in 24:19–20; the people still express their desire to worship God, and the covenant is finally entered into.

That both Joshua and Israel are depicted as having to complete the
words of God by interpretations that purport to make explicit what is
only implicit within them, and that they both agree on a retributive
interpretation which on the face of it appears far removed from the
comforting mercy so obviously emphasized by the final verses of the
LORD's account, are compositional aspects of this story which admirably
serve the ultimate semantic authority of the book itself.

The Ultimate Semantic Authority of the Book of Joshua

Our compositional analysis of Joshua has revealed it to be a sustained
meditation on what it means to interpret the word of God in general
and the book of the law in particular. By means of an account of the
Israelite occupation of the land, the narrator offers an account of Israel's constant application of the law. In the case both of law and of
land, gaps are emphasized. The distance between the commands of the
law and Joshua's (Israel's) fulfillment of them is the underlying theme
of Joshua 1–12. Similarly, the distance between the divine promises
about the land and God's fulfillment of them is the underlying theme of
Joshua 13–21. Finally, the distance between the divine word and
human interpretation is the underlying theme of Joshua 22–24 and the
general theme of the entire book as well.

Woven throughout the story are the dual threads of God's mercy and
justice on the one hand, and Israel's self-identity on the other. Israel's
traditional characterization of God as both merciful and just, and of
themselves as both citizens and aliens, is bound together in the
Deuteronomist's narrative of the events that comprised the occupation
of the land under Joshua.

It would be misleading to characterize the dominant ideological voice
of the text so far discovered as one simply of retributive justice. The
complicated nature of the various perspectives interrelated in the books
of Deuteronomy and Joshua shows clearly that such a simplistic characterization is not faithful to the compositional structure of these texts.
Thus the prevailing view of scholars on the overly mechanistic nature
of the Deuteronomic theology of history could not be further from the
compositional evidence that this study has attempted to describe in the
preceding pages. Standing behind God's account of his *gracious* giving
of the land in Joshua 24:2–13 is Moses' account of God's *merciful* giving
of the land in spite of Israel's many sins in Deuteronomy 9–10. The
very occupation of the land that is the subject matter of the entire book
of Joshua is dependant, from a compositional point of view, upon God's
merciful decision in Deuteronomy 10:11 to forgive Israel's disobedience
and give her the land:

Set out now at the head of the people so that they may enter and occupy the land which I swore to give to their forefathers.

There immediately follows in Deuteronomy 10:12–22 Moses' interpretive conclusions to be drawn from his historical review and signaled by the rhetorical term, $w^{ec}att\bar{a}h$, "now therefore. . . . " We find in Moses' exhortation here not only the necessity of obedience to God's law but also God's love and care for the "outsider," the widow, orphan and alien: "You too must love the alien, for you once lived as aliens in Egypt" (10:19).

Meditation, therefore, upon Israel's own identity as both citizen and alien provides the interpretive key to the dominant ideological perspective of the Book of Joshua. The constant concern of the text with "exceptional outsiders," be they Rahab, the exempted animals of Ai, the trickster Gibeonites, the women, dependants, Levites, or especially the transjordanian tribes of Israel, reveals their functional role throughout the story as *types of Israel.* The complicated relationship between God's mercy and justice is bound up with Israel's self-understanding as both citizen and alien within the community of the LORD. As the narrative describes Israel-the-community settling within Israel-the-land, it never ceases to emphasize how much of the "outside," both communally and territorially is "inside" Israel. Doubtless the Deuteronomic narrator's audience, which appears from the text to be situated outside Israel-the-land, was to take comfort in the realization that they had always been outsiders, even when inside the land. At the same time, the experience of the transjordanian tribes could provide a model for an Israel that was a community of *'ezr^{e}ḥîm* even though they lived outside the territorial limits of the land God had given to their fathers. And coloring all of the ideological aspects of the story was the amazing fact that in spite of all their deficiencies, the community of Israel was still alive. This startling fact was something that authoritarian dogmatism could defend but never explain. We shall see in the next chapter how the voice of critical traditionalism faces squarely its own ultimate inability to explain Israel's continued existence throughout the chaotic period of the judges.

Four

THE BOOK OF JUDGES

The Book's Introduction (1:1–3:6)

1. The exploits of the various judges who are the main characters of this book only begin to be narrated in 3:7 with the brief account of Othniel. What precedes this appears to be a double introduction—such would be a typical explanation of biblical scholars who have trained their historical critical sights upon this section of the text—whose segments have not been editorially unified very successfully. The results, we are told, are an introductory account of Israel's partially unsuccessful attempts to complete the occupation after the death of Joshua (1:1–36), followed by a second introduction which synthesizes the varied accounts of the judges in terms of a cyclical theology of history (2:6–3:6). Separating these two sections is a brief report of the words of the LORD's angel explaining why not all of the inhabitants of the land have been driven out (2:1–5).

It is easy to see why editorial layers have been "discovered" in 1:1–3:6: at first glance, these opening chapters do not read very well from a narrative point of view. The text begins, "After the death of Joshua . . ." (1:1), yet we read in 2:6 that Joshua dismisses the people, and in 2:8–9 that he dies and is buried. A significant amount of material in chapter 1 is almost a word for word repetition of portions of the Book of Joshua, and a unified outlook that would explain why the specific information recounted in this chapter has been selected is not readily apparent. Then, the LORD's judgmental explanation of the reason for only a partially successful occupation (2:1–5) seems to be unrelated to the more straightforward account in chapter 1 of the greater strength of some of Israel's enemies. An objective account devoid of excuses or moralistic explanations is followed by an ideological account: first history, then theology. But then one is struck by certain discrepancies between the ideology of 2:1–5 on the one hand and that of 2:6–3:6 on the other. In 2:1–5 the remaining inhabitants of the land are to be a decoy and a trap for Israel in punishment for their embrace of foreign gods, whereas in 2:6–3:6 the nations which the LORD left are to test Israel's continuing obedience to the law (2:20–23; 3:4) and to teach an inexperienced Israelite army how to make war (3:2). And finally, within 2:6–3:6 itself the LORD's words of 2:20–22 appear to be a punishment for Israel's worshiping of false gods after Joshua's death, whereas the narrator's comment upon these words in 2:23 refers them *to the previous generation's inability under Joshua* to drive out all the nations. One would therefore be foolish to deny categorically that there is evidence of editorial activity that resulted in the present text of 1:1–3:6. At the same time, too much historical critical theorizing about such editorial activity has not helped us much in our efforts to read the present text in relation to what precedes and follows it.

The first thing that strikes one in reading 1:1–36 is that it paints the same kind of picture of Israel's partial military victories *after* Joshua's death as Joshua 13–21 described *before* his death. There are military successes primarily by Judah and Simeon, but even these are partial (1:19, 21) and it appears to be the failures of Manasseh, Ephraim, Zebulun, Asher, Napthali, and Dan that are really emphasized (1:27–35). Another thing about the chapter is that it repeats, with only a few slight changes, information already given in the Book of Joshua: Jd 1:10–20 = Josh 15:13–14; Jd 1:11–15 = Josh 15:15–19; Jd 1:21 = Josh 15:63; Jd 1:27–28 = Josh 17:11–13; Jd 1:29 = Josh 16:10; and Jd 1:34 = Josh 19:47. If the entire Book of Joshua presented us with a balanced description of the partial occupation of the land as the actual fulfillment of God's promises (Josh 13–21), this first chapter of Judges repeats this complex picture for the period immediately following Joshua's death. Looked at in this way, we see that Judges 1 takes a central position described in the preceding book and applies it to the period following the death of that book's main hero, Joshua, with the help of an almost word for word repetition of many utterances from the previous book. But this was very much the case, as we have seen, with Joshua 1 vis-a-vis Deuteronomy. Largely by means of a number of literal or paraphrasing repetitions of utterances from Deuteronomy, Joshua 1 recapitulated the central position of the Book of Deuteronomy and applied it to the period following the death of that book's main hero, Moses. The effect is the same in both instances: the book begins by encapsulating a central position of the preceding book before or as it proceeds on with its own narrative. The past is reviewed as the narrated present interprets and applies it. The big difference between the open-ing chapters of these two books is that one does it with words alone (Josh 1) and the other with narrated actions (Jd 1). And as to the books themselves, the question in Joshua was not *whether* Israel under Joshua would occupy the land but how much or how little they would occupy; that they would indeed occupy the land had already been decided during Moses' lifetime, as narrated in Deuteronomy 9–10. The Book of Judges goes a step further. Now the question is not how much or how little land Israel would occupy during the period of the judges, but *why* they had not been able completely to drive out the inhabitants of the land. The Book of Judges, like Joshua, briefly recapitulates the previ-ous book before interpreting it further.

Although Joshua was intent upon emphasizing the limited nature of Israel's occupation of the land and connecting this up in some way with the limited nature of Israel's occupation of the law, the exact relation-ship between occupation of land and of law was never really explained in any explicit manner. That the Book of Joshua's account of the pro-gressive occupation of the land was at the same time a meditation upon Israel's continual attempts to occupy the book of the law was a funda-mental conclusion of the last chapter, but there is still a problem con-nected with this view. If the Deuteronomic History was intent upon dem-onstrating how blessing flows from obedience and destruction from disobedience, it first had to explain how and why Israel did in fact receive the land at all, given their disobedience immediately following Sinai. Deuteronomy 9–10 dealt with this problem and most of the Book of Joshua examined the implications of these chapters from Deuteronomy: Israel would occupy the land although they had not merited it. But given the dying off of the first generation of Israelites outside the land (Moses' contemporaries), and given the wickedness of the nations and the promise God made to the fathers, why was not the *entire land* given to Joshua's Israelites? For, although the first generation of Israelites grossly sinned against God, and although each generation under the judges did likewise, there is no account of the Israelites under Joshua seriously betraying the covenant as a community. Apart from Israel's timidity in sending out spies to Jericho, we cannot find a more exemplary community than that depicted in Joshua. Although Joshua 23 acknowledged the fact, it never really explained why there had to be "the peoples that are left among you." The Book of Judges, in its first chapters, now turns to the problem of why Joshua was not able to drive out *all the nations,* and it will examine the implications of its answer in the subsequent history of Israel during the judges.

2. We may get an idea of the literary composition of this opening section of Judges by first examining the various shifts in perspective on the psychological, spatial-temporal, and phraseological planes of the text.

On the psychological plane, the entire first section of the introduction, from 1:1–2:5, is narrated from a psychological point of view *external* to the characters of the story. The narrator displays himself here as one who has no special knowledge about "the internal processes (thoughts, feelings, sensory perceptions, emotions)" (Uspensky, 1973:83) of any of the characters of the story, God included. What we are told is what any onlooker could have experienced, known, or surmised were he present at the events described. At this point in the story the narrator does not reveal any of that privileged knowledge he has consistently displayed previously and will display once again. In other words, the narration in 1:1–2:5 is of a synchronic narrator while that of 2:6–3:6 belongs to a panchronic narrator (Uspensky, 1973:113–4). The effect of 1:1–2:5's psychological perspective is to shield us from any advance knowledge of how Israel's initial forays into battle after Joshua's death will turn out. This allows us to experience the same shifts in thoughts and emotions that the Israelites are described as experiencing as they live out the exploits described in 1:1–2:5. The book begins on a triumphant note by quoting God's words in response to the Israelites' question about which tribe was to attack the Canaanites first: "Judah shall attack. I hereby deliver the country into his power" (1:2). After the previous account in the Book of Joshua had made it clear that the Israelite occupation under Joshua was in no way complete, the effect of the LORD's words, after Joshua's death, is to raise Israel's expectations to new heights. Now finally, they would drive out the remaining nations! Indeed, Judah and Simeon roll up victory after victory until the bubble bursts in 1:19 where Judah, although in control of the hill-country, could not drive out the inhabitants of the vale who had chariots of iron. Much like the shift in emphasis between Joshua 6–11 and 12–21, the account in Judges after v. 18 details a much more mixed picture of Israel's military exploits. Caleb is successful in 1:20 but Benjamin fails with the Jebusites in 1:21. Joseph captures Bethel in 1:22–25 but the rest of the chapter does downhill as the narrative begins a staccato: "Manasseh did not drive out. . . . Ephraim did not drive out. . . . Zebulun did not drive out. . . . Asher did not drive out. . . . Naphtali did not drive out." The Danites are contained in 1:34, and the Joseph tribes have to struggle finally to dominate some of the Amorites in 1:35.

Then the account confirms what must have been the Israelite feelings of frustration in the face of defeat, by quoting the angel of the LORD's condemnatory words in response to (we are surprised to hear) Israel's disobedience:

> So I said I will not drive them out before you; they will decoy you,
> and their gods will shut you fast in the trap. (2:3)

The Israelites now weep and wail, and offer sacrifice to the LORD. By means of a realistic, externalized, psychological perspective, the synchronic narrator has allowed the reader to accompany the Israelites as they descend from high hopes to final discouragement and a realization of further troubles. Like the Israelites of this section, the reader gradually but powerfully realizes that the generations of Israelites after Joshua will be no more successful in driving out the nations than were the generation before them.

But the psychological perspective of the next section, 2:6–3:6, is not so clear-cut. It begins by continuing the external point of view of the preceding section, but we soon realize that the narrator has now become an omniscient panchronic observer who is permitted to penetrate the consciousness of all his characters, God included. Sweeping statements about the fidelity of Joshua's generation and the sinfulness of its successors, about provoking the LORD's anger, about the LORD bringing disaster upon Israel and then relenting when he hears their moans and cries, all show that the narrator is now as all-knowing as God himself. He is one who presents his story from a psychological perspective internal to many or all of his characters. The account then concludes by alternating psychologically between an internal (3:1, 2, 4) and external (3:3, 5, 6) point of view.

There are shifts in temporal perspective that more or less parallel those of the psychological plane. Up to 2:6, the temporal perspective matches that of the characters in the narrative. Most of the exploits after Judah's initial forays are narrated in such a way as not to imply strict sequence, but the temporal effect still allows the reader to experience the *basic sequence* of initial success followed by more and more failures that culminates in a definitive explanation by the LORD in 2:1–4. By 2:5, the reader wonders with the Israelites themselves how and why the situation could have deteriorated so. The vagueness of the LORD's accusation,

> You have disobeyed me. Look what you have done! (2:2),

forces the reader to ask what the Israelites, we would think, must have asked themselves: what was done to anger the LORD so? Now comes a temporal shift that brilliantly responds to the author's psychological and temporal perspectives in 1:1–2:5. The narrative in 2:6 shifts back to the moment described in Joshua 24:28 when Joshua dismisses his people and, using this moment as a starting point, begins a panoramic temporal overview of the entire period covered by the Book of Judges. In sweeping temporal terms, a cyclical sequence is presented which explains not only the incidents of Judges 1 but *all* the events to follow in the book.

The time-line of 1:1–2:5 is schematically linear while that of 2:6–3:6 is circular. The events of 1:1–2:5 begin shortly after Joshua's death and terminate with the angel's journey to Bokim and his condemnatory explanation of Israel's intervening military failures. The angel's accusation, "But you did not obey me and look what you have done!" (2:2), cries out for explanation, and the flashback at the beginning of 2:6–23 provides just such an explanation—and more. By rewinding the narrative tape and bringing us back to the incidents already reported at the end of the Book of Joshua (Jd 2:6–9 = Josh 24:28–31), we are presented with a parallel account of what Israel did following Joshua's death. Judges 2:10–15 now narrates events within the same time-frame as Judges 1:1–2:5, but now Israel's exploits are not only military but idolatrous: they forsake the LORD and worship the Baal and Ashtaroth (2:10–13) so that their military failures are caused by the LORD's anger (2:14–15). But Israel's disastrous experiences immediately following Joshua's death are not to be unique. 2:16–22 now depicts with broad narrative strokes the entire period to be covered by the subsequent narrative in Judges. God raises up judges who bring temporary relief but not repentance, and with the death of a judge comes even deeper corruption. The LORD angrily states in 2:20–22 that he will not drive out one single man of the nations which Joshua left at his death.

Up to this point (2:22), the narrative is cyclical but not circular. Israel's subsequent history under the judges simply repeats what the first generation after Joshua's death experienced. The narrative in 2:6–22 simply states that Israel under the judges was condemned to repeat, over and over again, the same destructive pattern that was depicted in vivid detail in 1:1–2:5. However, the main problem with which both the Book of Joshua ends and the Book of Judges begins has not yet been addressed: if it is understandable that the generations of Israelites after Joshua's death continually walk the tight-rope between victory and defeat as a result of their repeated breaking of the covenant, *we still have no adequate understanding of Joshua's inability to occupy the entire land before his death.* Both Joshua 24:31 and Judges 2:7 state categorically that, as long as Joshua and his elders were alive, Israel worshiped the LORD.

Moreover, our compositional analysis of the entire Book of Joshua made abundantly clear how impressively Joshua and the Israelites went about occupying the law even as they endeavored to occupy the land. Given the limits according to which legal application, like hermeneutic interpretation, can only *approximate* yet never attain the full meaning of the law, there is absolutely nothing in Joshua's generation like the previous failures of Moses' generation on the one hand, or those of the subsequent generations of the judges (2:10–22) on the other. While Moses was alive, Israel seriously broke the covenant, and even while the judges were bringing them temporary protection Israel continued to sin, as 2:17 makes perfectly clear.

The Deuteronomic narrator confronts this problem head on, and in one terse statement provides an answer which transforms the explanation of 2:6–22 from a cyclical into a truly circular narrative:

> So the LORD left those nations alone and made no haste to drive
> them out *or give them into Joshua's hand.* (2:23; emphasis added)

The reference to *Joshua's* failure to complete the occupation is totally unexpected, and profoundly influences the significance of 1:1–2:22 on the one hand, and everything that follows on the other. If we were content to think that 2:6–22 was a cyclical explanation of Israel's experiences from the death of Joshua on through the period of the judges, we now realize from 2:23 why 2:6 so unexpectedly began with a reference to Joshua. The narrator reaches back into the core of the preceding book's narrative, and for the first time explicitly states what our compositional analysis of Joshua revealed in great detail: the Mosaic covenant is not a mechanistic predictor of success or failure whereby an adherant's obedience unequivocally brings blessing, and disobedience or inimical opposition necessitates failure. Rahab and Gibeon, Caleb and Othniel, Reuben and Gad, the dependent daughters of Zelophehad and the unique tribe of Levi, the anonymous man of Bethel who founded Luz and Adoni-bezek who preserved his life and dies in Jerusalem, even the animals of Ai and of the northern cities that were spared destruction in spite of the ban—all of these characters function in the narrative in precisely the same way as "the nations which the LORD left alone." They are all "aliens" in some sense and are to be a continual reminder that Israel the "citizen" is also an alien of the land:

> I gave you land on which you had not labored, cities which you had
> never built; you have lived in those cities and eat the produce of
> vineyards and olive-groves which you did not plant. (Josh 24:13)

It is no exaggeration to state that Judges 2:23 reaches back on the temporal plane of the text and embraces the entire Book of Joshua, even as it provides the evaluative background for the entire Book of Judges.

Because of 2:23 and its reference to Joshua, the temporal composition of 3:1–6 is to be interpreted in as sweeping a fashion as 2:1–22. The section's first statement, "These are the nations which the LORD left . . ." (3:1), refers back even to Joshua's generation, and its final statement, "they took their daughters in marriage and gave their own daughters to their sons; and they worshiped their gods" (3:6), looks forward to the specific time span covered by the Book of Judges.

The spatial composition of the narrative also shifts significantly, mostly in concurrence with the psychological and temporal planes of the text. When the psychological plane takes an external point of view and when the temporal plane is accordingly limited and specific, the spatial composition follows suit, as we would expect. Thus, in 1:1–2:5, we find a spatial perspective according to which the narrator seems to be moving along with his characters as they act out their assigned tasks from specified place to place. On the other hand, although the spatial perspective of 2:6–3:6 begins and ends in specificity with the place names of 2:9 and 3:3, 5, in between we find a vast no-man's land where place cannot be specified and where we have only "bands of raiders," "plunderers," "enemies," and "nations" as the anonymous adversaries of Israel. There is an abundance of proper names for Israel's enemies in 1:1–36, as opposed to the panoramic shift of 2:6–3:6 in which the national enemies of Israel are all generically referred to, until 3:3, 5 when the narrative needs to shift gears down again to the specific stories beginning in 3:7. Thus, the first occurrence of the LORD's condemnatory explanation fits the general composition of 1:1–2:5 by being located for us spatially (the angel travels from Gilgal to Bokim), whereas the reported words of the LORD in 2:20–22 which *repeat* this condemnation in the panoramic context of 2:6–3:2 float in a vague spatial nowhere. And even though it is clear that 2:20–22 is to be understood temporally as uttered by God after Joshua's death, 2:23 extends *its* efficacy back into Joshua's time in the panoramic fashion of this section. The spatial vagueness of the reported word is here matched by its partial detemporalization.

The Ideological Problem of 1:1–3:6

The phraseological composition of these introductory chapters of Judges, by revealing the mutual influence of reported and reporting speech, helps us sort out the ideological perspectives of 1:1–3:6. If we look first at the reported speech of God, we notice that it functions differently in the two sections of 1:1–2:5 and 2:6–3:6. In the first section, God's words in 2:1–5 function *as an explanation of the preceding reporting narrative of Israel's partial failures.* Thus the inability of Israel to drive out all their enemies, so objectively described in 1:1–36, finds an authoritative explanation in the reported words of God in 2:1–4. Notice that the reporting words of 2:5 do not comment upon or interpret God's speech, but simply describe Israel's tearful reaction to them. On the other hand, God's words in 2:20–22 are introduced characteristically in the narrative as God's angry reaction to Israel's continual disobedience, and are fundamentally interpreted and semantically extended by the narrator's reporting words in 2:23. On the phraseological level, therefore, whereas in 1:1–2:5 the reporting speech of the narrative is interpreted by the reported speech of God, in 2:6–3:6 the reported speech of God is interpreted by the reporting speech of the narrator. And the two sections are not entirely in agreement in the interpretations they give.

At first glance it would appear as if God's words in the first section support a kind of mechanistic ideology that would allow one to have predicted the mixed results of Israel's military expeditions, given their disobedience to God's laws. But the narrator, even in 1:1–36, anticipates in subtle ways the sweeping reinterpretation of these mechanistic divine words that we find in 2:6–3:6, where his reporting speech appropriates and subordinates them to an ideological point of view clearly at odds with the predictive aspects inherent in them. What 2:6–3:6 boldly opposes, 1:1–2:5 only questions subtly, namely, that one can predict the specific turns in Israel's destiny by examining their success or failure in observing "the commands which the Lord had given to their forefathers through Moses" (3:4). Let us see how these two sections variously state their cases.

The three anecdotes about Adoni-bezek, Caleb, and the man of Bethel do tend to cast some doubt upon the sweeping ideological claims of 2:1–4. If failure follows from the breaking of covenant, Israel is surprisingly successful even though, contrary to the law of *ḥerem,* they spare Adoni-bezek's life. Their fortunes do not turn until later in the chapter, so that Judah himself is not nearly so unsuccessful as many of his brother tribes. Similarly, Caleb vows to give Debir to whoever captures it, and does so even though Othniel, his kinsman, is not strictly speaking an Israelite; then considerations of blood give Achsah more than Caleb had bargained for. Finally, like Joshua's spies with Rahab at Jericho, the Josephite spies spare the life of the man of Bethel, yet Joseph is still allowed successfully to take the city. All of these practices are not directly and clearly against the law of Moses, as we have already seen countless times in Joshua. Yet their combined weight, as in Joshua, forces, as it were, the reader to soften any universal mechanistic understanding of God's words in 2:1–4. No matter how clear-cut and obvious the word of God appears to be, the preceding events of 1:1–36 will not allow one to invest 2:1–4 with the predictive certainty one might be tempted to see in them.

On the other hand, the sweeping circularity of 2:6–3:6 explicitly neutralizes the dogmatic pretensions of 2:20–22. For the narrative of 2:6–19 makes it clear that even though there is often a causal connection between Israel's failures and their disobedience, it is still the case that God's compassion will continually protect Israel even when they continue to give their allegiance to foreign gods. Thus, during a judge's lifetime, and even while Israel persists in disobeying God, he will persist in protecting them. Not only that, 2:23 forcefully reminds us, as Joshua itself did, that even a relatively sinless generation such as Joshua's can suffer periodic defeat and failure. Joshua's failures in the Book of Joshua thus illustrate that if the Mosaic law of Deuteronomy 24:16 ("Fathers shall not be put to death for their children, nor children for their fathers: a man shall be put to death only for his own sin") represents retributive principles with regard to individuals, it does not do so for the destiny of generations.

The cyclical preview of the entire period of the judges found in 2:6–3:6 is not, therefore, a recurring pattern of disobedience/repentance, but rather one of punishment/mercy. What is emphasized throughout the book is an unrelieved picture of Israel's continual disobedience to the way of the LORD. Although the Israelites continue to cry out to the LORD, they also "continue to do what was wrong in the eyes of the LORD," as 3:12; 4:1; 10:6; and 13:1 attest, as reaffirmations of the bleak picture introduced by 2:17. The question is, given Israel's persistent idolatry, how long will this cycle of punishment/mercy continue before the very nation itself will be blotted out? An even more important question, perhaps, is whether the critical traditionalism that has provided the necessary ideological perspective of Deuteronomy and Judges can withstand the profoundly disintegrating perspective of 2:6–3:6. For if the retributive point of view of the preceding books allowed the mercy of God to operate at crucial turning points in the story, it never ceased to emphasize the stipulations of the Mosaic covenant and the obedience due them as the governing force behind the destiny of Israel and the fundamental explanation of their successes and failures. With the Book of Judges and the panchronic explanation of 2:6–3:6, even the critical traditionalism of the preceding books is put to the test.

Othniel, Ehud and Shamgar (3:7–31)

1. With the short account of Othniel's judgeship in 2:7–11, we have a perfect embodiment of the cyclical paradigm described in 2:6–3:6. In place of general terms we now have the names of a specific judge and of a specific foreign king, as well as chronological information about the length of time of Israel's subjugation and subsequent peace. In fact, this story mirrors so perfectly the pattern it immediately follows that it appears almost redundant. Certainly it tells us that the cyclical key to the entire book was validated in at least one case, but so perfect a narrative confirmation, if continued, could only result in the most banal of histories. It is almost as if the narrative immediately presents us with an example of what the coming story about the judges will *not* look like. We already have had some indication that Judges is to be concerned with the ambiguous, the unpredictable, the unexpected. The gradual frustration of reader and Israelite alike in the failures of chapter 1, the central symbol of the remaining nations as a *decoy* and a *trap* in 2:3, the nature of the historical paradigm of 2:6–3:6 in which alternating peace and subjugation will be the fate of a continually disobedient Israel, the utterly unexpected assertion of 2:23 that the relatively obedient genera- tion of Joshua's was made to suffer for the sins of subsequent genera- tions, the strange explanation of 3:2 that the nations were left to teach subsequent generations of Israel how to make war—all of this does not prepare us for the predominantly prosaic account of Othniel's judge- ship.

Ehud's exploits, on the other hand, are filled with all the colorful details that Othniel's account lacks. The beginning of the story, "The Israelites continued to do what was wrong in the eyes of the Lord" (3:12), reinforces the beginning of the preceding story, "The Israelites did what was wrong in the eyes of the Lord" (3:7); one of these two formulations will continue to be found at the beginning of individual stories in the book (4:1, 6:1; 10:6; 13:1) just as it occurred in the beginning of the paradigmatic introduction to the book (2:11). The Israelites do, and continue to do, what is wrong in the eyes of the Lord. In fact, the generations of Israelites under the judges were as continu- ally disobedient as Joshua's generation was obedient. The recurring notices of continual disobedience are already prefigured in the cyclical pattern of 2:6–3:6. But what kind of testing by the remaining nations is this, whose conclusion is so foregone? And how can the story of this testing of Israel exploit the unexpected when the results of the testing are already divulged at the beginning? No matter how colorful and detailed the Ehud story is, we already know how it will end as we had already known how it would begin: Israel continually sinning, but as long as their victorious judge is alive, remaining at peace. But once their judge is dead, they will again be subjugated to enemies from within and without. Let us look at the Ehud story to see how it succeeds in exploiting the unexpected in spite of the predictable framework in which it has been placed.

2. The phraseological composition of the story reveals it to be concerned with the difficulty with which the word of God is interpreted. There are only five reported utterances in the story, and all but the last have to do with the unexpected and ambiguous nature of the word of God. After Ehud, the left-handed one, had fashioned his two-edged sword, he approaches Eglon and says, "My lord king, I have a word for you in private" (3:19). We already know that this "word" is Ehud's hidden, two-edged sword, so that Eglon's response, "Silence!" (3:19), is ironic, since he unknowingly characterizes this secret word as one which will not be heard, but somehow felt. Then, alone with Eglon in his private chambers, Ehud reveals the *source* of his silent word: "I have a word from God for you" (3:20). Ehud then thrusts this two-edged word of God deep within Eglon's belly, locks the doors of the chamber from without, and flees. When Eglon's servants come, they find the doors locked, and say, "Surely (*'ak*) he is relieving himself in the closet of his summer palace." The contrast between the certainty with which they utter their interpretation of the situation (*'ak*) and the obvious error of their judgment is underlined and symbolized in the story by the image of the locked doors. Only after they were "ashamed to delay any longer" do the servants open these doors and discover what the word of God here signifies—not Eglon's relief but Israel's release. Only with the final utterance of the story, Ehud's command to the Israelites, "Follow me, for the LORD has delivered your enemy the Moabite into your hands" (3:28), do we encounter reported speech that can be termed a "correct" interpretation of a situation. Ten thousand Moabites are killed, Moab becomes subject to Israel, and there is peace in the land for eighty years.

There are also some illuminating temporal shifts in the story. When Ehud approaches Eglon in his summer palace, the narrative shifts to a more deeply synchronic point of view emphasizing the perspective of the participants: "He [Eglon] was sitting (*yošēb*) in the roof chamber" (3:20). But after the word of God was announced, Eglon rose from his throne as if to foreshadow that this word of God signified the end of his rule. Then, after the murder, a second shift to a more synchronic viewpoint emphasizes the central image of the locked doors; "the doors being locked (*dal^etôt n^{ec}ulôt*)" (3:24). Finally, a series of three synchronic verb-forms describe from within, as it were, the gap between the servants' interpretation of the situation and the true state of affairs, and positions the cause of this distance between them, so that the sequencing of the narrative mirrors its semantic content:

error:	"Surely he is relieving himself (*'ak mēsîk hû'*)" (3:24)
cause of error:	". . . and behold there was no one to open the doors . . . (*w^ehinnēh 'ênennû potē^aḥ*)" (3:25a)
true state of affairs:	"there was their master lying on the floor dead (*nopēl . . . mēt*)" (3:25b)

These shifts to imperfective verb-forms enable "the author to carry out his description from within the action—that is, synchronically, rather than retrospectively—and to place the reader in the very center of the scene he is describing" (Uspensky, 1973:74).

When we turn to the spatial composition of the story, we are immediately hindered by certain semantic ambiguities that seem to be a built-in feature of the narrative. Where in fact is the summer palace of Eglon? Is it in Israel or Moab? The story is deliberately vague on this point. It may be, of course that this information was presumed to be known by the Deuteronomist's audience; but my impression is that this is not so since this same type of spatial ambiguity plays an obvious compositional role in the Gideon story as well, where extra-textual information would not seem to be able to resolve the difficulty. At any rate, because of this basic ambiguity in the Ehud story we are not able to tell, at the end of the story, in which direction the pursuing Moabites are going when the Israelites "seized the fords of the Jordan against the Moabites and allowed no man to cross" (3:28). Even the crucial references to the idols of Gilgal (3:19, 26) do not allow us to situate the story any more clearly. Even if Eglon's summer palace were in Moab, Ehud's initial turning away from these *p^esîlîm* in 3:19 and his "passing through them" in 3:26 after the crime, would make perfectly good sense. We think therefore that no amount of extra-textual information would clarify this feature of the story, neither the exact location of Palm-city nor that of Seirah, to which Ehud eventually flees.

3. It is almost as if the spatial ambiguity of the story serves a deeper ideological purpose. It is all the same, whether the assassination at the summer palace took place in Moab or in Israel, and one's suspicions about this are heightened by the contrast between this glaring ambiguity and the overwhelmingly specific emphasis of the rest of the narrative. The story begins with Moab invading the land of Israel, with God's permission—a fact immediately complicated by the reader's recollection of Israel's original by-passing of Moab during the journey toward the Jordan (Deut 2–3). Surely Israel's plight is now the result of their continual sinning; but we have no information about the relation of Moab's sudden ill fortune and *their* standing with Yahweh. If they also were presently at odds with Yahweh for some reason, then the story is about the fluctuating fortunes of two nations, both of whom deserve punishment. On the other hand, if Moab is to be considered an innocent party in the story, simply a tool of Yahweh, then we have a story about Moab's undeserved loss of their king and ten thousand soldiers. We have therefore the impression that *retribution* is really not what is at stake here in the story, but rather the inability of man always to predict his destiny, whatever may be his current relationship with the LORD. What is important here is on the one hand the ever present condemnation of Israel's apostasy, and on the other hand the paradoxical fact that subjugation or deliverance equally may be Israel's experience during their continued apostasy.

But the story does not allow its denial of a mechanical view of divine retribution to soften its condemnation of Israel's idolatry, and here we see how this first crucial story about an Israelite judge allows us to gain important insight into the ideological perspectives of the book. For we now must return to our initial reflections on the paradigmatic explanations of 2:6–3:6 as foreshadowed by the words of the LORD's angel in 3:1–3. In what sense are the nations a decoy to Israel and their gods a trap? What is the narrative's purpose in emphasizing the nations' testing of Israel throughout the Book of Judges when we are told from the beginning that Israel continually would fail that test? And what does it mean that God's purpose was to teach succeeding generations of Israelites to make war?

> By their means [the remaining nations] I will test Israel to see whether or not they will keep strictly to the way of the LORD as their forefathers did. (3:22)

This explanation of the LORD's, mirrored by the narrator's own words, only makes sense (in the light of what has already been narrated in Deuteronomy and Joshua, and of what is to be told subsequently) if one assumes that the retributive nature of the Mosaic covenant still allows, in specific cases and according to God's mysterious workings, the guilty to go unpunished and the innocent to endure unmerited suffering. Even though it is the case that adherence to foreign gods often brought convenient and often lucrative marriage alliances for their sons, and in spite of the fact that rejection of these gods often meant the continual disruption of war with the surrounding nations, Israel must nevertheless discount these consequences and strive continually to walk in the way of the LORD.

Contrary, therefore, to widespread scholarly attitudes about the overly mechanistic attitude of the Deuteronomic History with respect to the retributive aspects of Israelite religion, our compositional analysis has revealed strong evidence of a predominant point of view that critically rejects such a simplistic explanation of Israel's self-understanding vis-a-vis the LORD. The Deuteronomist is, for example, much more obviously united with the basic viewpoint of the Book of Job than scholars, including myself (1977:58), have heretofore allowed.

Finally, we find in the Ehud story intimations of a theme that will grow in importance in the book, until it reaches an imposing climax in the story of Samson: the characterization of a judge who carries out, either symbolically or effectively, the LORD's designs in an apparently unknowing fashion. In our present story, the reference to the idols at Gilgal in 3:19, and to the idols in 3:26, provide us with an important ideological frame to Ehud's deliverance of Israel. The deliverance itself is not just a matter of the defeat of Moab and the subsequent eighty years of peace for Israel. For Ehud's decisive action begins when he "turns away from the idols at Gilgal" and his escape is successful when he "passed" the idols and fled to Seirah. Ehud is not portrayed as a particularly likeable judge; in fact he comes across in the narrative as someone who is repugnant, deceitful, and cruel. In spite of this, it is he whose decisive actions for Israel begin with a characteristic "turning away from the idols (*šûb min happᵉsîlîm*)," as one "turns away from the evil way (*šûb midderek harāᶜāh*)" (1 Kg 13:33; 2 Kg 17:13) and "returns to Yahweh" (Deut 30:10). Similarly Ehud's deliverance of Israel is signaled successful in the text by the ambiguous phrase, "he passed [or crossed over] the idols (*ᶜābar happᵉsîlîm*)," which might alternately be understood as, "he transgressed or broke the idols" in a narrative recuperation and restoration from the apostasy of Israel described by the typical Deuteronomic phrase, "to transgress my covenant (*ᶜābar bᵉrîtî*)" (Jd 2:20; Deut 17:12; Josh 23:16; 2 Kg 18:12). It is in this way that the semantically ambiguous nature of the spatial elements in the story perform specific ideological functions, and that specific information about the exact location of these idols becomes largely irrelevant. We shall soon see how the narrative develops this symbolic technique, centered on wordplay, especially in the Samson story. What is clear already is that a judge may be depicted as unknowingly "walking in the way of the LORD."

With the incomplete reference to Shamgar's success over the Philistines in 3:31, the text turns the story away from the dangers of external nations, toward Israel's ongoing conflicts with one of the nations the LORD left, the Canaanites. The Deuteronomist's previous concern with the "alien" within Israel now finds expression with the story of the only judge in the book who is a woman, Deborah.

The Story of Deborah (4:1–5:31)

1. The crucial feature of the opening verse of the Deborah story is the placement of the notice of Ehud's death *after* the formulaic statement that the Israelites continued to do what was evil in the eyes of the LORD. By this we learn that the eighty years of peace mentioned in 3:30 are not to be construed as dependent upon any supposed repentance of Israel, but solely upon the length of Ehud's life. This is in line with our interpretation of 2:6–3:6 as not involving repentance as one of its cyclical elements, in spite of the ambiguous use of *sārû* and *yāšubû* in 2:17 and 2:19 respectively. Israel's quick turning away from the paths of their fathers (2:17) and their turning and acting more wickedly than their fathers (2:19) denote a process that began with the generation following Joshua's death and continued almost unabated throughout the various turns of their fortunes recounted in Judges. It is quite clear that the term, "fathers," mentioned in 2:17, 19, refers primarily to the immediately preceding generation of Joshua's time. With Joshua's death, we enter a period of Israel's history in which, because of Israel's constant apostasy, they clearly deserved each set back they experienced but not the years of peace their judges' lives and God's compassion brought them. The evaluative gaze of the Deuteronomist, so intent upon the principles of divine justice in the Book of Deuteronomy, then measurably softened by the actual account of God's merciful giving of the land in the Book of Joshua, now confronts the awesome fact of God's continued compassion on Israel in spite of their continual weakness. The task that faces the Deuteronomist is to make some ideological sense of the chaotic period of the judges. Nothing in Israel's history is more remarkable than that they continued to exist in spite of their sustained apostasy in the days between Joshua's death and the establishment of kingship. The main task facing the author of Judges is to explain why the Deuteronomic History did not in fact end with this book. Each of the traditional stories selected and fashioned for this period explores and deepens the mystery of Israel's existence. The narrative skill that so convincingly described the relations of God and Israel during the lifetime of Moses and Joshua now reveals that such clarity was simply the prelude to mystery and obscurity. The Book of Judges is a major turning point in the narrative because it self-consciously reveals the weaknesses and limitations of all ideologies, however necessary and unavoidable they may be.

It is no wonder, therefore, that exegetes have continually given in to the temptation of adding an element of repentance to the cyclical paradigm of 2:6–3:6 in order to salvage the overwhelmingly retributive perspective of Deuteronomy and, to a lesser extent, of Joshua. The hard-won insights of the retributive ideology so painstakingly arrived at in these two books can instill a comfortable confidence in one's ability to occupy and master the word of God. However, once authoritarian dogmatism has been effectively neutralized, and principles of critical traditionalism have been allowed to command and control the narrative, the reader is now allowed to experience doubts about the foundations of the very critical certainty the author had maneuvered him into embracing. The genius of the Deuteronomic storyteller lies in the depths of his self-reflection and in his ability to force his reader to reexamine the deadening effect of believing one finally understands. To be so deluded about such complex affairs means that one ceases to read, no matter how many pages he continues to turn; the Deuteronomist wants us to know that his story is not yet finished.

2. We have seen how the very perfection with which Othniel's story fits the explanatory paradigm of 2:6–3:6 paradoxically underlined the weaknesses of such explanations; the banality of reading a story one feels he already knows, yet whose unexpected twists and turns one cannot re-create, makes it extremely difficult to keep on reading. Such a narrative is self-defeating. With the story of Ehud, interest was once again kindled because the very predictability of its beginning (apostasy, divine compassion, and the raising up of a judge) and end (the judge's military success and subsequent peace within the land) was effectively set off against the story's emphasis upon misunderstanding the word of God. But even there, the misunderstanding of God's word was limited to Eglon and his servants—opponents of Israel. Ehud and the reader know from the beginning that the word of God is a two-edged sword, for the narrator took us into his confidence very early on in the story when in 3:16 we were told about Ehud's concealment of the sword upon his person. So it was relatively easy for the Israelites and the reader to believe Ehud when he told us and them in 3:28 that God had delivered Israel's enemies into their hands: did not Eglon already lie dead within his summer palace? We knew this even before his servants found it out.

With the story of Deborah, the obscurity of God's word is deepened not only by the narrated events but also by the narrator's refusal to bring us into his confidence early on in the story, as he had done in the preceding story. The point of that story, like a favorite fairy tale that is continually reread, is the reader's ability to relive the unexpectedness and uncertainty that not only belong to the characters as they act out their parts but also were part of the reader's experience the first time he confronted the story. The literary effect of "estrangement" is deepened in the Deborah story: not only is the reader's ignorance of what is to take place protracted as long as possible, but the Israelite characters, Barak and Deborah, experience the unexpected together with the reader and, in Barak's case, even beyond him. The story's composition on various levels brings this out very well.

On the temporal level, certain shifts from the retrospective (though not necessarily panchronic) point of view to a strictly synchronic perspective help to characterize the participants in the story. Deborah sits (*yošebet*) and judges (*šopᵉṭāh*) over Israel (4:4–5); Barak is the pursuer (*rōdēp*) of Sisera (4:22) and is characterized by Deborah as one who travels (*hōlēk*) a road (4:9) and by Jael as one who looks for (*mᵉbaqqēš*) a man (4:22); Sisera is described as the fallen dead (*nopēl mēt:* 4:22); and Heber is the one separated (*niprād*) from the Kenites (4:11). We thus have Deborah the sitting judge, Barak the go-getter, Sisera the fallen dead, and Heber the Israelite apostate (cf. 1:16). Yet the narrative succeeds in reversing the roles of these characters so that its synchronic and retrospective descriptions of them are deliberately opposed to each other. Because of Barak's unexpected response to God's commands (4:8), Deborah, the one accustomed to sit and judge, is constrained to get up and go with Barak to Kedesh. Barak the go-getter walks a path of glory but does not attain it, pursues Sisera but only finds him too late. And Sisera the fallen never "fell" at all, since he was lying asleep when Jael killed him.

The phraseological composition of the story intensifies the reader's feeling that the story is all about how things are not what they seem. The relation between reported and reporting speech is so consistently nonconcurrent that one must see equivocation and obfuscation as major themes of the story. The LORD, Deborah, Barak, Jael, and Sisera are directly quoted in this story as uttering commands and/or predictions, and in all cases the reporting speech of the narrator provides an unexpected twist to the fulfillment of these reported utterances. Both God (4:7) and Deborah (4:14) are quoted as predicting that God would give, indeed has given, Sisera into Barak's hands, yet the ensuing narrative does not bear out this prophecy in the strict sense: Sisera's army falls to

Barak but Sisera himself escapes to be killed later by Jael. When Barak finally gets his hands on Sisera, the latter is already a corpse. Deborah's prediction to Barak, that Sisera will fall into the hands of a woman (4:9), is sufficiently equivocal to mislead Barak, the reader, and perhaps even Deborah into believing that Deborah herself is that woman; yet it turns out to be Jael, the wife of Heber, who has been prophesied. Moreover, the prophecy of 4:7 is obviously at odds with 4:14, which itself repeats the prophecy of 4:7 that Sisera will fall into Barak's hands. Then, when we come to the dialogue between Jael and Sisera (4:14–20) we find only commands or entreaties, and in all these cases the reporting narrative provides an unsuspected twist. The soothing sibilants of Jael's invitation to Sisera, "Turn aside my Lord, turn aside to me (*sûrāh 'ªdonî sûrāh 'ēlay*); dont' be afraid" (4:18), are followed by a chilling narrative that makes only too clear how afraid Sisera should have been to turn aside. Then, when Sisera requests water (4:19), the narrative reports that Jael gives him milk. And when Sisera commands Jael to stand at the tent door and, should she be asked, to answer that no one is in the tent with her (4:20), this command is not only contradicted by the facts but is obviously in double contrast to the subsequent scene in which Jael rushes out and, of her own accord, tells Barak that someone *is* in the tent (4:22). Jael's words, "Come, I will show you the man you are looking for," culminate in what is clearly designed to be Barak's surprise and disappointment, for what he finds is Sisera certainly, but Sisera dead. Finally, the only utterance in the story that seems to be unequivocally fulfilled is Barak's threat to Deborah early in the story, "If you go with me, I will go; but if you will not go, neither will I" (4:8). Yet, even though he achieves his purpose in getting Deborah to accompany him, he still does not succeed in apprehending Sisera. Barak's casuistic interpretation and application of the LORD's command is ultimately ineffective. We thus see how the phraseological composition of a story so surrounded by the certainty of Israel's victory and Sisera's defeat can still strongly suggest the inability of man, even God's elect, fully to understand either God's words or his own, or to predict his own destiny.

3. It is in reference to the psychological and temporal level of the text that we have perhaps the clearest indication of the story's ideological thrust. As with the previous story, there is a glaring alternation between two kinds of reporting utterance, one in which the narrator reveals himself as an omniscient observer who knows even the inner thoughts and feelings of his characters, including God himself, and another in which the narrator utters only what would be visible to an observer present at the action described. In general, the evaluative statements

that begin and end the stories belong to a kind of "panchronic" narrator who is able to tell us that the LORD sold the Israelites to the Canaanites (4:2), and that he gave victory to the Israelites over Jabin, king of Canaan (4:23). As we have seen, most of 2:6–3:6 belongs to this point of view. On the other hand, the contrast between these narrative utterances and the bulk of the Ehud and Deborah stories, with their almost obsessive attention to detail and their lack of internal psychological indicators, reveals a "synchronic" narrator who represents a perspective that is deliberately "objective," revealing only what would be apparent to the characters themselves or to an anonymous observer who, though he appears to be present at the events described, is not a party to any of the privileged information possessed by the panchronic narrator. (This distinction between types of narrative description is not precisely the same as that already discussed of synchronic versus retrospective points of view, indicated by the alternation between perfective and imperfective verb forms. A synchronic narrator may himself speak either synchronically or retrospectively.) When we read such statements as,

> The hilt went in after the blade and the fat closed over the blade; he did not draw the sword out but left it protruding behind. (3:22)

> But Jael, Heber's wife, took a tent peg, picked up a hammer, crept up to him, and drove the peg into his skull as he lay sound asleep (4:21),

we are hearing the voice of a synchronic narrator whose point of view is that of one of the characters involved, or of an anonymous observer present at the event described. In general, the temporal, spatial and psychological perspectives of this narrator are similar to those of one or more of the characters in the story, and are to be contrasted with the perspectives of the panchronic narrator who does not speak from an estranged or distancing point of view at least in the sense that he is able to reveal the inner lives of his characters.

When, therefore, we have a story that begins with the certainty of God's selling Israel into bondage, and ends with him always rescuing them from it, no matter how mysterious it is that God's continual compassion saves Israel again and again from utter destruction, we at least have the initial comfort of what might be called panchronic stability. On the other hand, a particular emphasis on concrete details and unexpected twists and turns in the story is able to portray, in a striking way, the instability of the psychological, spatial-temporal, and phraseological points of view of one or more of the characters in the story; and this is especially appropriate to a period of Israel's history when "every man did what was right in his own eyes" (17:6; 21:25). In other words, this greatly intensified alternation in the Book of Judges between panchronic narration, which appears necessary at this point in the history to preserve some semblance of stability as well as to continue the reader's confidence in the narrator, and synchronic narration, which tends to destroy one's sense of the stability of God's dealings with Israel, depends upon the present object of description, that is, the particularly chaotic period of Israel's history between Joshua's death and the establishment of kingship. The distanced and estranged viewpoint of the body of the stories about the judges, as opposed to the evaluative utterances that form their framework, puts the reader into the very experiencing of chaos and ambiguity that is portrayed as the inner experience of Israel during this period.

This is why the Deborah story is filled with equivocation and opposition. Deborah, the sitting judge, is no longer allowed to sit. She is a judge but is not said to deliver Israel. Barak, the go-getter, goes but does not get. Heber, the separated one, allies himself with Jabin. This means that Sisera is finally killed by an ally, Jael, the wife of Heber. But that ally is thus a woman and we are surprised that this woman into whose hands Sisera finally falls is not Deborah. Moreover, the woman is not even an Israelite. She is a heroine who offers milk instead of water, death in place of sleep, a corpse instead of a captive. The effect of all of these details provided by the synchronic narrator is to reinforce questions already raised by the apparently stable but still surprising point of view of the panchronic narrator first encountered in 2:6–3:6, and repeated with each of the stories of the judges. No one experiences more surprise than the reader—not Eglon, Deborah, Barak, or Sisera in their own affairs—when he is confronted with the panchronic description of Yahweh's compassion in not only preserving Israel's existence throughout this period, but in giving them more years of peace and prosperity than war and subjugation in spite of their continual breaking of the Mosaic covenant through apostasy and intermarriage with non-Israelites.

4. The song of Deborah and Barak (5:1–31) further exemplifies the author's strategy in this regard. From a compositional point of view, this chapter consists of the brief reporting speech of the narrator, "That day Deborah and Barak son of Abinoam sang this song. . . . The land was at peace for forty years" (3:1, 31b), within which is the reported speech of Deborah and Barak. And within this reported speech, we find embedded more reported speech of the LORD's people (5:12), of Ephraim

(5:14), of Sisera's mother (5:28), and of the wisest of her princesses (5:30). Attempts at reconciling the details of this chapter with those of the preceding chapter falter not only because of the profound lexical and grammatical difficulties of the text, but also through a serious misunderstanding of the song's function at this point in the narrative. We must assume that the song will continue the preceding chapters' role of engendering a feeling of confusion concerning the basic ideological positions of the preceding books. Thus, details about the war with Jabin both add to the picture of the previous chapter concerning information about the individual tribes' participation or lack of it in the war, as well as confuse us as to precisely what happened, as is the case with the deliberately repetitive words of 5:27. The flashback to Israel's early successes in 5:4–5 is deliberately contrasted with the later apostasy of Israel recounted in the flashback of 5:8. The lack of response of many Israelite tribes is contrasted with the final deliverance of Israel by Jael, the supposed ally of Sisera. And lest right, insight, and acclaim be mistakenly accorded to non-Israelite individuals or nations, the ironic question and answer of the Canaanite women in 5:28–30, so similar to the misunderstanding of Eglon's servants in 3:24, show how mistaken both sides are as to the true state of affairs recounted in these traditional stories. The final wish of 5:31a, "So perish all thine enemies, O LORD; but let all who love thee be like the sun rising in strength," strongly suggests that even Israel may be a part of the company of the LORD's enemies. But this penultimate irony of the song is deepened by a further irony that goes once more to the heart of the basic problem of the Book of Judges: the reporting speech of the narrator juxtaposes the suggestion that Israel is now the LORD's enemy with the report that "the land was at peace for forty years" (5:31b). How can even the critical traditionalism apparent in Deuteronomy and Joshua deal with such a situation? Why does apostate Israel not only continue to exist but more often than not exist in peace? For like the previous periods under Othniel and Ehud, the subsequent years of peace under the judge, Deborah, are far greater than the period of subjugation they replace:

Othniel:	8 years' subjugation	40 years' peace
Ehud:	18 years' subjugation	80 years' peace
Deborah:	20 years' subjugation	40 years' peace

The long and threatening list of curses in Deuteronomy 28 have begun to lose their credibility.

Gideon and Abimelech (6:1–9:57)

1. The Gideon story depicts the excessive concern men exhibit who seek by signs and tests to insure the success of their ventures. Even God is not immune from this story's critical eye. Yet, throughout all the venturesome incidents of the story, whether they involve successful enterprises or not, there is an aura of ultimate mystery surrounding the destiny of both man and nation, a destiny that is not finally predictable by any ideology, be it dogmatic or critical. Almost every incident in the story concerns its characters' attempts to solve hermeneutic problems through some sort of *test* that will illumine or explain aspects of their lives. Thus Gideon asks for a sign concerning who is speaking to him (6:17); Joash suggests that Baal himself will manifest his own divinity by taking care of the man who tore down his altar (6:31–32); Gideon twice uses a fleece of wool as a test to determine whether God will deliver Israel through him, as he has promised (6:36–40); Yahweh himself commands a water test to separate out, for His own glory, a dog-like three hundred men from the rest of Gideon's army (7:1–8); Gideon, at Yahweh's suggestion, uses the mechanism of a Midianite dream to shore up his courage (7:9–15); Gideon calms the men of Ephraim by appealing to their capture of Oreb and Zeeb as indicative, as it were, of the proverbial conviction that a bird in the hand is worth two in the bush (8:1–3); the men of Succoth and Penuel are concerned to give bread only to those who have passed the test of victory (8:4–9). And interspersed throughout all these testing incidents are a small number of conditional statements that emphasize the story's "iffy" situations:

Gideon: "if (*'im*) I have found favor in your sight. . ." (6:17)
Joash: "would (*'im*) you rescue him?" (6:31)
         "if (*'im*) he is a god. . ." (6:31)
Yahweh: "if (*'im*) you are afraid to do so. . ." (7:10)
Gideon: "if (*lû*) you had let them live. . ." (8:19)

Each of these questions, signs, and tests recalls the basic test of obedience already announced by God in 2:22:

> "By their [the nations'] means I will test (*nassôt*) Israel to see whether or not [*hᵃ*. . . *'im lo'*] they will keep strictly to the way of the LORD as their forefathers did."

Yahweh's test here suggests the limitations of the main ideological points of view of the preceding books of Deuteronomy and Joshua. For if peace or war are indiscriminate results sometimes of obedience to the

Mosaic covenant and sometimes of disobedience, and if, in spite of their faithlessness to Yahweh, Israel finds themselves more often than not at peace with their neighbors and relatively independent of them, then what motive is there for trying to walk in the way of the LORD? The various signs, tests, and questions apparent on the surface of the story appear to illustrate the basic ideological problems that lie beneath it. No wonder that the story revolves around repeated efforts to resolve ambiguity; ambiguity is the ideological theme of the entire book. The story of Gideon, like the previous stories, rehearses a mystery that is ultimately impervious to ideological clarification: even though Israel continued to betray Yahweh, before, during, and after his deliverances of them, he continued to have compassion on them.

The confusion and ambiguity engendered by the preceding stories actually increase with the traditions surrounding Gideon. In spite of the fact that the predictable pattern of a greater period of peace following a shorter period of subjugation is here once more the case (seven years of Midianite domination followed by forty years of peace under Gideon), and although Israel's disobedience is once again accompanied by the LORD's compassion for them, these mysterious yet stable elements within the book are accompanied by the opaque vision and searching state of mind of most of the participants in the story. This confusion is most obvious in the shifting perspectives of both the narrator and characters as they alternate the names of the hero and deity of the story.

The most obvious shift in naming concerns the hero of this section who is initially introduced to us as "Gideon" in 6:11 and most often referred to in this way throughout the story. But in 6:32 his father changes his name to Jerubaal, "Let Baal sue," and although he is subsequently still referred to as Gideon, we find "Jerubaal, that is, Gideon" in 7:1, "Jerubaal" in 8:29, and "Jerubaal Gideon" in 8:35. When we combine this information with the interesting fact that chapter 9 will consistently refer to him as Jerubaal (9:2, 5, 16, 19, 28), the vacillation in 6:1–8:35 takes on added significance. Somehow or other, the story means to emphasize through its hero's names a basic tension concerning his loyalty towards Yahweh. Since the Book of Judges has already emphasized how Israel continually worshiped Baal and the Ashtaroth throughout the period of the judges, we are in no way surprised by this split characterization of our hero. We simply need to know how such a literary feature fits in with the other phraseological elements in the story.

In addition, there are also periodic shifts in the name of the deity throughout the story, as throughout the whole book, and it is difficult to avoid the impression that this instability in naming the deity has a compositional relationship with the twofold name of Gideon/Jerubaal. Most of the time the deity is referred to as "Yahweh," or "Yahweh the God of Israel," or "Yahweh your (their) God." But there are a number of places where the generic title, "God ([*ha*] '*elohîm*)," is used. First, even though the person who speaks to Gideon in 6:11–24 is mostly referred to as "Yahweh" or "the angel of Yahweh," once, in 6:20, he is called "the angel of God." Then, after the spirit of Yahweh comes upon Gideon and he calls out the Israelite tribes against Midian (6:33–35), the incident of the double fleece (6:36–40) finds the narrator referring to the deity exclusively as "God" (6:36, 39, 40). The next occasion when "God" is used occurs when Gideon overhears someone in the Midianite camp say, "God has delivered Midian and the whole army into his [Gideon's] hands" (7:14). Then, when the men of Ephraim reproach Gideon for not summoning them, Gideon refers to "God's" deliverance in 8:3. Other references to "God" are when Joash says, "If Baal is god. . . let him take up his own cause" (6:31), and when the narrator reports, "The Israelites. . . made Baal-Berith their god" (8:33), after the death of Gideon.

Why does both the reporting speech of the narrator and the reported speech of various characters vacillate between "Yahweh" and "Elohim" when referring to the deity? It seems likely that this feature of the story, like the Gideon/Jerubaal alternation, depicts in a graphic manner not only the indecision of Gideon and the Israelites whether to worship Yahweh or one of the gods of the Canaanites, but also and more fundamentally their inability to distinguish at times who the god was who was delivering them from the Midianites, Yahweh or another. To be sure, the alternation between divine names is not a feature peculiar in Judges to the Gideon story, for it occurs elsewhere in the book and in the history, but it serves a more obvious ideological purpose here than perhaps in any other story in Judges. If then one assumes that "Yahweh" and "God" are employed in a purposeful manner in the Gideon story, the result is, in my opinion, an interesting and appropriate reading not only of 6:1–8:35 but also of the Abimelech story that follows. Even as the narrator here makes clear that it is Yahweh who saved Israel from the Midianites, Amalekites, and Qedemites, he subtly portrays the manner in which Gideon and the Israelites exemplify the indictment of God in the beginning of the story:

> I said to you, "I am Yahweh your God: do not stand in awe of the gods of the Amorites in whose country you are settling." But you did not listen to me. (6:10)

2. The story of Gideon portrays how Israel even in the very process of being delivered by Yahweh vacillates between allegiance to him and allegiance to another god. More than this, it develops the irony that the result of Yahweh's deliverance through Gideon is Israel's transition from partial to total worship of Baal-Berith after Gideon's death (8:33). If the previous stories work out the theme of Israel's inability to predict their destiny by interpreting and applying the word of God, the present story goes even further: it depicts Israel's confused efforts to decide which god, Yahweh or one of the gods of the Amorites, would deliver them from their oppressors and ensure them peace. As before, Yahweh's concern and care for Israel remain constant; the tests (6:39) and traps (8:27) of the story involve Gideon's and Israel's confusion and intermittent inability to understand what is going on around them, and who it is who is acting in their behalf. Let us see how the story reads from this point of view.

The narrator leaves no doubt that it is the angel of Yahweh, even Yahweh himself , who is speaking with Gideon in 6:11–24. This contrasts sharply with the narrator's depiction of Gideon as ignorant of the identity of his interlocutor until after the miraculous fire upon the rock, when Gideon exclaims, "Alas, my lord Yahweh" (or perhaps, ". . . my lord is Yahweh") in 6:22; he had needed a sign before recognition came. Confident of Yahweh's commission, but not enough to allay fear of his clan's reactions, Gideon destroys Baal's altar by night and sacrifices a whole-offering upon the altar of Yahweh which he had built following the angel's apparition. Because of this action against Baal, Joash changes his name to Jerubaal. Joash, the Baal worshiper, is convinced that Baal is god enough to defend his own interests: "If Baal is God, let him take up his own cause" (6:31). Yahweh then takes possession of Gideon, who gathers his army for battle. It is precisely here that the narrator recounts Gideon's double testing not of "Yahweh" but of "God" with the fleece of wool (6:36–40). Since Gideon, like his fellow citizens, has been a Baal worshiper who was recently put to the test by Yahweh, it may be that Gideon is now intent upon putting his own god to the test—whoever he may be, probably Baal—in a time of crisis. With Yahweh *and* "God" on his side, how can he lose? The reporting speech of the narrator shifts, therefore, at this point to the perspective of Gideon who, as the newly proclaimed Jerubaal, asks his god to take up his own cause and deliver Israel as he had promised. The twofold miracle indicates to Gideon that this "god," whoever he may be, *also* is prepared to claim the loyalties of the Israelites and defend his own interests against those of Yahweh's. Notice that this incident and the Midianite's explanation of his companion's dream are the only cases in the story in which the deity is described as sending a communication without any divine words being reported: in both cases that deity is ambiguously named "God" rather than "Yahweh." Yahweh speaks directly to Israel whereas *elohim* communicates in signs and dreams; this distinction has first a synchronic significance rather than the diachronic significance attributed to it by the old documentary hypothesis. Now that Gideon has successfully tested "God," now that "God" has successfully taken up his own cause, the text immediately refers to our hero as "Jerubaal, that is, Gideon" (7:1).

After Yahweh uses the water test to reduce Gideon's army from 32,000 to 300, and thus ensure that Israel will attribute the coming victory to him rather than to themselves (7:1–8)—even Yahweh is depicted here as overly concerned with a "sure thing"—Gideon still needs to be convinced that victory will be his. It is Yahweh himself who suggests what will finally give Gideon courage enough "to go down and attack the camp" (8:11). Thus Gideon sneaks into the Midianite camp and hears a Midianite explain his companion's dream with the words, "God has delivered Midian and the whole army into his [Gideon's] hands" (8:14). To the Midianite here, as to Adoni-bezek in 1:7, to Eglon in 3:20, and to the narrator in 4:23, "God" refers to a deity whose identity, from the point of view of the speaker uttering his name or in view of the speaker's audience, is not Yahweh himself, or else a deity unable to be recognized as Yahweh in a particular instance of communication. This distinction is crystal-clear in the exchange between the two Midianites. One must assume that, since Yahweh is not explicitly referred to in the conversation, as indeed he could have been—Rahab, the Canaanite, for example, is privy in Joshua 2:10–12 to *Yahweh*'s intervention in behalf of Israel—what the interpreting Midianite is described as referring to, and what his companion heard being referred to, is certainly not Yahweh, whoever else this "god" may be. In this way, Gideon's courage is increased: not only has Yahweh pledged Israel's deliverance but the "god" referred to by the Midianite has prophesied the same assistance in a dream. Only now has Gideon enough confidence to proclaim to his small company, "Up, the LORD has delivered the camp of the Midianites into your hands" (7:15).

In 8:1–3, Gideon himself attributes the capture of Oreb and Zeeb by the Ephraimites to "God," not Yahweh. Once again this is an indication that the Ephraimites, or perhaps even Gideon himself, put more store in the help of a deliberately obscure "elohim" than in the help of Yahweh himself. That Gideon and the Israelites continue to profess allegiance not only to Yahweh but to the worship of another is made clear by the incident of the golden ephod in 8:24–27:

> All the Israelites turned wantonly to its worship, and it became a
> trap to catch Gideon and his household. (8:27)

This is a clear reference back to the words of Yahweh's angel:

> So I said, I will not drive them out before you; they will decoy you
> and their gods will shut you fast in the trap. (2:3)

The trap does close fast upon the Israelites as they make Baal-Berith
their god and forsake Yahweh (8:33–34). The story ends with a reference to "Jerubaal, that is, Gideon" (8:35).

The ideological perspective of the Deuteronomist continues to manifest itself. By portraying the inability of his Israelite heroes often to
understand Yahweh's words or even to recognize his salvific intervention, and by emphasizing their overreliance on tests and signs, the
Deuteronomist suggests to his audience the danger of putting too much
confidence in the ultimate test of an approved ideology, even that es-
poused by the author himself.

3. With the account of Abimelech in 9:1–57, the ambivalence of the
previous story toward its hero and his deity is no longer continued. This
new stance is signaled not only by a consistent reference to Abimelech's
father solely as "Jerubaal" (9:2, 5, 16, 19, 28), but even more significantly, in light of previous references to the deity in Judges, by the
exclusive use of *'elohîm* even where "Yahweh" might be not only appropriate but expected. Thus, both the narrator (9:23, 56) and Jotham
(9:7) refer to "God" rather than to "Yahweh." (Within Jotham's para-
ble, we also have two references to an anonymous "god" or "gods" [9:9,
13] and the narrator refers once to the Shechemites going to "the
temple of their god" [9:27].) There are, therefore, no references at all
to Yahweh in a chapter which clearly functions as a climax to the Gideon story, and this has a profound effect on our understanding of the
ideological composition of the entire pericope (6:1–9:57).

The Abimelech story is filled with characters who continually ask
rhetorical questions that imply the wisdom of the questioner and the
misguided ignorance of his interlocutors. Thus, Jotham's four questions in 9:16–17, 19, represent his conviction about his own grasp of
what is "fair and honest" (9:16, 19), in contrast to the errant sinfulness
of the Shechemites. Similarly, Gaal's three rhetorical questions in 9:28
underline his smug certainty of superiority over Abimelech in contrast
to the foolishness of the Shechemites who had unwisely given their
allegiance to him. Then, after Zebul was able to convince the
perspicacious Gaal, for a time at least, that an oncoming enemy was but

a shadow, the former turns the latter's prior questions back against him with a rhetorical question of his own, "Where are your brave words now?" (9:38). Gaal now has become the fool and Zebul the man of perception. But among all the shifting claims of those who "understand" versus those who do not, the Deuteronomic narrator clearly chooses twice, in 9:22–24 and 56–57, to confirm the point of view of Jotham as it is expressed in the reported speech of 9:16–20.

Thus, those who on one hand appear to know "what is going on" at this point in Israel's history are Jotham and the panchronic narrator of 9:22–24, 56–57; those who, on the other hand, are seriously misguided in their understanding of what they experience are everyone else in the story. And among those who are blind to events in the story, Abimelech himself is singled out at the end as the epitome of such ignorance. For, intent upon not having it said that a woman killed him, he has his armour-bearer finish him off, as if ironically to reveal his own ignorance that it really is neither man nor woman who kills him but God himself. Abimelech, like Samson after him, dies so obviously ignorant of the larger issues that surround his life and death that he aptly represents the ignorance of all the other characters in his story.

But the ideological point of this climactic story of Abimelech will be entirely missed unless the phraseological point of view indicated by the consistent naming of Jerubaal and Elohim is taken seriously. The exploits of Abimelech begin only after we are told that the Israelites again worshiped the *baalim* after Gideon's death, and made Baal-Berith their god (8:33); these exploits end with the destruction of Shechem and Abimelech, events that characteristically do not result in the Israelites' repentance and rejection of idolatry, but rather in their simply going back home (9:55). From beginning to end, all the characters in the story, Jotham included, exhibit no knowledge of or allegiance to Yahweh, the God of the Israelites. The only insight that Jotham and the narrator share, and all the other characters of the story lack, is the retributive nature of "God" who requited the crimes of Abimelech and the men of Shechem.

The recognition of Yahweh that was intermittently forced from Gideon has completely disappeared. Israel is now so much like the remaining nations that surround them that the names of any one of these nations could be substituted in the story wherever Israel is mentioned, and the story remain entirely intelligible. As in the Book of Deuteronomy where the theme of the similarity of Israel with the other nations tended to coalesce with the theme of retributive justice, so it is precisely here in the Abimelech story, *where for the first time in the Book of Judges just retribution finally is accomplished, that both Israel and the narrator lose their distinctively Yahwistic identities.* When we finally come upon someone who for the first time in the book receives the punishment he deserves, there is absolutely nothing Yahwistic in the entire story, not even the speech of the narrator himself. Neither Adoni-bezek, Eglon, Barak, Oreb, Zeeb, Zebah, or Zalmunnah had been portrayed as out-and-out scoundrels. They are all depicted as vaguely worthy of either punishment or blessing as Israel's judges are. But Abimelech is portrayed as a true villain, and it is not *Yahweh* who is said to have punished him!

These features contrast all the more with what we know of the preceding story, since the picture of man there, trying out his abilities to situate himself in his surroundings through the use of conditional alternatives (*'im, 'im lo', lû*), continues on into the Abimelech story, where Jotham twice employs the *'im. . . we'im 'ayin*, "if so . . . if not", idiom. Thus, if the Gideon story effectively illustrated the traps and dangers inherent in *desiring* too much ideological security and certainty, even that sought for by the Yahwistic reader of the book itself, the Abimelech story seems, on the other hand, to err by *offering* too much ideological security to the reader, except for one troublesome but saving aspect: such security seems to come only when Yahweh is completely ignored and forgotten. "Fairness and honesty (*'emet we'tāmîm*)" (9:16, 19), may be capable of illuminating the issues of retributive justice; they are relatively useless in clearing up the mystery of what happened to Israel during the period of the judges. Not the least aspect of that mystery consisted in the realization that, in all fairness and honesty, Israel should not have survived. So that if this thorny fact is to be honestly faced and the uncomfortable mystery of Israel's exploits continue to be embraced, the easy answer of the Abimelech account must be rejected. The author helps us to reject it by keeping away from it Yahweh's majestic stamp. Yahweh's lessons are more profound than those found in the story of Abimelech.

4. The phraseological point of view expressed by the various shifts in the naming of the deity has such crucial importance for understanding the ideological perspective of the Book of Judges that it will be opportune here for us to review the situation as we have so far construed it before going on to the story of Jephtah. It appears likely that in the Book of Judges the use of now "Yahweh," now "Elohim," has compositional implications, whatever might be previous assertions about the diachronic aspects of such an alternation. In those passages where there is a shift between "Yahweh" and "Elohim," the use of "Elohim" appears to signal a deity whose identity, from the point of view of the speaker uttering his name or in view of the speaker's audience, is either not

Yahweh himself or else a deity unable clearly to be recognized as or identified with Yahweh in a particular instance of communication. Thus, the Canaanite Adoni-bezek speaks about "what God has done for me" in 1:7. Because Ehud is addressing the Moabite king, Eglon, he speaks about "a word from God for you" in 3:20. The narrator tells us in 4:23 that "God gave victory to the Israelites over Jabin king of Canaan" because it was Jael, the wife of Heber, separated from the Kenites and allied to Jabin—that is, a non-Israelite woman—who had just killed Sisera. So also the Midianite in 7:14 talks about Elohim instead of Yahweh.

Using these examples of the narrative's precision in naming, we would make no great interpretive leap to assume that a shift in the naming of the deity elsewhere in the text will, more often than not, have a similar significance. The twofold test of the fleece in 6:33–40 concerns "Elohim" not "Yahweh" because what is being described here is Gideon's perception of the deity he was testing. Whoever this god was to whom Gideon spoke, it was not obviously or certainly Yahweh. The naming is deliberately ambiguous because Gideon's inner psychological perspective is thereby accurately portrayed. Similarly, we are to understand in 8:13 that either Gideon or the Ephraimites or both felt more comfortable attributing the capture of Oreb and Zeeb to a vague "Elohim" rather than to Yahweh himself. Finally, Israel's state of total idolatry noted in 8:33 is the background for the consistent use of "Elohim" in Judges 9 in contexts where "Yahweh" had previously been appropriate. We shall soon see how and why the Jephtah story returns to a consistent use of "Yahweh," before we move on to the Samson story, where the Israelite use of "Elohim" once more takes on an ideological significance. Compositional analysis does not illuminate every occurrence where the name of the deity occurs—the "angel of God" in 6:20, for example—but in many cases the precision of the narrative in the naming process is thereby illuminated.

Jephtah (10:6–12:7)

Yahweh returns to full view with the exploits of Jephtah. After a brief mention of the judgeships of Tola and Jair (10:1–5), we come upon the only reference in the book to Israel's repentance of their idolatry, banishment of foreign gods, and return to the worship of Yahweh (10:16). This conversion of Israel is absolutely unique in the Book of Judges, and it signals an important aspect of the Jephtah stories: if perhaps all the confusion and ambiguity that had hitherto characterized Israel's experience during this period of their history were thought to have been the direct result of their continual breaking of the

LORD's covenant, such an explanation may no longer be proposed. For in a verse that we must translate with some difficulty, we realize that despite Israel's unique repentance they still will be unable either to predict what the future has in store for them or to insure the success of their military ventures against the nations that surrounded them. That they did in fact defeat the Ammonites (11:32–33) after beginning to worship Yahweh once again (10:16) only underlines, from another viewpoint, the paradoxical relationship they enjoyed with their God. If previously they had cried out to the LORD in bold and unrepentant voice, confident that once more he would listen to them and deliver them, now when they finally call to him in repentance he has grown tired of their voice:

> They [Israel] banished the foreign gods and worshiped the LORD;
> and he grew annoyed [or impatient] with the troubled efforts of
> Israel (*wattiqsar napšô ba^{ca}mal yiśrā'ēl*). (10:16)

That the end of this verse is so often construed to refer to Yahweh's compassion, e.g., ". . . and he could no longer endure the plight of Israel," seems to me to be another example of the ease with which the cyclical pattern of 2:6–3:6 is thought to include the cause and effect principle of repentance followed by deliverance. In all the many places in the book where repentance is never mentioned but rather incorrectly assumed, for example, by mistranslations of *hôsîp la^{ca}śôt* as "once again to do. . . " instead of "to continue to do. . . , " the LORD's subsequent deliverance is thereby made comfortably intelligible. Here, where Israel's repentance is not assumed but clearly stated, it is just as comfortable to assume that the LORD's response will be positive. The Book of Judges offers no such security.

If we concentrate on the phraseological composition of the Jephtah stories as it manifests itself in mutual relations of reported and reporting speech, we find that there are five main episodes, at the heart of each of which is a dialogue between two main characters or groups in the story. Some sort of tension or conflict is either the subject of or the background for the dialogue of each episode in the story. Each conversation that follows the initial dialogue between Yahweh and Israel rehearses from another viewpoint some aspect of the original tension-filled dialogue. By the end of chapter 12, we have looked once more at the "test as a trap" theme from a number of provocative points of view.

Episode 1 concerns the subjugation of Israel to the Ammonites and Israel's subsequent repentance (10:6–16). The confrontation between Yahweh and Israel sets the tone for the following episodes. After Israel acknowledges their sinfulness in 10:10b, Yahweh reacts negatively in

10:11b–14, "therefore I will deliver you no more." Then comes Israel's impertinent, even presumptuous request:

> We have sinned. Do with us as you will; only save us *this day* we beseech you! (10:15; emphasis added)

After perhaps hundreds of years during which undiminished treachery on their part produced God's deliverance time and time again, it is easy to ask with sincerity for what is essentially a preposterous request: do whatever you want, only save us immediately! The reporting words of the narrator spell out the situation clearly: there are no further words of Yahweh promising deliverance, there is only a reference to instant repentance followed by notice of Yahweh's annoyance with an Israel who believes in the efficacy of a timely, even a desparate, repentance. 13:1 will attest to the brief life of Israel's newfound devotion. In any event, this episode ends with Yahweh's rejection of Israel's overtures. However one wants to interpret 10:16b, its very opacity is an integral feature of the story. What comes through quite forcefully in this dialogue are both Israel's rather self-serving conversion as an apparent attempt once more to use Yahweh to insure their peace and tranquility, and Yahweh's argument that a slighted and rejected God will be used no longer.

The negative notice of 10:16b is followed immediately by the second episode, the elevation of Jephtah as lord and commander of Gilead (10:17–11:11). The failure of the first test, in which Israel promised, "We will repent if you will save us," is followed now by Gilead's announcement of a second test to insure Israel's eventual victory:

> If any man will strike the first blow at the Ammonites, he shall be lord over the inhabitants of Gilead. (10:18)

Again the heart of this episode is, like that of the first, a confrontatory dialogue in which the very perspectives of the participants, here Jephtah and the elders of Gilead, are much too similar to those of Israel and Yahweh in the first dialogue to be accidental. Just as Israel had rejected Yahweh, so Gilead had rejected Jephtah and sent him to exile in the land of Tob. Threatened by the Ammonites, the elders of Gilead call out for help from Jephtah, just as Israel called out to Yahweh in episode 1. Jephtah responds precisely as Yahweh did in 10:11–14, with the bitter words of a rejected one:

> You drove me from my father's house in hatred. Why come to me now when you are in trouble? (11:7)

The elders of Gilead now repeat their offer of the prize by which they hope to insure their own success: they promise the lordship of Gilead to Jephtah. Unlike Yahweh with respect to Israel, however, Jephtah is influenced positively by the Gileadites' offer: *the test has now become a trap*. If the first episode ended on the negative note of the narrator's comment, the narrator appears in 11:11 to be at least neutral to the agreement between Jephtah and Gilead. If God refuses to be used by Israel, Jephtah has no such hesitation with respect to Gilead.

The third episode concerns the unsuccessful negotiations between Jephtah and the king of Ammon (11:12–28). Once more we have a dialogic confrontation that forms the core of the episode, and once again, as in the first episode, the narrator concludes the section on a negative note. As Yahweh rejected Israel's terms, so also does the king of Ammon:

> But the king of the Ammonites would not listen to the message which Jephtah had sent him. (11:28)

What unites the first and third episodes, as distinct from the second, is precisely this negative outcome to negotiations, as well as a precise line of argumentation that is explicit in the third and implicit in the first. When Israel makes its preposterous request in 10:15, what makes it credible are the hundreds of years during which Yahweh did exactly what Israel implored, even though they did not repent. Similarly, Jephtah appeals in 11:26 to the three hundred years in which Israel had lived in peace in the land now overrun by the Ammonites. In the first case, Israel appealed to the donor to return the land; in the second case, Jephtah appeals to the original inhabitants to return it. In both cases, an unsuccessful attempt to rectify the present is made by appealing to the past. And in both cases, failure to achieve the goals so forcefully argued for is followed by an attempt to capture success through the issuance of a promissory test. Yahweh's rejection of Israel's repentance is followed by Gilead's offer to crown the man who will dare to fight Ammon; the Ammonite king's rejection of Jephtah's arguments is followed by Jephtah's vow to sacrifice to the LORD who will insure him victory over Ammon.

In the fourth episode (11:29–40), Jephtah's vow is central, and it is almost as a minor incident that we find a mention of the rout of Ammon in 11:32–33, important more for what follows than in itself. The focus is once again on a dialogue, this time the tragic confrontation of Jephtah and his daughter, his only child whom he has anonymously but rashly vowed to sacrifice to Yahweh as the price to be paid for his victory over Ammon. Here more obviously than in the other episodes, the test by which Jephtah had insured his victory has become a trap that forces him to destroy his only progeny. Having unsuccessfully avoided military confrontation through negotiation, Jephtah has now insured the success of his military ventures through a promissory test in which the person who first comes out to meet him, the "outcome" of his vow, turns out to be his virgin daughter, whom he will soon have to sacrifice to Yahweh. So far, the first four episodes repeat a pattern in which a dialogic confrontation, mostly argument and assertion, ends unsuccessfully (episodes 1 and 3), followed by a dialogic confrontation at the heart of which is a promissory test devised to insure the success of a particular venture (episodes 2 and 4). These latter two episodes are concluded by the narrator with utterances that are, at the most, neutral in their evaluation (11:11, 39–40).

The fifth episode concerns the dispute between Ephraim and Gilead over the march against the Ammonites (12:1–6), and comprises two dialogic confrontations that repeat the pattern discovered in the previous four episodes. The dispute between Jephtah and the Ephraimites embodied in their dialogue of 12:1–3 cannot be resolved by words, and ends in a pitched battle between them (12:4). The Ephraimites are defeated and, to insure that no Ephraimites escape back into Ephraim, 12:5–6 narrate the famous shibboleth/sibboleth test, whereby Gilead assures continued protection against his fellow Israelites. 12:6 ends with the narrator's notice that 42,000 men of Ephraim lost their lives at that time.

An attempt to understand the spatial-temporal composition of these stories runs into the same semantic difficulties that were encountered in the Ehud story. Here, as there, the spatial ambiguity seems quite deliberate, even stylized. In fact, the Jephtah story develops to a much greater degree the spatial, ultimately ideological, ambiguities present in the Ehud story. The verbal play of *ᶜābar*, whereby Ehud "passed through, or crossed over, the idols" or perhaps even "transgressed or broke" them, as a verbal recuperation of Israel's "transgressing my covenant" (2:20), is brought to a climax at the end of the story, where we are unable to determine in which direction the Moabites are fleeing as the Ephraimites "seized the fords of the Jordan and allowed no man to cross" (3:28). The deliberate spatial ambiguity of the Jephtah stories, accompanied also by a now greatly increased play on the "pass through/transgress" dimensions of *ᶜābar*, similarly comes to an opaque climax at the fords of the Jordan, where it is now the Ephraimites who may not cross the river. Compounding the spatial problems in the text is our uncertainty whether the "Mizpah" of 10:17; 11:11, 34 is the same city as the transjordanian "Mizpah of Gilead," mentioned twice in 11:29.

There is so much "crossing over" and "passing through" in the story that the verbal disorientation appears to reinforce the ideological aims of the book as we have so far uncovered them: both covenantal and hermeneutic boundaries are being thoroughly and continually transgressed. Some form of the root *ʿābar* is found in 10:8, 9; 11:17, 18, 19, 20; 11:29 ter, 32; 12:1 bis, 3, 5 bis, 6. What does it mean, for example, that Ephraim, after crossing over to Zaphon, asks of Jephtah why he had "crossed over" to fight against the Ammonites? But Jephtah lives in Mizpah, east of the Jordan. Or does he? Or how can Jephtah "cross over to attack the Ammonites" (11:32) if he is already east of the Jordan (11:29)? Boling's translations (1975:207 and passim) fortunately recognize some of the problems involved and offer plausible suggestions. We will deal with the question in a slightly different way. It would appear that such examples of spatial disorientation produced by verbal plays and ambiguities are meant, on the surface of the text, to reinforce the semantic ambiguity that is so central to the ideological stance of the book. The period of the judges represents a period of Israel's history when the ideological categories previously helpful in understanding the Israel of Moses' and Joshua's times begin to dissolve into one another and produce no real insights into that stretch of time between the death of Joshua and the rise of kingship in Israel. We shall now see how the narrative continues this attack upon the idolatry of ideology itself, as it documents the further disintegration of Israel apparent in the exploits of Samson.

Samson the Nazirite (13:1–16:31)

1. Samson is *par excellence* the unknowing judge. Although he prays at times to Yahweh, e.g., 15:18; 16:28, he appears never to have had any concern for the interests of Israel, nor any knowledge of the role predicted for him by the angel of Yahweh at the beginning of these stories. If we begin our interpretation with an examination of the phraseological composition of chapter 13, the episode in which the angel of the LORD appears to Manoah and his wife, we shall have a much clearer understanding of the implications of the following episodes. We will concentrate in this chapter on *naming*; we have already seen its relevance in previous stories. Its importance as a formal element in compositional structure has been well expressed by Uspensky:

> The change of the authorial position as formally expressed by the use of elements of reported speech (specifically in the act of nam-

ing) occurs not only in literary texts but also in everyday story-telling and indeed in ordinary speech where the same compositional devices are in operation as in a literary work. Any speaker constructing a narration may change his position and assume in sequence the point of view of one or another of the participants in the action, or even of characters who do not take part in the action. (1973:20)

What is immediately obvious in Judges 13 is that the narrator, in contrast to both Manoah and his wife, knows from the beginning that the "man" who appears to them is "the angel of Yahweh": the narrator names him in 13:3, 15, 16 bis, 18, 20, 21 bis. We have here the panchronic narrator of the framework sections of the book that introduce and conclude either the book itself or the individual stories of the various judges. The narrator exhibits the same privileged information here that he revealed in the similar passage involving the angel's appearance to Gideon in Judges 6. It appears likely also, that just as the narrator of Judges 6 could call the messenger not only "the angel of Yahweh" but even once "the angel of God," so also the narrator here assumes that "Yahweh" and "Elohim" are to be identified:

> God heard Manoah's prayer, and the angel of God came again to the woman. . . (13:9)

On the other hand, the narrator tells us explicitly that Manoah did not know that he was talking to the angel of Yahweh (13:16) and only discovered this fact after the individual failed to appear to him again (13:21). This recognition comes almost at the end of the episode, as it had with Gideon in Judges 6. What is not so clear, however, is whether Manoah could identify Yahweh and Elohim as easily as does the narrator, for Manoah is reported as uttering the ambiguous statement:

> We are doomed to die, we have seen God [or a god]. (13:22)

If the narrator knows from the first, and Manoah eventually discovers, that each is speaking about or to the angel of Yahweh, there is no indication that Manoah's wife ever comes to such a conclusion. She is certainly aware that Manoah offers a sacrifice to Yahweh (13:23), but neither she nor the narrator say anything that indicates she has identified the messenger who appeared to her and her husband. Her response in 13:23 to her husband's enigmatic statement of 13:22 makes just as much sense if we assume that she believed the remarkable individual who gave her such wonderful news was not Yahweh but another god or one of his messengers.

What contributes to Manoah's temporary, but his wife's apparently enduring, ignorance about their interlocutor is this person's refusal to identify himself except by the cryptic remark of 13:18, "How can you ask my name? It is 'wonderful (*peli'y*).'" He never *tells* Manoah or his wife that he is the angel of Yahweh, and speaks only of "God" in the content of his speeches. Similarly, the messenger's reticence to reveal his own name is matched by the narrator's reticence in informing us about the name of Samson's mother. Throughout this chapter she is always called "Manoah's wife," and it is not difficult to see how her lack of a name complements the fact that in the story she neither asks for (13:6) nor apparently discovers the name of the messenger or his master. She who is nameless receives valuable information from one who from her point of view remains nameless. This paradox is intensified when we examine the *content* of the messenger's speech as it is reported directly by the narrator and indirectly by Manoah's wife herself.

The narrator reports to us in 13:3–5 that the angel of Yahweh predicts the miraculous birth of a son and prohibits both the mother from eating and drinking certain things and the son from coming in contact with a razor. He explains how the boy will be a nazirite consecrated to God from his birth to his death and will begin to deliver Israel from the power of the Philistines. But when the woman then reports this to her husband in 13:6–7, *she does not tell him about the prohibition of the razor nor about her son's destiny as deliverer of Israel*. Moreover, even the angel himself in 13:13–14 repeats to Manoah only the alimentary prohibitions, and rephrases the remaining message in general terms: "Your wife must be careful to do all I told her. . . . She must do what I say." Thus Manoah never appears to find out about his son's destiny as a razorless deliverer of Israel.

We see, therefore, how the knowledgeable Manoah remains ignorant, and how his unknowing wife becomes knowledgeable. This is nowhere better seen than in the dialogue between the two in 13:22–23. Manoah prays to Yahweh, offers up sacrifice to him, and eventually recognizes his messenger. Yet it is the faithful and knowing Yahwist who remarks that contact with Yahweh or his messenger means death, whereas the unknowing wife is presumptuous enough to believe that their contact with "God" is acceptable and harmless, since Yahweh had accepted their sacrifice in spite of such contact. The situation in which the woman, ignorant of her interlocutor's identity, was kept ignorant of Samson's future, is related to the basic paradox according to which this story is to be interpreted. As it progresses, we shall see that Samson himself appears to remain ignorant of his delivering role, in spite of the fact that his mother must have told him at least about the prohibition of the razor.

2. Even more to be emphasized than the mutual contrasts between Manoah's and his wife's knowledge is the contrast between the narrator's omniscience and these characters' limited knowledge of their situation. Manoah knows who it is who speaks, but is deliberately kept from a crucial part of his message. His wife receives the entire message, but does not know who delivers it or on whose behalf it comes. The narrator, however, is in full control both of the message and its source, and appears intent upon underscoring his characters' limitations of knowledge and understanding. This intention becomes even more obvious with the episode of Samson's disappointing marriage, recounted in chapter 14. The panchronic narrator underlines his characters' ignorance with the following explanation of why Samson's parents were opposed to his marrying a Philistine woman:

> His father and mother did not know that the LORD was at work in this, seeking an opportunity against the Philistines who at that time were masters of Israel. (14:4)

Implicit in this explanation of the parents' ignorance is the ignorance of God's plans exhibited by Samson himself, whose own reason for choosing the Timnite woman had already been given us by the narrator's report of Samson's command, "Get her for me for she pleases me" (14:3). Samson is here depicted by the narrator in a negative fashion as the typical Israelite of this period, for the very words used here by Samson and echoed by the narrator in 14:7, "for she pleases me," and "she pleased him" (literally: "to be right in the eyes of . . ."), are used by the narrator later on in the book to typify the treacherous norm according to which Israelites conducted their business before the coming of the monarchy:

> In those days there was no king in Israel and every man did what was right in his own eyes. (21:25)

However, if the narrator makes clear how misguided are Samson and his parents, he also reminds his readers of *their* ignorance and dependence on his omniscience, when, for example, he deems it necessary to point out to them in 14:4 that the Philistines were "at that time masters of Israel." This is an aspect of the story's background of which even the characters themselves, in seeming contrast to the narrator's audience, were well aware. By conveying to the reader both information which was normally available to the participants in his story as well as information which only a panchronic and omniscient observer could have known, the Deuteronomic narrator thus allows his audience periodically to share his omniscience as the story progresses. He has in fact been alternately revealing and hiding his omniscience as his larger story-line has developed. Just as there is among the stories a variation in the amount of insight he allows the characters who act out their parts within them, so there has been a constant alternation in the amount of insight and prescience he allows the readers as the stories follow upon one another. The Deuteronomist thereby manipulates his readers so that they may identify at times with the struggling characters and at times with his all-knowing narrator. The ideological perspective according to which man is not able always to predict his destiny or insure the success of his efforts is felt by the reader who, like the story's participants, at times must struggle to see what lies ahead, yet is forced at times to experience the unexpected. And when the narrator does reveal hidden knowledge to the reader, it is paradoxically to increase his own plausibility at the same time as the Deuteronomist intends to put limits on it.

Armed therefore with the knowledge given him by the narrator in 14:4, the reader is able to understand the irony that is at the center of chapter 14: whether one has been visited by Yahweh's own messenger, as had been Samson's mother and father, or is led to do what is right in his own eyes, as was Samson's wont, whether one knows the answer to a riddle as does Samson, or discovers the answer in the way his wife and her kinsfolk do, all man's attempts to grasp the truth and understand his situation can painfully miss the mark.

The reporting speech of chapter 14 presents us with a series of four dialogues, together with an utterance coming between the second and third dialogues. All five of these verbal encounters illustrate man's continual struggle with alternative solutions through the employment of rhetorical questions and conditional propositions. As we have seen, the previous stories contained numerous examples of this, notably the Gideon and Abimelech accounts; the present story intensifies such illustrations. Samson's riddle, and the other questioning tests of the chapter, illustrate the central ideological stance of the book as it is foreshadowed by Yahweh's angry words of 2:20–22: an ideological test becomes a trap if too much confidence is placed in its hermeneutic and existential capabilities. Whether Israel walks in the way of the LORD must not depend on the blessings and curses they endeavor respectively to assure and avoid.

Thus the dialogue between Samson and his parents in 14:1–3 includes a rhetorical question emplying *ha'ên;* there is an immediate contrast between the parents' confident position (Are there not so many

Israelite or Danite women, that it is foolish to choose a Philistine!) and their ignorance of God's plans. The second dialogue, between Samson and the thirty men (14:12–14) contains the famous riddle of the honeyed lion. Samson in 14:12–13 sets out the terms of the contest he proposes in precisely the verbal alternatives used in the book's prototypical test of 2:22: "if . . . or if not (*'im . . . weᵉim lo'*)." The story soon shows how he was erroneously confident of the riddling contest's outcome. After the second dialogue, the narrator reports in 14:15 what is said to Samson's wife by her thirty kinsmen. Once again their rhetorical question explores possibilities and assumes the truth of one alternative by using the questioning words, "Have you or have you not invited us to dispossess us (*ha. . . haᵉlo'*)?" The irony is that their avoidance of dispossession by forcing a deceitful answering of the riddle is in reality the first step in Samson's series of successful acts of revenge against their people. We the readers have been warned by the narrator that what they want really will not be in their own best interests. The third dialogue, between Samson and his wife, occurs in 14:16 and contains Samson's rhetorical question, "I have not explained it even to my father and mother, and am I to tell you?" He who utters such a word professes confidence in the correctness of his position; yet he then changes his position out of love (or the persistence of his wife's nagging) only to lose the contest. The final dialogue of the chapter is between Samson and the thirty men to whom he had proposed the riddle (14:18). Here not only do the men give the answer to the riddle by means of a double question, but Samson reacts to their perfidy with a conditional (*lûle'*: "if not") proverb: "If you had not ploughed with my heifer, you would not have found out my riddle!" Little does Samson know, as we do, that he is Yahweh's heifer in this case.

Man confident in his own knowledge as he steps forward toward failure and disaster is the condensed message of the reported speech of this chapter. We would be tempted to say that the panchronic vision apparent in the reporting speech of the narrator stands in stark contrast to these reported words of man's ignorance, if it were not for the fact that the narrator's omniscience has all along been serving a paradoxical purpose in the book: the undermining of our excessive confidence in just such ominscience. Using the confusion that results from man "doing what is right in his own eyes" as the central theme of the book's stories, the Deuteronomist turns his critical gaze back upon himself and his narrator, so that he may illustrate the confusion that results from idolizing ideologies, which are, after all, man-made. However much critical traditionalism is to be preferred over authoritarian dogmatism, even the former has its limitations, and it is the main purpose of the Book of Judges to bring these out. Only then can the

Deuteronomist's arguments for the necessity of a continually critical testing of God's words avoid becoming for him and his audience an idolatrous trap.

3. The incidents narrated in chapter 15 are clothed in a dazzling display of verbal dexterity that may appear to be merely fanciful wordplay, but actually serves the Deuteronomist's plan of deliberate ideological obfuscation. Most of the reported utterances in the chapter are either questions, answers, or statements of intent, all of which are meant to provide, on the surface, an explanation for past or proposed courses of action. However, this reported speech as contextualized by the narrator is strangely effective in calling into question man's ability to justify his actions or to understand why he has been acted upon in certain ways. The chapter culminates in the words of the narrator in 15:19b–20, of themselves innocently explanatory, but ultimately vertiginous in their effect because what precedes them powerfully calls into question the very confidence with which they are uttered.

In keeping with the book's theme of man's struggle to understand what is happening to him and about him, many of the utterances in the chapter involve question-answer interchanges. The dialogue between the Philistines in 15:6 is the first such interchange and allows them to discover not only who burned their fields but why. The narrator at the end of this verse immediately relates the upshot of this discovery:

> The Philistines then went up and burned her [Samson's wife] and her father's household.

We have only to recall the threat issued by the kinsfolk of Samson's wife in the previous chapter to realize that these poor Philistines of Timnah were doomed whichever course of action they chose:

> Coax your husband and make him tell you the riddle, or we shall burn you and your father's house. (14:15)

Had she not coaxed the riddle's answer from Samson, the same fate would have come to the Timnite woman and her household that eventually came to them because she *did* unravel the riddle. For this led to Samson's anger and withdrawal, which led to her remarriage, which led to Samson's angry burning of the Philistine fields, which culminated in the very fate she had avoided in the first place. The similarity of the phraseology is too close to be accidental:

> *niśrop 'ôtak wᵉet bêt 'ābîk bā'ēš* (14:15)
> *wayyiśrᵉpû 'ôtāh wᵉet 'ābîhā bā'ēš* (15:16)

In 15:10 we have a second question-answer interchange between the men of Judah and the Philistines, followed immediately by a third interchange in 15:11–13 between the three thousand Judahites and Samson. In both cases (15:10 and 15:11) it is the Judahites who ask questions, attempting to find out in the first instance why the Philistines had attacked them, and in the second why Samson had acted so foolishly in slaughtering the Philistines. The answers the Judahites receive are in part remarkably similar:

> Philistines: ". . . to do to him [Samson] as he did to us." (15:10)
> Samson: "As they [the Philistines] did to me, thus I have done to them." (15:11)

Moreover, part of the answer of the Philistines mirrors the Judahites' later statement to Samson:

> Philistines: "in order to bind Samson we have come up." (15:10)
> Judahites: "in order to bind you [Samson], we have come down." (15:12)

The final example of a question-answer interchange occurs at the end of the chapter when Samson asks Yahweh in 15:18 whether he had given him this great victory only to have him die of thirst. The narrator then recounts God's answer through the miraculous flow of water in 15:19.

All of these questioning examples in the chapter reveal the unforeseen, ironic, or obscure results that flow not from the refusal but from the giving of answers. After the Philistines' question was answered, the Timnites suffer a doom they could not have avoided. The Judahites' reasonable questioning of both the Philistines and Samson involves them in answers that float in the narrator's almost endless morass of who first did what to whom: the Philistines want Samson for slaughtering their own people; but he had done this because they had killed his wife and father-in-law; but they had done this because he had burned their fields; but he had done this because his father-in-law had given away his wife; but he had done this because Samson had gotten angry and left; but he had done this because his wife had given the riddle's answer to her kinsmen; but she had done this to avoid being burnt up by them—and so we have circled back once again to the unavoidable fate of Samson's Timnites. Similarly, Samson's answer in 15:11 leads to the Judahites' ironic decision to bind over to their enemy their kinsman for certain death, just as the Philistines had ironically killed their own kinsmen, the Timnites, when they learned of the destructive actions of their enemy Samson. Finally, God answers Samson's questioning cry for help with a miracle that is as ironic as all the other actions by which Samson is delivered. For no character in the story is less deserving of deliverance and victory than Samson himself. In short, all the reported and reporting answers provided in the chapter are unsatisfactory from the point of view of the ideologies that have vied for dominance in the preceding books. Neither authoritarian dogmatism nor critical traditionalism, nor any systematic model of divine mercy and justice help fully to explain the fate or justify the actions of Israelite and Philistine alike.

The reported speech of the chapter also contains statements of intent or assurance that underline how precarious is man's ability to assess his own situation. In 15:1 Samson's cohortative statement, "Let me go in to my wife" is immediately contradicted by his father-in-law's explanation that he no longer has a wife to go to. This very explanation in 15:2 contains two examples of Hebrew infinitive absolute plus finite verb, whose function is to express very emphatic declarations, *'āmor 'āmartî kî śāno' śᵉnē'tāh* "I must insist that you certainly divorced her!" The Timnite's certitude, however, resulted in his own death. But this very killing of his father-in-law and wife causes Samson to exclaim to the Philistines, "If you do things like this, I swear I will be revenged upon you and then I will quit!" (15:7). The truth of such an oath is marred by the story's emphasis on his continuing acts of destruction: previously after his killing in anger of thirty men of Ashkelon, Samson had revealed the ongoing nature of his destructive actions with the words, "This time I will be innocent concerning the Philistines" (15:3); yet contrary to his oath, he continues to perform acts of destruction (15:15, 30) until his death. No one in the story appears so misguided as Samson. He believes that each act of destruction will be his last; that belief is finally justified only when he destroys himself in the process.

If the story undoubtedly emphasizes how those within it who appear to have all the answers are naively mistaken and misguided, the narrator who apparently displays an omniscient control of the story then deliberately undercuts his own omniscience by his careful use of ambiguous phraseology. To delight in wordplay and to establish and reveal etiologies imply a certain control over the significance of words and objects. The narrator prepares us for his own verbal dexterity by first describing Samson as one who exults in wordplay and etiological naming. After Samson slays a thousand men, he is described in 15:16 as composing a couplet that plays upon the identical words for donkey and heap, *ḥmr*. Samson then names the height upon which he jawboned his enemies, "Jawbone Hill" (15:17). Undoubtedly all this wordplay pleased the Deuteronomist's audience; it is not only delightful but comforting to know that the reason a certain town is called Jawbone is because once Samson slew there a thousand Philistines with the jawbone of an ass. To name something, to know its name, is to have power over it, at least the power that comes from knowledge. Even Samson, who is depicted as ignorant of his own destiny, possesses such knowledge and power, and is described as using it. How much more so the narrator under whose verbal control even Samson is. Thus, just as Samson is described as establishing an etiology, ". . . and he called that place Jawbone Hill" (15:17), so also the narrator can reveal an etiology: "That is why its name is called En-hakkore to this day" (15:19). Stepping momentarily out of his role as narrator, he establishes direct contact with his audience by referring to the "now" of his act of communication rather than the "then" of his story. Only because an audience has confidence in a narrator's grasp of the situation do they listen to him. But if the narrator begins to play with this confidence, his audience has to reassess what they are hearing. And this is what takes place in this chapter through a play upon the root *qr'*, which is used in the story in its various meanings of (1) "to meet, encounter"; (2) "to call, name, give a name to"; and (3) "to call upon or cry aloud to." The Philistines, in 15:14, come out shouting to meet Samson (*liqrā'tô*); Samson, in 15:17, "named (*wayyiqrā' l^e*)" that place Jawbone Hill"; "he called upon or cried out to Yahweh (*wayyiqrā' 'el*)" in 15:18; and the miraculous spring's name "is called (*qārā*) the crier's spring (*ᶜên haqqôrē'*)" in 15:19.

Two of these meanings of *qr'* have important hermeneutic implications for our story. One meaning of *qr'*, "to name, give a name to," emphasizes the power that comes from knowledge of something. On the other hand, when, for example, Samson "cries out to" or "calls upon" or "appeals to" Yahweh in 15:18, as he will again do in 16:28, he is in fact being described as one who needs to test the truth of his own knowledge ("shall I now die of thirst?") or power ("give me strength only this once, O God"). In the one case, *qr'* means having power through knowledge; in the other it means a questioning of knowledge and power. So far, Samson may be accurately described as fulfilling both of these conditions.

But when the narrator steps out of his narrator's role and speaks to us directly in 15:19, he invites us to meditate upon the very ambiguity of explanation itself, by employing *qr'* in an unavoidably ambiguous way. In the very uttering of an explanation of why a certain spring is called by its name, the narrator insures that the very name of the spring casts doubt upon the ultimate value of the explanation it is meant to convey. For since Samson has been described as both naming (*wayyiqrā'*) a place and calling upon (*wayyiqrā'*) Yahweh, *ʿên haqqôrēʾ* may mean "Crier's Spring" or "Namer's Spring." So that when the narrator's explanation tells us *why* the spring is so named, is he emphasizing Samson's previous knowledge and power whereby he had named the hill after his victorious slaughter of a thousand men, or is he referring to Samson's weakness and ignorance wherein he had just called out for help from Yahweh? The very naming of *haqqôrēʾ* cries out for ambiguity over certainty, obscurity over clarity, in the nature of the explanation itself. We do not really know from the chapter whether "naming" explains and subdues "crying out," or whether "crying out" gives one the power "to name." We find ourselves in the midst of obscurity because the Deuteronomist has led us there, as he has been doing all along in the Book of Judges. Turning away from his subject matter for a brief moment at the end of 15:19, he invites us to meditate upon the fact that if we cannot arrive at a clear picture of the role of Samson in Yahweh's plans, neither should we invest too much in the explanatory role of the narrator himself. For in addition to the voice which names names and explains events, there is the voice which cries out to Yahweh for understanding. In this regard, Samson and the Deuteronomist are one.

We cannot say very much about the enigmatic incident involving Samson and the prostitute of Gaza (16:1–3). Like Samson's mother and wife, and unlike Delilah, the prostitute has no name. As before, the reported speech illustrates how the confidence with which one proposes a course of action is ill conceived. The people of Gaza wait for him at the barred city-gate saying to themselves:

> When day breaks, we shall kill him. (16:2)

The security behind this statement rested upon the security of a locked city-gate which supposedly barred Samson from escaping from their grasp. But Samson wrests this security from them at midnite by hoisting upon his shoulders the city-gate's doors, door-posts, and bar and carrying them to the safety of a hilltop at Hebron. That which in its own locale symbolized security and certitude for the Philistines of Gaza and certain death for Samson is transplanted to the anomalous locale of Hebron where it foreshadows Samson's and the Philistines' death in its original city, Gaza.

4. The story of Samson and Delilah enlarges upon the testing theme that has been found throughout the book. If Delilah is to obtain the silver promised her by the Philistine lords, she must somehow persuade

Samson to divulge the secret of his strength; she must find out what that secret is. Three times she asks him and three times the conditional tests he suggests turn into traps that deceive her:

> If they bind me . . . then I shall become like any other man. (16:7)

> If they really bind me . . . then I shall become like any other man. (16:11)

> If you weave the seven locks of my head . . . (16:13)

Each time Delilah carries out Samson's instructions, the narrative describes how Samson is still able to exercise his superhuman strength and frustrate Delilah. But on the fourth day, after he tells her,

> if my head were shaved . . . then I should become weak like any man (16:17),

the narrative departs from the previous pattern wherein Delilah had not known if Samson was telling the truth until she carried out his instructions. We are now informed by the narrator that no sooner had Samson uttered this explanation than "Delilah saw that he had revealed to her his secret" (16:18). What is immediately obvious by this departure in the narrative is that Samson's words are not tested in this case before their veracity is recognized by Delilah: the truth of what Samson says in 16:17 is immediately recognized not just by the reader, who has been privy to the information since chapter 13, but, the narrator tells us, by Delilah herself, who had already been burned three times by Samson's false statements. What the narrator emphasizes at this crucial point in the story is Delilah's immediate recognition of Samson's secret even before she put this new knowledge to use. Her subsequent actions were no longer a *test* of Samson's veracity; Delilah immediately knows that Samson has truly revealed the secret of his strength even before she has a man shave off his locks. She even knows that his strength has left him before Samson does. For the narrator informs us that, after his haircut, "she began to overpower him (*leʿannôtô*) and his strength left him" (16:19). On the other hand, upon Samson's awakening, "he did not know that the LORD had left him" (16:20).

There is a reversal, therefore, in the Samson-Delilah story that has important implications for our understanding of how this story fits in with what has preceded it in the Samson cycle, and in the larger context of the book itself. When Delilah three times follows Samson's conditional instructions, there is no indication that she either believes or disbelieves him. Her subsequent actions alone are depicted as revealing to her whether Samson's words are truthful or not, that is, they put his words to the test. And in all three cases, she fails to achieve her goal of becoming rich by helping to overpower Samson. But when he gives a fourth conditional explanation, she is depicted as immediately knowing that he had spoken the truth. Thus her subsequent actions are portrayed as consequent upon her apprehension of the truth, and do not therefore function for her as the putting of his words to the test. And it is on this occasion that she finally attains her objective. Delilah is portrayed by the narrator as successful precisely when she is no longer dependent upon putting Samson's words to the test. Somehow or other, the truth of Samson's words become self-evident to her and are not subject to a critical testing before she accepts them.

A test is meant to give some kind of assurance, proof, or certitude to him who administers it. Ehud does not ask the Israelites of Ephraim to follow him and believe that the LORD has delivered their enemy into their hands (3:28) until he has successfully assassinated Eglon. Barak is not willing to obey Yahweh's command until he has the surety of Deborah's company at Mount Tabor (4:8). Gideon wants a sign to know who it is who is speaking to him (6:17). He twice has to give God a wooly test (6:36–40) and then he has to hear his enemy interpret a dream in his favor (7:9–15) before he can believe with confidence that Yahweh has given Midian into his hands. Even Yahweh (7:1–8) is depicted as using a winnowing water test to assure that the Israelites will attribute their coming victory to him rather than to themselves. Jephtah has to insure his victory over the Ammonites with a rash and ultimately tragic vow to Yahweh (11:30). Manoah informs the divine messenger that it will be when his words come true that he will honor him (13:18) and Manoah's wife is sure that Yahweh will not kill her and her husband since she considers his acceptance of their sacrifice a test of his good will toward them. Even Samson testily appeals to Yahweh's previous deliverance of him as an argument that he should not let him die of thirst (15:18). That Delilah is portrayed as departing from her usual practice of a cautious critical testing of Samson's words, that she is described as confidently sending word to the Philistines immediately upon hearing Samson's fourth explanation, and that she is indeed correct in her immediate recognition of the truth of Samson's words contrasts greatly with the predominant hermeneutic attitude of most of the characters in Judges, be they Israelite or not. Delilah is the one outstanding exception to this pattern so far in the book, and stands for the limitations that are inherent especially in an ideology such as critical traditionalism. Paradoxically, in this respect her apprehension of the truth of Samson's words is much more closely related to the intuitive implications of an authoritarian dogmatism than to the testing process of critical traditionalism. Yet even the ideology of authoritarian dogmatism is not what Delilah's intuitive grasp of the truth exalts here, for she apprehends the truth from within herself, whereas a dogmatic ideology imposes it from without.

Once again, the point of all this is not right or wrong, success or failure. Many of the judges are depicted as successful after they had administered such tests as we are discussing, and even after they had appeared to put too much store in them. Conversely, even Israel is depicted during this chaotic period as eminently successful in spite of the fact that by their continual sinning they fail the Mosaic test for success so critically set out in the Books of Deuteronomy and Joshua. Except that the fatal test they now lived by, throughout all this unrelieved disobedience, was that so aptly expressed by the unknowing Samson:

> Thou hast let me, thy servant, win this great victory, and must I now . . . fall into the hands of the uncircumcised? (15:18)

Such an attitude dramatically shows that unless the value of critically testing God's words is put into proper perspective, it too can become a trap as much to be rejected as the dogmatism rejected by the Deuteronomist in the Book of Deuteronomy.

In the final scene of the story, Samson's physical blindness is an emblematic climax to the blindness whereby he never understood the reason why Yahweh had so far delivered him from his enemies. His words to Yahweh before bringing down the pillars of the temple upon himself and the Philistines (16:28) reveal the same egocentric obliviousness to the affairs of Yahweh and the welfare of Israel that had characterized him throughout the story. The very egocentrism of his words explains why it is ironically appropriate for him to want to die with the Philistines: *their* words of praise and rejoicing before Dagon are as excessively egocentric as Samson's. We refer here to the narrator's direct reporting of their prayers in 16:23–24, in which the possessive pronoun "our" is repeated eight times in two utterances that comprise a total of only sixteen words (fourteen words if *'et* is not counted): *our* God, *our* enemy, *our* hands, *our* land, *our* dead.

The Samson stories are an attempt to burst structure by calling it into question, and Samson himself consequently inhabits the interstices of a number of basic Israelite categories. Who is an Israelite, and how should one live like one? Who is a judge, and how should one act like one? Most pointedly, Samson inhabits the no-man's land between a critical and a dogmatic ideology. Almost never does he ask critical questions about his role as Israelite and judge, nor does he ever appear intuitively to know what that role is. If the Book of Judges aims principally at attacking the idolatry of ideology, the oblivious Samson represents the negation of ideology. Perhaps these two extremes comprise the limits of the book's horizon: neither the overvaluing nor undervaluing of ideology can sabotage Yahweh's inscrutable plans for Israel.

Micah and the Danites (17:1–18:31)

1. In spite of some indications of textual disarray in this section (e.g., 17:3b: "But now I will return it to you," seems to belong to the end of Micah's statement in 17:2), Judges 17–18 exhibits an intricately worked out compositional structure. Chapter 17 is easily seen as background for the following chapter, and within the background chapter itself, its shifting perspectives form an obviously recognizable structure. The kernel of Judges 17 is v. 5 which forms a perfect summary of what precedes and follows it in the chapter. Both 17:1–4 and 17:7–13 employ inclusions which not only mark off the extent of these sections, but also indicate their subject matter. In addition, since the evaluative statement of 17:6 is so closely tied with the preceding nuclear verse of 17:5, it forms an inclusion with its repetition at the very end of the book in 21:25 in such a way that chapter 17 serves both as background material for the following story of the Danite migration and as an introduction to the entire last section of the book (17:1–21:25).

Since Micah and his priest are an essential part of the Danite story, Judges 17 tells us who Micah is and then who his priest is. Their stories are summarized beautifully in 17:5:

> The man, Micah, owned a shrine. And he made an ephod and teraphim, and installed one of his sons to be his priest.

This summary is so phrased that its beginning (*wᵉhāʾîš mîkāh*) not only refers to the beginning section on Micha, but also corresponds to the inclusions that mark off that section (17:1: *wayhî ʾîš . . . ûšmô mikāyhû*, and 17:4: . . . *bᵉbêt mikāyhû*). Similarly, its final words (*wayhî lô lᵉkohēn*) not only refer to the following section on Micah's priest, but also help form the inclusion for 17:7–13 (. . . *hāyāh lî hallēwî lᵉkohēn*). Finally, just as the two main sections of the chapter focus first on Micah's background, then on his priest's, and just as the summary statement of 17:5 begins with the words, "the man, Micah," and ends with the word, "priest," so the entire chapter is framed by its first noun, "a man," referring to Micah, and its last noun, "priest," referring to, as we later learn (18:30), Jonathan.

There then follows the story of the Danite migration, introduced by the statement, "In those days there was no king in Israel" (18:1), which marks it off as a story about the anarchy of the times, just as the same statement in 19:1 marks off the following story (19:2–21:24) as another illustration of that same anarchy.

A brief look at the temporal composition of 17–18 confirms the background nature of Judges 17 in relation to the following chapter. The narrator's speech in Judges 17 consistently employs only perfective verb forms with their retrospective point of view, in contrast to its frequent use of the imperfective participial forms in Judges 18, thus emphasizing the synchronic perspective of much of this chapter. The Danites were in search of (*m^{e}baqqĕs:* 18:1) territory in which to live; the Laishans are characterized in 18:7, 9, 27 with the use of four different participial forms; in 18:16–17, the six hundred Danites and the Levite are described as "stationing themselves (*niṣṣab/niṣṣabim*) at the entrance of the gate"; and in 18:28, there was no one to deliver (*maṣṣîl*) Laish. This shift in the temporal perspective of the narrator's speech—that is, from the constant retrospective viewpoint of Judges 17 to the frequent synchronic perspective of Judges 18—helps us recognize these authorial frames used to distinguish background from foreground elements in the story.

There is another feature that characterizes the phraseological composition of 17–18. The reporting and reported speech of the story combine to present us with an unusual number of repetitions in the narrative, whose function must somehow be important since they continue to occur throughout the story. It is almost as if the narrator is intent upon emphasizing certain aspects of his story. In 17:3–4, the narrator informs us twice that Micah returns the money that he took from his mother, and both these reports follow Micah's own words, presumably in v. 2, that he would return the money. Then in 17:7–9, we have a similar tripartite repetition in which the narrator twice gives us the same information about the future priest's background (17:7–8), followed by the man's own words to Micah (17:9) repeating most of the same information. In 18:2 we have the narrator's reporting that the Danites sent five men "to reconnoiter and explore the land," followed immediately by the reported words of the Danites, "Go and explore the land." (18:14, 17 further characterize these men as those "who were going to reconnoiter the land," even long after they had done so!) The end of 18:2 and the beginning of 18:3 give us the following repetition in the reporting speech of the narrator, ". . . they came . . . to the house of Micah and lodged there. They were at Micah's house when they recognized. . . ." In 18:17–18, the narrator curiously reports twice that the five men "took the idol, ephod, teraphim and image." Finally in 18:30–31, the narrator concludes his story by reporting that "the Danites erected for themselves the idol" (18:30), and "they set up for themselves the image . . ." (18:31).

If all these repetitions seem to solidify certain aspects of the story for us, other features, that is, shifts in naming, tend to blur some of its details. Most obvious of all is the identity of "the things Micah had made" (18:27). They are called: "a molten figure (*pesel ûmassēkāh*)" by Micah's mother and the narrator in 17:1–4; "an ephod and teraphim" by the narrator in 17:5; "ephod, teraphim, and molten figure" by the five men and the narrator in 18:14, 20, with a variation of this in 18:17, 18; "my gods(god) which I made" by Micah in 18:24; "what Micah had made" by the narrator in 18:27; and "figure (*pesel*)" by the narrator in 18:30, 31. Micah, his mother, and his priest refer to the deity as "Yahweh" in 17:2, 3, 13; 18:6, and the Danites call him "God" in 18:5, 10. Then in 18:12 the narrator reports that Qiriath-Jearim's name was changed to "Dan's camp," and in 18:29 that Laish's name was changed to Dan. Finally, Micah himself is named *mikāyhû* in 17:1, 4, and *mikāh* afterwards in the story, while Micah's priest is not given a name by anyone until the narrator calls him Jonathan in 18:30.

2. It is not difficult to see how the utterances of chapter 17 reach their immediate climax in the confident words of Micah after he has installed the Levite as his priest to care for "the things Micah had made":

> Now I know *for sure* that Yahweh will make me prosper for I have the Levite as priest. (17:13)

Not only do these words continue, in a most explicit way, the theme that we have shown to be so central to all of the stories of the judges that have preceded them, they also represent the manner according to which chapter 17 is designed to be the introduction to the entire concluding section of the Book of Judges. That chapter 18 concludes with Micah's priest and *pesel* installed far away from Micah's shrine in the newly named city of Dan illustrates how fragile was the confidence with which Micah in 17:13 interpreted his previous efforts.

It would be wrong to assume that the shattering of Micah's confidence has a retributive function in the story. It is true that the narrator uses the full spelling of Micah's name in 17:1, 4, to emphasize an irony: what Micah called "my god" (18:24) was made *by* one whose name means "who is like Yahweh?" and *with* money which had been consecrated to Yahweh. It is also ironic that what is stolen from Micah represents somehow the abominable use of stolen money that had been returned to its rightful owner. Perhaps it is even fitting that the Danites, who do not call upon the name of Yahweh in the story, come to possess the "god" which Micah the Yahwist should not have rightfully made or possessed. Nevertheless, the events of chapter 18 make all such retributive interpretations inappropriate, since these events soon make obvious that the fate of all the story's main characters does not depend upon their being "right" or "wrong": success or failure comes mysteriously to whomever it will.

The ultimate unpredictability of a man's or a tribe's destiny is well brought out in the dialogue between the five Danite spies and Micah's priest in 18:5–6. Once again, what has been a central concern of the entire book is made explicit by the reported speech of its characters. But even more than this, the central message of ambiguity that represents the ideological perspective of the entire book is succinctly articulated in this interchange:

> They [the Danite spies] said to him, "Inquire of God, please, that we may know whether the path that we are on will be a complete success." And the priest said to them, "Go in peace, the path you pursue is *nokaḥ* Yahweh." (18:5–6)

The semantic range of *nokaḥ* extends from "opposite" to "in front of," so that the priest's words may here mean that the Danites' mission is either "agreeable" or "disagreeable" to Yahweh. Since the Levite has been and will be further depicted in the story as an arch-opportunist, his response, or better yet the narrator's report of his response, rivals a Delphic oracle in ambiguity. If in fact Israel, throughout the period of the judges, enjoyed many more years of peace than of subjugation in spite of her continual idolatry, it is not difficult to believe that the prophesied peace with which the priest blesses the Danites will come to them in spite of the tragic manner by which they will establish that peace: they will cruelly slaughter the calm, confident, and carefree Laishans. One man's priest betrays his father and becomes priest to a tribe. Micah refuses to repossess what is his because of the Danites' superior strength. And the fate of the Laishans comes finally to the Danites and the descendants of Jonathan (18:30). Success or failure falls mysteriously to whomever it will.

The repetitions of 17–18 now can be seen to fit into a pattern whereby each of the main characters of the story, Micah, his priest, and the Danites, is pictured as unscrupulous or scrupulous—depending on one's point of view—opportunists. 17:3–4 concentrates on Micah, and emphasizes how the returning of stolen money is the prelude to the idolatrous making of a molten figure. An opportunist's correction of one evil act can lead to a more evil act. 17:7–9 concentrate on Micah's priest and help to emphasize how this Israelite, who is ready to sojourn wherever he may in another tribe's territory, is already a type of the perfect opportunist. Then, all the repetitions of Judges 18 emphasize how carefully the Danites work to insure the success of their endeavors. The chapter begins (18:2) and ends (18:30–31) with repetitions so that the story is doubly framed, first with the Danite tribe's exploratory steps to insure the successful takeover of a territory, and then with its idolatrous steps to insure the permanence of that takeover. In the midst of the chapter, 18:2–3 and 17, 18, emphasize how the five Danite spies begin their dispossession of Micah as guests *within* his house, and then complete it by *forceably entering* that house and taking the carved figure, ephod and teraphim.

Functioning as a counterpoint to all this focused striving after success are the ambiguously characterized people of Laish, who from opposite points of view are either "confident" or "unsuspecting (*boteᵃḥ*)," "peaceful" or "idle (*šoqēṭ*)." Are the men of Laish depicted as careful or careless? This obfuscating characterization of Laish through words that shift in meaning even as one reads them helps us to see how both the repetitions we have been discussing and the more obvious shifts in naming in the story serve the same equivocating function. If we are not quite sure what *mîkāh*, or *mikāyhû*, made (molten figure, ephod, teraphim, or gods), if we are not quite sure who deserved these things more (or less) (the explicit Yahwist Micah or the implicit Yahwists the Danites), we always have the example of the narrator, who shows us here how easy it is for a Judahite town, Kiryath-Jearim, to be called "Dan's Camp," and for "Laish" to be changed to "Dan."

As with the Samson story of Judges 15, the Deuteronomist once again uses his characters' and his narrator's efforts at securing the success of their own enterprises as the starting point for a meditation upon the limitations of explanatory and predictive ideologies. There is no pattern to be perceived in all these exertions. However much they strive, these characters and their narrator sometimes succeed, sometimes not. Ultimately, the Deuteronomist is calling attention to the narrator himself and asks his reader to apply the same evaluative criteria to that narrator as to the characters he introduces. The narrator, like one of his characters, might repeat so as to be better understood; yet sometimes these repetitions obscure rather than clarify. The narrator, like one of his chief characters, may shift his point of view; yet the change in perspective may not incite insight but vertigo. As with the characters so

with their narrator: success or failure appears mysteriously where it
will.

The Benjaminite Outrage and Israel's Moral
(Dis-)solution (19:1–21:25)

I do not intend to go into a detailed compositional analysis of the last
three chapters of Judges. Rather I shall selectively deal with only a few
aspects of the narrative that appear to have the greatest bearing on the
major perspectives we have already uncovered. Since we are at the
finale of our stories about Israel's exploits during the period of the
judges, we would expect that it provide us with a fitting climax to the
major themes so brilliantly worked out by the Deuteronomist in the
course of this book, and we are not disappointed. If the book's first
chapter began with an effective psychological portrait of the process
whereby Israel, after Joshua's death, progressively went from certainty
to confusion concerning the high expectations of victory guaranteed
her by the Mosaic covenant, the book's finale now completes with a
flourish the paradoxical picture of confusion within certainty, obscurity
in clarity, that has occupied its pages from the start.

1. The story of the outrage itself is most interesting from a compositional point of view. We are given first of all in chapter 19 the narrator's
detailed presentation of how the Levite and his concubine came to suffer
the horrible fate that befell them at Gibeah, while spending the night at
the home of an Ephraimite sojourning in Benjamin, and of how the
Levite reacted to such an experience. Then in 20:4–7, the narrator
gives us a story within a story by including therein the Levite's own
account to his fellow Israelites of what happened to him that night, and
what he did in response. If we compare the narrator's long and detailed
reporting speech of the incident with the short reported speech by the
Levite of the same occurrence, it may be that the most outrageous
aspect of all is constituted neither by the base actions of the men of
Gibeah who rape and abuse the concubine, nor by the crass reactions
both of the old Ephraimite host who was ready to throw concubine and
daughter to the dogs and of the Levite who actually did cast his concubine to them, nor by the unbelievably insensitive manner with which
the abused concubine is greeted at the door the next morning by her
husband, nor even by the shocking dismemberment of the concubine by
an outraged husband. Perhaps the most outrageous thing of all is that
neither the story itself nor the following story within a story clarifies for
us whether the concubine was alive or dead when the Levite dismembered her.

It is true that where the Massoretic text is vague, the Septuagint immediately adds, "for she was dead" (19:28a), as if to exemplify *someone's* recognition of this outrageous feature of the story. Be that as it may, we will leave such an "addition" to historical considerations that do not concern our initial literary analysis of the Hebrew text. It remains for us to interpret the story without this questionable narrative clarification. When the Levite returns home and cuts up his concubine limb by limb into twelve pieces, the *kāzo't*, "such a thing as this," of the message that accompanies the pieces takes on an eerie ambiguity:

> Has such a thing as this happened or been seen from the time the Israelites came up from Egypt till today? (19:30)

Do we have an angry man murdering his abused concubine by dismemberment, or simply (!) the dismemberment of a corpse to constitute a bloody message about a bloody crime? The narrator is obscure on this point.

When we look at the story within a story, that is, the Levite's own explanation of what happened, we have the following reported speech:

> They intended to kill me . . . and they raped my concubine and she died (*wattāmot*). I took her and cut her in pieces . . . (20:5–6)

Here the Levite's explanation appears to clear up the ambiguity by proposing the sequence: rape, death, dismemberment. Yet we are already struck by the self-serving tenor of the Levite's words which had also proposed the alternatives, murder of himself or rape of his concubine, in such a way that his concubine's rape would appear to have been the lesser of two evils. His use, however, of the word, *wattāmot*, "and she died," rather than, say *waḥ*ᵃ*mittîhā*, "they killed her," does not allow us completely to dispel the suspicions that the narrator's account had engendered. It is of course possible that the reported words of the Levite are to be understood as "they raped her until she died," but once again we wonder if the use of the *qal* form of *mût* is chosen by the narrator to depict the Levite as covering up, without actually lying, his participation in her death, if not by dismemberment itself, then at least by a cowardly unconcern for her fate until he opened the door that morning and stumbled upon her prostrate form. It appears likely, therefore, that the Levite's reported speech of this incident is as deliberately vague on this crucial point as was the narrator's reporting speech:

> He said to her, "Rise up, let us go," and there was no answer. (19:28)

If then the dismembered body turns out to be an outrageously one-sided and vague message about an outrage—an outrage that is described by the narrator as the cause of a headlong decision of Israel to exact just retribution from Gibeah and ultimately Benjamin—we once again find ourselves concerned with a narrative that is intent upon emphasizing not just the inability of its characters to determine clearly and exactly what takes place around them and which of them is guilty, but even the inability of the reader to piece together crucial aspects of the events in which these characters are enmeshed. It may very well be that the ambiguity of the narrator is as deliberately orchestrated as that of the Levite himself. Perhaps it is the exegete as well as an outraged Israel that rushes headlong into the specious clarity of restorative action, that is, of interpretation. Perhaps we are being told by the Deuteronomist what the narrator says of the Levite:

> . . . but there was no answer. (19:28)

2. The story of the outrage is simply background for the civil war between Israel and Benjamin described in chapter 20. And here the narrator is intent upon intensifying the doubt and confusion in Israel with which he began his story in Judges 1. He does this first of all by emphasizing in 20:8–11 Israel's precipitous decision to exact retribution before inquiring of Yahweh. Then in 20:18, in deliberate contrast to chapter 1 where the Israelites inquire of *Yahweh* who shall first go to battle against the *Canaanites,* the narrator informs us:

> They arose and went to Bethel to inquire of *God* . . . "Who of us shall go first to the battle with the Benjaminites?" (20:18)

In both cases the narrator tells us that *Yahweh* says, "Judah will go first," and it is clear that if the narrator here knows that Yahweh decides these matters, the Israelites, like Gideon, do not call upon the name of Yahweh as consistently as they should. The impact of 20:18, seen in the light of the defeat that follows and the subsequent inquiries at Bethel, seems to emphasize both the neutral power of the generic name, *'elohîm,* and the error of the Israelites in *assuming* too much about war with their brothers. The subsequent oracular attempts in the chapter will successfully correct these misapprehensions.

The narrator's and the Israelites' shift in naming helps us understand how intricately this chapter is constructed. If the narrator tells us that Israel inquired of "God" in 20:18, we are told that they inquired of "Yahweh" in 20:23 and 20:26–28. Corresponding to this shift in the naming of the deity between the first and the following inquiries is a shift in the naming of the *inquirers* between the second and the third instances. In 20:18 and 23, the narrator speaks simply of the Israelites (*bᵉnê yiśrā'ēl*), but in 20:26 the narrator expands his reference to "all the Israelites and all the people." Corresponding also to these shifts in naming is the narrator's increasingly more detailed account of what the Israelites *did* when they went up to Bethel to seek guidance. In 20:18 they simply inquire; in 20:23 they lament before the LORD and inquire; and in 20:26–28 they lament, fast, offer-up sacrifices, and inquire of the LORD.

Changes toward more detail in the reported speech of the inquiries themselves correspond to the changes in the narrator's reporting speech. In 20:18 the Israelites already assume that they should attack Benjamin; in 20:23 they simply question whether they should continue to approach for battle with Benjamin; but in 20:28 they inquire whether they should again enter into battle *or desist*. There is also a notable shift in naming between 20:18 and the following instances: in the first instance the Israelites refer to "Benjamin," but in the following two they refer to "Benjamin my brother." The response of Yahweh also increases in its oracular content in the last instance, where he not only tells Israel to go up, but adds that he has given Benjamin into Israel's hands.

3. The build-up of dramatic tension by this succession of oracular questions is very much like the series of questions in which Delilah seeks to discover the secret of Samson's strength. In both cases the series ends in the successful attainment of the questioner's goals. Samson was captured by the Philistines, and Benjamin is almost annihilated by Israel. But in the last chapter of Judges, Israel asks one final question, the narrator tells us, of "God":

> They said, 'O LORD God of Israel, why has it happened in Israel that one tribe should this day be lost to Israel?' (21:3)

Israel's use of *ḥerem* against Benjamin, and their vow to refuse their daughters to Benjamin, threaten his extinction. The rest of the chapter recounts in an almost grotesquely comic fashion how Israel, in the absence of any direct response from Yahweh, proceeds to insure that Benjamin not be lost to Israel. By their destruction of all the inhabitants of Jabesh-Gilead, except those women who were still virgins, and by their allowing Benjamin to kidnap as many Shilonite daughters as he needed, Israel insured that Benjamin would regain his former strength. By detailing for us Israel's planning and justification for the cruel slaughter of the inhabitants of one of their own towns, and for the kidnapping of some of their own daughters, the narrator scarcely conceals his scornful condemnation of the inhumane manner in which Israel solves the problematic state of affairs that began with the Benjaminite outrage. The conduct of the Levite, the Benjaminites, and all Israel throughout this entire affair, is portrayed as outrageously abominable. If the Israelites are finally able to articulate their god's full name, "Lord God of Israel" (21:3), the narrator shows in his own speech that they are really speaking only to *'elohîm*. The irony of the Yahwist, Micah, making an idolatrous molten image to secure his own safety, is continued here as the Israelites, who now call upon the full name of Yahweh, cruelly slaughter and kidnap their own brothers and sisters to help secure tribal completeness.

In a verse which looks forward in hope toward Israel's kings, and backwards toward their judges in sadness, the Deuteronomic narrator ends the book:

> In those days there was no king in Israel and every man did what
> was right in his own eyes. (21:25)

It remains to be seen whether the narrator's apparent optimism about the coming monarchy is borne out in the subsequent books of the Deuteronomic History.

SOME REMARKS ON APPLICATION

If it is true, as Gadamer argues (1975:274–278), that understanding, interpretation, and application all comprise one unified process instead of a sequence of hermeneutic operations, then this postscript must be recognized as partially artificial. Nevertheless, it seems worthwhile to reflect upon my reading of the Deuteronomic History (up through Judges) and to make explicit some aspects of it that concern the present situation. Whether the Deuteronomic message actually influences my understanding of the present state of biblical studies or whether I have read the present situation back into the biblical text is not within my ability to say; and even if it were, the direction of influence is relatively unimportant. As I reflect upon my reading, what stands out are a number of correspondences whose overall insight must not be postponed by instituting a quest for origins.[1]

The Voice from the Book of Deuteronomy
It is possible to drive home one truth by shouting out its denial. This was the case with the main ideological position in Deuteronomy. The Deuteronomist composes a powerful testament to the unique prophet, Moses, in such a way that the more authority he invests in his hero, the more he will take to himself in the following books of his history. The more exalted Moses is, the less he becomes. He portrays Moses as promulgating a lawcode that so tightly weaves together God's word and man's that each is finally indistinguishable from the other. The necessity for subsequent interpretation of Moses' word is secured by its prior merging with God's word. The boundaries between God's word and Moses' interpretation have been deliberately blurred to illustrate the condition of all interpretation. On the one hand it is always necessary; on the other it is finally impossible to distinguish what part of an interpretation is of the interpreter and what part of the one interpreted. We called the voice that drives home this point, while allowing the opposite to be spoken, "critical traditionalism." In Deuteronomy it is

heard as a still small voice, but will speak more loudly in the Book of Joshua. In Deuteronomy, however, its relative stillness silences a voice that unsuccessfully clamors for attention on the surface of the text, a voice of authoritarian dogmatism. "Here is the word of Moses," it says. "Do not add to it or take away from it." The word is transparent; there is no need for constant reinterpretation down through time. Immediacy, transparency, and univalency characterize the word of Moses. There is one meaning to it, not many. Come to that meaning, however difficult it may be, and you are blessed; avoid it, fail to uncover it, and you are doomed. Word and interpretation are one when the one authentic meaning is uncovered. As transparent and immediate, the word *is* its own interpretation. Difficulty in recognizing its transparency is the result of an opaque interpretive instrument. Separation in time and space may cause difficulties, but these are external problems not a condition inherent in the word.

If we leave aside the main concerns about which these two ideologies speak—God as merciful or just, the uniqueness of Moses and Israel, the relationship between God's promise to the fathers and his covenant at Sinai—and concentrate upon the hermeneutical aspects of the dialogue, the Book of Deuteronomy is a statement against the transparency, immediacy, and univalency of the Word. Moses performs the central interpretive task of the book—he goes to the heart of the matter—not when he quotes God's ten words directly in chapter 5, but when he promulgates God's further words in chapters 12 through 26 in such a way that (his) word and (God's) Word are indistinguishable. In the lawcode, Word and interpretation are inseparable; God's utterances are no longer transparent, direct, and univalent. The style of the ten words approximates the directness of the Word: God and the Israelites are face to face and all actually hear God speaking. The style of the lawcode obliterates this apparent immediacy and establishes the main hermeneutical perspective of the book: subsequent revisionary interpretation is necessary not in order to recover the original word of God—for the narrative makes clear this is impossible—but because Moses himself establishes the precedent by immediately *applying* God's further commands even as he is transmitting them to the people.

It is impossible for me to avoid seeing a reflex of this Deuteronomic dialogue in the present situation concerning literary hermeneutics. The lines are presently drawn so sharply that one is confronted with a clear choice, and for the implied author of the Book of Deuteronomy, at least, it is clear what that choice must be. It is in this sense that modern hermeneutics can be put to the test using biblical scales.

Do we cast our critical allegiance toward the perspective of a fundamental distinction of meaning and significance so forcefully argued for by E. D. Hirsch (1967), or do we reject it in favor of the Heideggerian position perhaps best represented by H. G. Gadamer (1975)? The situation extends far beyond the hermeneutic struggle that can be documented in the writings of these two scholars and their followers, and the issues are much more complicated than this brief impressionistic picture can adequately convey. Nevertheless, for those who are sufficiently conversant with the present dialogue,[2] it should be clear that the Book of Deuteronomy does have something relevant to say, at least insofar as my reading of it is concerned. The Deuteronomic History, I maintain, does take a stand concerning the crisis that biblical studies finds itself in, and the Book of Deuteronomy begins to suggest a remedy for a crisis that is simply symptomatic of a larger hermeneutic struggle.

If interpretation involves distinguishing the meaning an original author intended from the multiple significances given a text by subsequent interpreters, then there is a fundamental stability and univalency to the literal sense of a text invested in it by its original author. Any significance attached to this text by later exegetes is essentially dependent upon and subordinate to this literal meaning. The voice reflected in the views of Hirsch commands of the literal meaning what a subordinated voice of Deuteronomy unsuccessfully commands of the Deuteronomic lawcode: "you shall not add to it or take from it (13:1; Heb)." Whatever is added to or taken away from an original author's intent constitutes not a meaning that is fundamental but a significance that is subordinate. Meaning in Hirsch's view is transparent (at least to the author), stable, and univalent. Otherwise we are all reduced to a situation of pure relativism. Thus, the views of Gadamer, allowing as they do the simultaneous validity of multiple and contradictory interpretations, are to be rejected. But the main ideological voice of Deuteronomy will not allow this.

When we turn toward a consideration of biblical hermeneutics, we find that modern historical criticism, understanding its authenticating commission and responsibility to be the recovery of the literal sense of a biblical passage—that meaning it had for its original audience and author—must give its allegiance to a Hirschian hermeneutics, even if it has rarely reflected on its role in these terms.[3] Modern biblical historicism, no matter how frequently it has cautioned us about the immense difficulties involved in recovering a unitary original sense, has always assumed that it is there nonetheless. What the present literary reading of Deuteronomy has to say about the nature of the subsequent historical analysis that must now follow upon it is crucial: a "scientific," historical critical approach, motivated by Hirschian hermeneutical principles, would confront a text which condemns such principles as inadequate for an understanding of the Word. If this modern view on interpretation is to be retained, then the main ideological perspective of Deuteronomy must be rejected. Moses is portrayed by the implied author of Deuteronomy as interpreting God's word *and* applying it to Israel's present and future situation. Concerning God's further words (Deut 5:27) as they are transmitted to us in the lawcode of chapters 12 through 26, his *meaning* and the *significance* Moses gives them (using here Hirsch's understanding of these terms) are indistinguishable *de facto* and *de jure: de facto* because of the style of reported speech Moses uses here, and *de jure* because the whole point of the lawcode's synthesized composition seems to be the setting up of a paradigm wherein the subsequent reinterpretations of Moses' words, which constitute the subject matter of the following books of the history, are made necessary. Only if divine meaning equals human significance in the lawcode, can the Deuteronomist's significance equal Moses' meaning in the history as a whole. We can now turn to the Book of Joshua in which the Deuteronomist's continuing reinterpretation of the law of Moses casts serious doubt on the Hirschian distinction of meaning and significance.

The Voice from the Book of Joshua

The voice of critical traditionalism reverberating through every page of the Book of Joshua presents us with a sustained meditation on what it means to interpret "the book of the law." Appropriation of the law through constant reinterpretation and occupation of the land through continual struggle are themes woven together so inextricably in the book that each is finally an interpretant for the other. The distance between the divine word and human interpretation, in the case both of law and of land, is the general theme of the entire book. Utterly to be rejected in the Deuteronomist's retelling of the Israelite occupation of the land are simplistic statements of fulfillment by man of God's law and by God of his own promises—statements like Joshua 21:43–45 which are deeply ironic, given the literary context in which the Deuteronomist places them. The dominant hermeneutic ideology of Joshua, as uncovered by the literary approach of the preceding pages, promotes the validity of multiple and contradictory interpretations as a primary paradigm for understanding God's intervention in the affairs of men. If such an assertion is taken to mean that a Heideggerian hermeneutic simply predisposes one to describe a text's ideology as sympathetic to such an approach—a kind of self-fulfilling prophecy— so be it. The Book of Judges will help to show how limited such a criticism is in coming to grips with the problems raised by attempting to read Joshua in a committed way.

Reflection on the hermeneutic stance of the implied author of Joshua reveals that interpretation must involve a historical axis, even if a Hirschian brand of literary historicism appears incompatible with such a stance. The Deuteronomist's response, as I read it, to the present crisis in biblical studies outlined in chapter 1 of this book would be to call for a historical approach to the Word that understands it by constant reapplication to the present situation in which the interpreter finds himself. In concrete terms, the Book of Joshua presents us with a narrative whose dominant ideological perspective cannot be reconciled with a theoretical distinction between meaning and significance (Hirsch), but which is sympathetic to concepts such as effective historical consciousness (Gadamer). Yet when we look at the main currents of modern biblical criticism, although there are sharp differences between Old and New Testament scholarship, theoretical discussion and practical exegesis are remarkably sympathetic to a basic separation between meaning and significance, yet irreconcilable with a concept like effective historical consciousness. By and large, present-day biblical scholarship is the application of a Hirschian hermeneutic to a text that reveals itself—admittedly only in the reading I have imposed upon it—to be virtually opposed to such an approach. Thus when Joshua interprets the Mosaic law on the ban by exempting Rahab, when the Israelites finally decide to allow the Gibeonites to live, or whenever the Mosaic law is constantly applied in the book, it is not the distinction between meaning and significance, but an insight such as effective historical consciousness which, though a modern theoretical construct, is more congenial to the biblical picture.

If there is one characteristic that appears to separate Old and New Testament scholarship—it is the degree to which Heideggerian hermeneutics is readily apparent in certain strands of New Testament scholarship while being practically nonexistent in Old Testament studies. Even to one as profoundly ignorant of New Testament studies as I am, the work of Barth, Bultmann, and the post-Bultmannians has implicit and explicit connections with a Heideggerian hermeneutics, connections which find no counterpart in the Old Testament field. Nevertheless, in both testamental branches, the crisis in scholarship about which I wrote in chapter 1 above is present in its own way. If in Old Testament studies the theoretical issues that separate a Hirschian and a Gadamerian hermeneutics have never been effectively faced, much less resolved, the same cannot be said for New Testament scholarship in which the issues have been widely discussed for over fifty years. However, even in the latter case, they appear to have been unsatisfactorily resolved in debates such as that over "the new quest of the historical Jesus," wherein an explicitly Heideggerian hermeneutics has been used to forge a curious historical critical path to "the very selfhood of Jesus," with all the transcendental overtones such a project implies. This mix of two apparently irreconcilable hermeneutic paradigms means that, for all their emphasis on Heideggerian principles, the proponents of the new quest never completely rejected a Hirschian role for historical criticism. In fact, in some cases historiography was elevated to the level of kerygma as an alternate route to the very person of Christ.[4] If, as Perrin asserts (1976:184), the movement toward "a new quest" has lost its momentum and its unity, this may be seen as a result of their resolve to recover the original sense behind the biblical text.

If the application of Heideggerian insights in New Testament studies may be characterized as mostly idiosyncratic and ultimately self-defeating, one of the reasons for this may be that these proponents of a new historicism, like their colleagues who have remained wedded to the old historicism of the last century, failed to assign a proper role to literary critical analysis of biblical material.[5] In this respect Old Testament and New Testament studies suffer from the same defect. Scholars such as Norman Perrin in the last years of his life (e.g., 1976) and those in New Testament associated with the journal *Semeia*[6] have only recently begun to correct an imbalance in New Testament scholarship that is scarcely even recognized in Old Testament studies. Dan O. Via's earlier mix of Bultmannian phenomenology and literary critical sensitivity (1967) was uniquely perceptive. If the talents and insights of the Bultmannians and post-Bultmannians had been as sensitive literarily as they were phenomenologically, perhaps they would not have arrived at the impasse their sympathetic colleagues (like Perrin) have described. We can now turn to a consideration of what the Deuteronomist's attitude might be toward a new historicism that would successfully wed phenomenological and literary principles of interpretation. Needless to say, we now enter the realm of an ideal situation in our attempt to put modern hermeneutical principles to a biblical test.

The Voice from the Book of Judges

The Book of Judges begins on the firm ideological footing established for it by the Book of Joshua; but the situation immediately begins to disintegrate. The chaotic period of the judges is surveyed by the Deuteronomist in a sustained reflection on the limitations of any ideology to test reality or to understand the historical vicissitudes man encounters in his lifetime. Man's overreliance on belief-systems in all their

religious, theological, and hermeneutic dimensions results in the dissolution of the systems themselves. The book begins with God putting
Israel to the test; "[The nations] were for the testing of Israel, to know
whether Israel would obey the commandments of the LORD which he
commanded their fathers by Moses (3:4)," and proceeds methodically
to tear down any confidence one may have had in the ability even of a
critical traditionalism to make sense of Israel's history during this period, or to predict her destiny on the basis of her obedience or disobedience to the Mosaic law. In spite of her continual disobedience, she
survived and, more often than not, thrived. Both authoritarian dogmatism and critical traditionalism falter here as reliable theological or
hermeneutic frames of reference. The mystery of God's dealings with
man and the comedy of man's efforts to overpower and master the
events that make up his existence form the core theme of the
Deuteronomic History up to this point. What lies in store for the literary
analyst of Samuel and Kings is beyond the scope of this present volume,
but if the totally unexpected turn of the Book of Judges is any indication of what awaits us, it would be a foolish exegete indeed who would
attempt a forecast, given the paucity of adequate literary readings of
these four books. In this respect my description of the Deuteronomist
as implied author of the Deuteronomic History is a half-finished portrait, a provisional statement. In addition, everything I have laboriously
built up about the ideological perspective of the history remains open-
ended, subject to revision not only in the sense that a critical
traditionalism would understand this term but also according to the
critique of such an ideology found in the Book of Judges.

Actually we find here another modern analogue in the hermeneutics
of Hans Georg Gadamer. As David Hoy points out (1978:165),
Gadamer explicitly recognizes that all hermeneutic theory, including
his own, must inevitably be superseded historically. Not to admit this
would be to sink back into a transcendental perspective. Thus, even
though Gadamer argues forcefully for a historically conditional hermeneutic that has a "critical" rather than a "dogmatic" function (471),
and in spite of our adaptation of Bakhtin-Voloshinov's terminology to
set up the Deuteronomic dialogue as one of "critical traditionalism"
versus "authoritarian dogmatism," the hermeneutic implications are
themselves historically provisional. Similarly, the dogmatic aspects of a
biblical hermeneutics that anchors its activity in the meaning of an
original author and audience as opposed to subsequent signification
may very well be presently opposed as unproductive and even detri-
mental to understanding of the biblical text. Yet such opposition must
itself remain provisional and open-ended if there is any value to this

book's application, as a synthesis of an ancient biblical hermeneutics with one that is modern and humanistic. If both the word itself and the hermeneutics by which it is interpreted are to avoid the idolizing tendencies of a universalist and transcendental method, readings, like the frames of reference that put them in focus, ought to remain provisional. And for those who, like Hirsch, fear that such an attitude submerges us in pure relativism, the constraints and constancy imparted by intersubjectivism in Heideggerian theory (Magiola:186ff) may offer some comfort. More than this the present incomplete reading of the Deuteronomic History is unable to offer.[7]

NOTES

Chapter One
Criticism and Crisis within Biblical Studies

1. As Robin Lakoff writes, "the notion that contextual factors, social and otherwise, must be taken into account in determining the acceptability and interpretation of sentences is scarcely new. . . . But the idea has not merely been forgotten by transformational grammar; rather it has been explicitly rejected" (Lakoff, 1972:926, n. 12). Lakoff's essay presents convincing arguments for the linguistic necessity of understanding language in context.

2. John Dominic Crossan (1977) defends a similar sequence of analysis in his discussion of the future of biblical studies.

3. Although my attempt in this chapter is to articulate hermeneutical problems that today confront the scholarly interpretation primarily of the so-called Deuteronomic History, i.e. that section of the *Hebrew Bible* extending from the Book of Deuteronomy through 2 Kings, the precise manner in which I have formulated these problems cannot fail to recall an enormous body of New Testament research over the past fifty years centered on "the new quest of the historical Jesus." James M. Robinson's classic study (1959) succeeded admirably in synopsizing the perspectives and contributions of Bultmannian and post-Bultmannian scholarship as they then signaled a crucial turning point in New Testament scholarship. To an Old Testament scholar such as myself, standing as I do outside this impressive and long-standing discussion of key hermeneutical problems affecting the study of the New Testament, it remains a mystery how and why no discussion of comparable depth and scope has taken place in Old Testament scholarship. At any rate if a similar Old Testament quest was in fact initiated in Germany, it certainly did not make itself felt in North America. All the more unfortunate, for what Barth, Bultmann, and their progeny have had to say on the relation of historical critical study to the biblical message has unavoidable implications for Old Testament studies.

Granting all this, I nevertheless am convinced that my third assertion would still be necessary had Old Testament studies taken the precise turn mapped out by the post-Bultmannian solution to hermeneutical problems. Even though influential schools of New Testament scholarship present us with a new historical criticism supposedly purged of the Kantian principles infecting nineteenth century historiography, and imbued with the existential concerns emphasized in the twentieth century by Heidegger, I am not convinced that this brand of scholarship fully escapes the criticism it had leveled against its predecessors. If Robinson can confidently conclude concerning the new quest that "the selfhood of Jesus is equally available to us (apparently both *via* historical research and *via*

the *Kerygma*) as a possible understanding of our existence (1959:125)," it seems
to me that the hubristic enterprise of the nineteenth century historian has now
been .superseded by an enterprise even more hubristic in scope. Criticism that
once was believed able to lead us to a Christ of veritable chronology now claims
to have the power to present us with "the selfhood of Jesus." Historical criticism, as it never did, now *applies* the biblical message, but with a vengeance!

4. Once again the New Testament critic will hear echoes here of the rejection
of the old quest of the historical Jesus argued for on theological grounds by
Karl Barth, as it was argued on historical grounds by Rudolf Bultmann (cf.
James Robinson: 1959:74). Limited as my knowledge is of Barth's contributions
to New Testament scholarship, and however much Bultmann and his followers
have taken center stage since the 1950s, it seems to me that Old Testament
scholarship now needs to hear—in some quarters perhaps for the first time—
Barth's voice on the role of historical criticism.

5. It is precisely here in the persistent use of questionable diachronic guidelines that I find much of New Testament interpretation so unconvincing. If the
phenomenological perspectives of Bultmannians and post-Bultmannians offered a much needed corrective to the dispassionate and "objective" scholarship
of a past century, their decision to use the historical critical method not as an
end in itself (as they claimed was the case in the nineteenth century) but as a
means of distinguishing, say, Jesus' message from the Church's *Kerygma* brings
them back to the same dilemma that faced their predecessors. More than this,
in New Testament studies there is practically no serious literary critical interpretation informing present research (apart from an esoteric brand of French
structuralism). It seems to me that the Bultmannians' use of Heideggerian
phenomenology has been highly idiosyncratic in its hermeneutic thrust. One
must here recognize that paradoxically post-Bultmannian hermeneutics
has taken a decidedly Hirschian turn. The prospect of a hermeneutics in New
Testament studies that may be described as Hirschian-Heideggerianism does
not bode well for its methodological clarity. Whatever advances New Testament
scholarship may be said to have made with respect to historical critical self-
reflection, it is at present as literary critically unsophisticated as its Old Testament counterpart.

6. This study owes much to the writings of a number of Russian scholars
belonging to the "formalist" and "sociological" schools in the study of literature,
as they have influenced present-day literary studies. These scholars include
V. N. Voloshinov (1973), M. M. Bakhtin (1973), and B. Uspensky (1973). In addition, I have benefited greatly from the rhetorical insights of Wayne Booth
(1961) and the frame-analytical insights of Erving Goffman (1974).

7. The work and influence of Bultmann in New Testament studies would be
an example of such a sustained reflection, but with severe literary critical
deficiencies.

8. In this case it seems to me best to respond to historical critical concerns by
at least recalling the stated positions of some of those who have fashioned the
literary tools utilized in the present study. This tactic is not at all an attempt to
"prove" the opposing viewpoint, after the manner of an argument from authority; rather it is meant simply to present another view to the problem without
attempting to *prove* the position it takes. What the following words exemplify, at
least, is that some fashioners of the literary approaches that form the inspira-
tion of my own study are aware of, and have taken account of, the theoretical

implications of some of the main issues just raised, e.g., literary unity versus editorial variance. Bakhtin, for example, writes:

> In this sense, every utterance has its author who is heard in the utterance as its creator. We can know absolutely nothing about the actual author as he exists outside the utterance. The forms of actual authorship can be very diverse. A given work can be the product of a collective effort, can be created by the successive efforts of a series of generations, etc.—in any case, we hear in it a unified creative will, a specific position to which we can react dialogically. A dialogical reaction personifies every utterance to which it reacts. (Bakhtin, 1973:152)

And as to cross-cultural utility, one may simply point out that Uspensky (1973) routinely gives examples of compositional structure from such diverse sources as the New Testament (149), Irish Saga (171), Homer's Iliad (170), and G. K. Chesterton (13), even though the bulk of his examples are derived from Tolstoy and Dostoevsky (7).

9. I share Uspensky's caution concerning the wholesale application of this assumption; "In respect to literature and contrary to some widely held opinions (that trace the description constructed from a plurality of viewpoints to the beginnings of the realistic novel) the use of several different viewpoints in narration may be noted even in relatively ancient texts" (Uspensky, 1973:171).

10. I often make use of this assumption in the present study in spite of my awareness that we have comparatively little knowledge of the conventional expectations of the biblical text's original audiences. But what we do have, within the biblical text and outside it, is a wealth of information on the continuing reinterpretation of what is understood to be the word of God. A detailed knowledge of these successive reinterpretations, especially in its precritical phases—that area most typically ignored by modern biblical scholarship—would serve to inform the historical critical analysis of the text that must follow up and readjust a preliminary literary analysis such as I am presently undertaking. And to those who would claim that biblical form critical research has taught us much about generic biblical conventions, I can only reiterate the perceptive remarks of Robert Alter (1978) about the limitations of such research for the purposes with which I am now concerned.

11. I understand "implied author" in a different way than Wayne Booth does in *The Rhetoric of Fiction* (1961:passim), that is, without his Hirschian presuppositions.

12. My goal, therefore, is to begin the task of literary interpretation programatically outlined by Uspensky (1973:153–54).

13. For those who question the validity of putting the genres of novel and history together in the same semantic boat in regard to the concept of monologic/dialogic structure, it should be noted here that, apart from the ambiguities of calling the Deuteronomic History "history," this study proceeds in wholehearted agreement with the views of Hayden White (1973) and Roland Barthes (1970) on the nature of historical discourse and its relation to literary interpretation. Both authors underline, from different perspectives, the similarities between the interpretive elements and imaginative constructions found in historiographic works and those found in other genres such as the novel.

14. Indeed, the basic issues that I am raising here have been set out by Wayne Booth in *The Rhetoric of Fiction*. Booth's discussion, in the manner with which he

exemplifies his conclusions with countless examples from modern western literature, complements the more methodologically oriented analyses of Bakhtin (1973) more than thirty years earlier.

15. Confer on this point Bakhtin (1973:160–61) and Uspensky (1973:8–16). I should point out here that when I write of the implied author's *intention*, I use this term in its phenomenological sense. The intentionality of the text is as much my own reconstruction as the implied author of a text is.

16. The Russian structuralists have already worked out many of the implications of the fact that "within a single utterance there may occur two intentions, two voices" (Bakhtin, 1973:153ff).

Chapter Two
The Book of Deuteronomy

1. I use the term "voice" sometimes to refer to a text's own distinction between reporting and reported speech. In this instance the expression-plane of a narrative itself distinguishes the voice or words, say, of its narrator from those of various characters in the story. At other times in this book I will use "voice" to refer to distinguishable perspectives on the ideological plane of the text. In this instance I am concerned with the implied author's ideological position as I have reconstructed it from the interrelationships discovered between the utterances of narrator and characters in the text. This stance of the implied author may be complex enough to warrant talking about two or more ideological voices and the specific order of subordination and/or equality apparent among them. Distinction of voice on the expression plane is the construction of a text's author. Distinction of voice on the ideological plane is the construction of the interpreter; this construction is what we call "the implied author."

2. Here "voice" is used to refer to the expression plane of our narrative; it is not a reconstruction as "voice" on the ideological plane would be.

3. In Uspensky's perspectival scheme (1973) the phraseological, spatial-temporal and psychological levels are on a text's surface or plane of expression; the ideological level refers to the deep structure or composition of a text.

4. It should be pointed out here that this work was probably written by Voloshinov's teacher, M. Bakhtin. Cf. V. V. Ivanov, 1974.

5. Voloshinov writes, "Regardless of the functional orientation of the given context of reported speech—whether it is a work of fiction, a polemical article, a defense attorney's summation, or the like—we clearly discern these two tendencies in it: that of commenting and that of retorting. Usually one of them is dominant. Between the reported speech and the reporting context dynamic relations of high complexity and tension are in force. A failure to take these into account makes it impossible to understand any form of reported speech" (1973:118–19).

6. "The stronger the feeling of hierarchical eminence in another's utterance, the more sharply defined will its boundaries be, and the less accessible will it be to penetration by retorting and commenting tendencies from without" (Voloshinov, 1973:123).

7. With regard to the "further" words of God found in the lawcode of 12–26, I make no judgments concerning the knowledge or lack of knowledge of its contents on the part of the audience or audiences that span the scope of its composition, be it centuries, generations, years, or perhaps even months. I embrace no historical judgments concerning the relative antiquity or novelty of

the various legal formulations found within it. What is important from a compositional point of view is that these further laws of God are presented within the book itself as privileged material which only Moses himself could have communicated to his hearers since only he had been commanded in 5:23–31 to stand beside the LORD to hear them. Similarly, I am arguing that the "further" words of Moses found in the books of Joshua through 2 Kings are also presented within the Book of Deuteronomy itself as privileged material which only the narrator could have communicated to his hearers since only he had been prophesied in 18:16–19 as a prophet like Moses in whose mouth God's words would be put. The historical critical investigations that have already established the relative antiquity of much of the material found both in Deuteronomy and Joshua–2 Kings are too well documented to be denied. They are, nevertheless, beside the point at this preliminary stage in the compositional analysis of the Deuteronomic History. The important fact that the lawcode is presented as esoteric, privileged material needing a prophet like Moses to convey its message to the people has a compositional impact on how the material in Joshua–2 Kings is to be understood from a literary point of view: as an explanation of why Israel's history shaped itself as it did, it too is privileged information needing a prophetic voice to convey its detailed interpretive message to the people.

8. This is, for example, the case in Jeremiah 26:2 where God is quoted in direct discourse saying, "You shall tell them everything that I command you to say to them, keeping nothing back." For in Jeremiah's case, once he has conveyed God's words to his listeners, there is nothing to prevent him from responding to and commenting upon the words of the LORD, as he in fact does in Jeremiah 26:12–15.

Postscript
Some Remarks on Application

1. I constructed an implied author, the Deuteronomist, who led me on an ideological and hermeneutical quest. I emerge from this constructive experience a different scholar. Whether I am a better one depends upon the scales of values one may bring forward. But the accuracy and utility of one ideological norm over another has been an integral theme of the quest itself. For good or ill the story these pages have uncovered already tips the scales.

2. A most valuable survey of the present situation in literary hermeneutics may be found in the autumn 1978 issue of *New Literary History*. This volume admirably sets out the alternatives of "Kantian" and "Hegelian" historicism in modern humanistic studies. To avoid misunderstandings about my use of the term "Kantian," I want to emphasize that I borrow this adjective from Richard Rorty (pp. 141–60 of the just noted issue of *NLH*) and restrict its meaning to the sense he gives it there.

3. This sweeping assessment will have to be modified below when we will have occasion to spell out some differences between Old and New Testament critical scholarship. Nevertheless, as we shall see, even when biblical hermeneutics has professed distinctly Heideggerian perspectives, it has rarely been able to reject its prior convictions, and ends up embracing Kantian historicism with a vengeance.

4. Leander Keck has perceptively criticized this result of the new quest (134). Keck's discussion of the historical Jesus is a remarkably clear presentation of the issues at stake here.

5. There are of course notable exceptions to this assessment. Dan O. Via, (1967) has correctly emphasized the *literary* dimensions of a Heideggerian hermeneutics.

6. Robert Funk, Dan O. Via, Dominic Crossan, Norman Petersen, and Daniel Patte all have emphasized in their own distinctive ways the literary dimension of the biblical material.

7. The limitations I place on my own literary efforts both in the opening chapter and here are meant to be more than rhetorical window-dressing suitable for a supposed academic humility. Just as I think it has been especially unfortunate that modern historical criticism of the Bible emphasized the value of historical perspectives and then proceeded paradoxically to ignore the centuries of interpretation that separate the biblical world and the rise of modern historiography, so it would be unfortunate if the "effective historical consciousness" which forms the theoretical underpinning of my literary approach to the Deuteronomic History would be effectively neutralized by a conviction, however implicit, that my reading is anything more than a serious but open-ended application of the text.

The recent study of John J. Collins (1979) reached me too late to incorporate into my manuscript; Collins provides an excellent analysis of some of the issues I raised above in chapter 1 and in the postscript.

WORKS CITED

Alter, Robert
    1975   "A Literary Approach to the Bible." *Commentary* 60:70–77.

    1978   "Biblical Type-Scenes and the Uses of Convention." *Critical Inquiry* 5:355–368.

Bakhtin, Mikhail
    1973   *Problems of Dostoevsky's Poetics.* Ann Arbor: Ardis Pubs.

Barthes, Roland
    1970   "Historical Discourse." Pp. 145–155 in *Structuralism: A Reader,* ed. Michael Lane. London: Jonathan Cape.

Booth, Wayne
    1961   *The Rhetoric of Fiction.* Chicago and London: University of Chicago Press.

Collins, John J.
    1979   "The Historical Character of the Old Testament in Recent Biblical Theology." *Catholic Biblical Quarterly* 41:185–204.

Cross, Frank M.
    1973   *Canaanite Myth and Hebrew Epic.* Cambridge, Mass.: Harvard University Press.

Crossan, John D.
    1973   *In Parables: The Challenge of the Historical Jesus.* New York: Harper and Row.

    1977   "Perspectives and Methods in Contemporary Biblical Criticism." *Biblical Research* 22:39–49.

Culley, Robert
    1976   *Studies in the Structure of Hebrew Narrative.* Missoula and Philadelphia: Scholars Press and Fortress Press.

Doty, William G.
    1973   "Linguistics and Biblical Criticism." *Journal of the American Academy of Religion* 41:114–121.

Frei, Hans
1974   *The Eclipse of Biblical Narrative: A Study in Eighteenth and Nineteenth Century Hermeneutics.* New Haven and London: Yale University Press.

Gadamer, Hans-Georg
1975   *Truth and Method.* New York: Seabury Press.

Goffman, Erving
1974   *Frame Analysis: An Essay on the Organization of Experience.* Cambridge, Mass.: Harvard University Press.

Hirsch, E. D.
1967   *Validity in Interpretation.* New Haven and London: Yale University Press.

1976   *The Aims of Interpretation.* Chicago: University of Chicago Press.

Hjelmslev, Louis
1961   *Prolegomena to a Theory of Language.* Madison, Wis.

Hoy, David Couzens
1978   "Hermeneutic Circularity, Indeterminacy, and Incommensurability." *New Literary History* X: 161–173.

Ivanov, V. S.
1974   "The Significance of M. M. Bakhtin's Ideas on Sign, Utterance, and Dialogue for Modern Semiotics." Pp. 310–367 in *Semiotics and Structuralism,* ed. Henryk Baran. White Plains, N.Y.: International Arts and Sciences Press.

Kaiser, Otto
1975   *Introduction to the Old Testament.* Minneapolis: Augsburg Publishing House.

Keck, Leander E.
1971   *A Future for the Historical Jesus: The Place of Jesus in Preaching and Theology.* Nashville and New York: Abingdon.

Koch, Klaus
1969   *The Growth of the Biblical Tradition.* New York: Scribner.

Krentz, Edgar
1975   *The Historical-Critical Method.* Philadelphia: Fortress Press.

Krieger, Murray
1976   "Introduction: A Scorecard for the Critics." *Contemporary Literature* 17:297–326.

Lakoff, Robin
1972   "Language in Context." *Language* 48:907–927.

Lord, Albert B.
1968   *The Singer of Tales.* New York: Atheneum.

Magiola, Robert R.
1977   *Phenomenology and Literature: An Introduction* West Lafayette, Ind.: Purdue University Press.

Maier, Gerhard
1977   *The End of the Historical-Critical Method.* St. Louis: Concordia Publishing House.

Miles, John
1977   "Gagging on Job." *Semeia* 7:71–126.

Molina, David Newton de
1976   *On Literary Intention: Critical Essays.* Edinburgh: University Press.

Noth, Martin
1967   *Überlieferungsgeschichtliche Studien.* Tübingen: Max Niemeyer Verlag

1972   *A History of Pentateuchal Traditions.* Englewood Cliffs, N.J.: Prentice Hall.

Patte, Daniel
1976   *What is Structural Exegesis?* Philadelphia: Fortress Press.

Perrin, Norman
1976   *Jesus and the Language of the Kingdom.* London: SCM Press.

Polzin, Robert M.
1977a   *Biblical Structuralism.* Missoula and Philadelphia: Scholars Press and Fortress Press.

1977b   "John A. Miles on the Book of Job: A Response." *Semeia* 7:127–133.

Pomorska, Krystyna
1971   "Russian Formalism in Retrospect." In *Readings in Russian Poetics,* trans. L. Matejka and K. Pomorska. Cambridge, Mass.: MIT Press.

Rad, Gerhard von
1966   *The Problem of the Hexateuch and Other Essays.* New York: McGraw-Hill.

Robertson, David
1977   *The Old Testament and the Literary Critic.* Philadelphia: Fortress Press.

Robinson, James M.
1959   *A New Quest of the Historical Jesus.* Studies in Biblical Theology. Naperville, Ill.: Allenson.

Said, Edward W.
1976   "Roads Taken and Not Taken in Contemporary Criticism." *Contemporary Literature* 17:327–348.

Saussure, F. de
1966   *Course in General Linguistics.* New York: McGraw-Hill.

Soggin, J. Alberto
1972   *Joshua. A Commentary.* Philadelphia: Westminster Press.

Soter, Istvan
1970   "The Dilemma of Literary Science." *New Literary History* 2:85–100.

Strickland, Geoffrey
1977   "The Theory of Criticism." *Encounter* 49:86–91.

Stuhlmacher, Peter
1977   *Historical Criticism and Theological Interpretation of Scripture.* Philadelphia: Fortress Press.

Tsevat, Mattitiahu
1975   "Common Sense and Hypothesis in Old Testament Study." *Vetus Testamentum Supplements* 28:217–230.

Uspensky, Boris
1973   *A Poetics of Composition.* Berkeley: University of California Press.

Via, Dan O., Jr
1967   *The Parables: Their Literary and Existential Dimension.* Philadelphia: Fortress Press.

Voloshinov, V. N. (= Bakhtin, M.)
1973   *Marxism and the Philosophy of Language.* New York: Seminar Press.

Weinfeld, Moshe
1972   *Deuteronomy and the Deuteronomic School.* Oxford: Clarendon Press.

Wellhausen, Julius
1965   *Prolegomena to the History of Ancient Israel.* Cleveland and New York: Meridian Books.

Wette, W. M. L. de
1805   *Dissertatio critico-exegetica, qua Deuteronomium a prioribus Pentateuchi libris diversum, alius cuiusdam recentioris auctoris opus esse monstratur.*

White, Hayden
1973   *Metahistory.* Baltimore and London: Johns Hopkins Press.

DETAILED STORY-LINE

Chapter 1
Criticism and Crisis Within Biblical Studies
Immediate Context: present tension between historical and literary criticism a healthy sign, 1; outcome of struggle already indicated within literary studies itself, 2; necessity of historical critical analysis, 3; prior necessity of literary analysis, 5; opposition between Bible and "scientific" criticism the real crisis, 7; book of Deuteronomy as example of biblical view of hermeneutics, 9; implications for modern criticism, 11; limitations of the present study, 12—*Historical Critical Work on Deuteronomic History:* disappointing because of questionable diachronic criteria, 13; also because of inadequate literary analysis, 15—*Modern Literary Criticism and Ancient Israelite Narrative:* possible objections to their usefulness for biblical text, 16—*Deuteronomic History:* literary approach as compositional, 18; relationship between Deut and Josh–2 Kgs, 19; distinction between reporting and reported speech applied, 19; central problem as identification of Deuteronomist's main ideological stance, 20; is Deuteronomic History a monologue or dialogue?, 21; why this is first a literary question, 23; compositional analysis as means of locating implied author's stance within narrator's and characters' utterances, 24.

Chapter 2
The Book of Deuteronomy
Moses and Narrator as Hero and "Author" of Book: Deut as book of utterances within utterances, 25; Moses and narrator as privileged declarers of God's word, 26; Moses' words and narrator's words as equal or subordinate, 27; as conveyors of implied author's stance, 28—*Narrator's Direct Utterances:* comprise only fifty-six verses, 29; first function of narrator to situate words of Moses, 29; other function is to serve as frame-breaks, 30; narrator's frame-breaks in Moses' first address call attention to himself rather than Moses, 32; in Moses' following addresses, frame-breaks undermine unique status of Moses, 33; as subtle counterclaim to narrator's own assessment of Moses in 34:10ff., 35; as hint of two Mosaic voices in Deut, 36—*Reported Speech in Deut: First Address of Moses:* utterances questioning his own unique status, 36; Mosaic dialogue on unique status of Israel, 37; and on characterization of God, 39; surface composition of first address as model for entire Deuteronomic History, 40; chap. 4 as representative of two ideological voices in book, 41—*Second Address of Moses:* Deut 5:1–5 as

illustration of complicated relationship of surface and ideological composition of text, 44; surface composition of second address blurs boundaries between God's words and Moses' words, 47; and exalts Moses' privileged position as mouthpiece of God, 49; ideological problems of second address: overwhelming emphasis on retributive justice and covenant of law, 50; on Moses' unique status, 50; and on Israel's, 51; but some utterances challenge Moses' and Israel's unique status, 51; how utterances on God's mercy and promise to fathers are neutralized in second address, 53; lawcode (Deut 12–26) as Moses' direct address obliterates practical importance of distinction between God's word and Moses', 55; how reader's perception of Moses thereby affected, 56; Moses as pre-eminent model for Deuteronomist's narrator: blurring of God's-Moses' words in lawcode prepare for blurring of Moses'-narrator's words in Josh–2 Kgs, 57; Deut 13:1–6 and 18:15–22 as representative of two main ideological voices of book, 57; 13:1–6 as implied author's ironic presentation of authoritarian dogmatism, 59; 18:15–22 as representative of critical traditionalism, 59; 13:1–6 as rejection of Deuteronomic History and vice versa, 63; compositional evidence for implied author's stance on these two pericopes, 64; summary of second address: how content and composition of utterances interact to provide ideological position, 65; namely a neutralizing effect on God's unconditional covenant, a diminution of Moses' and Israel's unique status, and a rejection of voice of authoritarian dogmatism, 67; Deut is so far a hermeneutic monologue in defense of critical traditionalism, 68—*Third Address of Moses:* surface composition, 69; ideological composition, 70—*Collection of Moses' Final Sayings:* 71—*Postscript and Preview,* 72.

Chapter 3
The Book of Joshua

Deut predominantly discourse, Josh now predominantly narrative: implications, 73; *Josh 1: A Paradigmatic Illustration* taken up by voice of critical traditionalism, 74; as a pastiche of previous utterances from Deut, 75—*Josh 2–12:* detailed polemic vs. simplistic picture of how Israel fulfilled God's commands, 80; reported speech of God and Joshua as portrayal of law of God in dynamic and changeable light, 80; interpretation involves articulation of command's intent, of subsequent event's meanings, and of principle of *epiekeia,* 82; reporting speech as story of occupation: unifying theme as series of events in which narrator highlights a number of *cruces interpretationis* concerning "book of the law," 84—*Spying of Jericho and Encounter with Rahab:* exemplifies two hermeneutic problems, viz., how to interpret and apply God's command to put complete trust in him and how to interpret Mosaic rules for holy war, 85; main voice here is of critical traditionalism, 87; meditating on Deut 9:4–5 from dispossessed nations' perspective, 88; Rahab represents both dispossessed nations and Israel herself, 88; Rahab story as preview of entire book, 90—*Crossing of the Jordan:* literary analysis and difficulties of passage, 91; liturgical narrative as framing device in Josh, 92; special attention given to this first cultic narrative of book, 94; puzzling temporal shifts in crossing narrative, 94; five episodes in narrative, 95; function of retrospective and synchronic view points in story, 97; the spatial stability of Ark and priests, the spatial mobility of people, 98; spatial perspective of characters, 99; of narrator, 101; the "omniscient" narrator, 102; episodes one to three as internal to participants of crossing, episodes four and five internal to dispossessed nations, 103; the antiphonal pattern of reporting

Chapter 4
The Book of Judges